Canadian Economic Forecasting

Canadian Economic Forecasting

In a World Where All's Unsure

MERVIN DAUB

McGill-Queen's University Press
Kingston and Montreal

© McGill-Queen's University Press 1987
ISBN 0-7735-0621-7

Legal deposit 3rd quarter 1987
Bibliothèque nationale du Québec

Printed in Canada

This book has been published with the help of a
grant from the Social Science Federation of Canada,
using funds provided by the Social Sciences and
Humanities Research Council of Canada.

Canadian Cataloguing in Publication Data

Daub, Mervin, 1943-
  Canadian economic forecasting
  Includes index.
  ISBN 0-7735-0621-7
  1. Economic forecasting–Canada.   2. Canada–
  Economic conditions.   I. Title.
  HC115.D38 1987   330.971   c87-094036-8

CARTOONS: p. 12: Reprinted with special permission
of Kings Features Syndicate, Inc., © Kings Features
Syndicate, Inc.; p. 17: By permission of Johnny Hart
and News America Syndicate; p. 42: Reprinted with
permission of Universal Press Syndicate, © Universal
Press Syndicate; p. 66: Drawing by Mankoff, © 1981
The New Yorker Magazine, Inc.; p. 78: Reprinted
with permission of Universal Press Syndicate,
© Universal Press Syndicate; p. 111: Reprinted
with permission – Toronto Star Syndicate; p. 156:
Drawing by Stevenson, © 1983 The New Yorker
Magazine, Inc.; p. 162: Published with permission of
the Regina Leader-Post

For Father, Mother, and the Soph

"Now, for instance, can ye charm away warts?"

"Without trouble."

"Cure the evil?"

"That I've done – with consideration ..."

"Forecast the weather?"

"With labour and time."

"Then take this ... 'Tis a crown-piece. Now, what is the harvest fortnight to be? When can I know?"

"I've worked it out already, and you can know at once ... By the sun, moon, and stars, by the clouds, the winds, the trees, and grass, the candleflame and swallows, the smell of the herbs; likewise by the cats' eyes, the ravens, the leeches, the spiders, and the dungmixen, the last fortnight in August will be – rain and tempest."

"You are not certain, of course?"

"As one can be in a world where all's unsure ... Shall I sketch it out for 'ee in a scheme?"

"O no, no ... I don't altogether believe in forecasts, come to second thoughts on such."

Thomas Hardy, *The Mayor of Casterbridge* (1886), chapter 26

Contents

Preface

I remember always being interested in what the future would bring.
No doubt most of us would say the same thing. But with me, for a
number of reasons most directly linked to an overfull childhood, it
became second nature; it is not surprising, in retrospect, to find that
I have spent nearly 20 years of my professional life working on
various aspects of it.

As I will argue below, the interest of any era in the future, and
hence of any individual living in such an age, is, like many other
things, as much sociologically based as personal. Thus growing up
in the late 1940s and the 1950s, one was inevitably infected for life
with the sense of importance and hope that that era attached to the
future. If not exactly articles of faith, predicting and managing the
future were at the very least passed on to the young of that time as
major requirements to living the appropriately modern way.

Being thus doubly star-crossed, and given the perspective of those
20 years, I have chosen to set down what I think I've learned about
the subject – not, mind, about all of it but rather about the narrower
subject of economic forecasting as it relates to Canada. This is not
so restrictive as it might seem. For one thing, barring strictly political
and weather forecasting, most activity with respect to this "futurism"
in our age has been focused on economic matters. Moreover, Canada
has in no way been exempt from more general influences; indeed,
it has helped to shape those influences.

For another thing, there is a certain disregard for my own self-
chosen boundary in what follows. Forecasting is not so completely
"dismal" as certain readers might expect. Nor is it as esoteric as others
might crave. This is not a book on the philosophy of "futurism." It
might have been. Rather it is closer to Landes's (1983) recent book
on time, albeit not so broad. Viewed this way, forecasting is a re-

sponse to natural concerns about the future much as clocks are a response to concerns about time. Just as understanding about clocks tells us a good deal about how we think about time, so understanding forecasting tells us much about how we think about the future.

Because no one, except in the rarefied realms of pure theory, ever drops neatly or cleanly an entire body of thought on an unsuspecting public, much of what is presented here draws on various studies, papers, addresses, chats, and other sources previously done, written, and given. A good deal has been rethought and redone for this work. Some, where it still seems right, has been used directly.

Among those whose continued interest is appreciated, I want to thank explicitly Victor Zarnowitz of the University of Chicago, Don Daly of York University, and Mike McCracken of Informetrica. As well, Don Akenson of McGill-Queen's University Press encouraged me at the outset to do the book and has helped to show the way throughout. John Parry's editorial contribution was most welcome. Finally, Annette Chiasson has carried the secretarial load with much grace.

There are others, including many in the business and my university colleagues, who are unfortunately too numerous to mention but who have contributed substantially over the years. Any errors that might be discovered are no fault of theirs. Rather they are mine alone, any small accomplishments those of a kindly fate.

Canadian Economic Forecasting

CHAPTER ONE

Introduction

All of us have at one time or another seen those wonderful, early, black and white movies. In some, Stanley, or another adventurer, is deep in the jungle surrounded by natives, led by a sinister type with much hair, and even more bones. We all know who he is. He is the witch doctor! We also all know the purpose of that bone rattling: dire consequences, not so much for the adventurer, who will be saved by the credits, but rather for the tribe.

In other movies there is the equally well-known scene in which the Indian shamans under their huge masks are hard at work calling up the spirits to reveal what is to come. In still others, the dashing Errol Flynn has his doom foretold by that marvellous gypsy fortune-teller with her crystal ball and hypnotic eyes.

As familiar to us are those horror movies in which the black arts of alchemy and entrails, witches and symbolism are portrayed. The Bard himself could not resist witches. Recall that wonderful cauldron scene in *Macbeth* where the future is so brutally foreseen. There are also fantasy stories and films such as *Conan the Warrior*, science fiction epics like Hebert's *Trilogy* and *Star Wars*. All are full of people like the priests of Styx or Obi Wan Kanobe who have wonderful powers to see into the future.

Consider also the Bible. Was it not Joseph who predicted from the Pharaoh's dream that Egypt would have seven fat years and seven lean ones? Did not at least two of the major prophets foretell that one day a Messiah would come to the Jews?

Certainly less romantic, but generally as well known, are the likes of Nostradamus with his predictions of catastrophic doom or Marx and his forecast of the inevitable demise of capitalism. At the level of the completely mundane, there are the myriad social, political, economic, and other "foretellers" (to say nothing of those predicting the weather), who regularly bombard us with forecasts of the rise and fall of nations, nuclear winter, drought, and other disasters large and small.

No doubt many people ask themselves from time to time why all of this takes place. Why did Xerxes, for example, have to consult the Delphic oracle before his great battle with Alexander? Why does the minister of finance *have* to talk with the Conference Board, or other "forecasters," before bringing down his budget? Why do we have to know what the weekend's weather will bring?

What is it about the human spirit that regularly down through the ages has required this looking forward in time, this "need to know what will be" before it is? Is forecasting the result of obscure Jung-style deeper forces running in the human psyche, a holdover perhaps from man's earliest fear of the dark, or of the "unexpected dinosaur behind the next rock"?

To shed some light on this very puzzling aspect of human behaviour, it is tempting to go off in quite a number of directions all at once. One could, for example, look at the practice in some philosophically precise way, considering, again for example, what language is used to describe it, or how it is portrayed. Alternatively one could study its history, or how it is carried out in certain circumstances.

Before considering several of these suggestions, we should realize, in this case from a historical perspective, that while forecasting is never entirely absent as a practice, it seems noticeably age-dependent; certain "ages" are more future-oriented than others. Our own is one of them, the Renaissance was another. To see this distinction, one need only compare today's collective psyche to a more present-oriented time such as the Middle Ages. We are unquestionably in one of those periods when the future seems more relevant than it does at other times.

A number of explanations might be advanced for this cyclical character of the concern for the future. For example, following Landes (1983), perhaps certain "technological" factors help determine the distinctive time-orientation of an age. The availability of large amounts of relevant information about one's environment, and the ability to process it economically, might help make an age future-oriented.

Yet another explanation may well be cycles in the accuracy of forecasters. A particularly disastrous run of forecasting could well lead to its rejection. In time those failures are forgotten, and the practice comes creeping back in. Alternatively, perhaps the more rapid is technological change in an age, the more that age's collective anxiety requires concern for the future.

The latter suggestion is a particular favourite of sociologists such as Toffler (1970) and my maiden aunt. I incline more to the first, technological explanation, for several reasons. First, changes in the speed of technology's change are always difficult to judge. Second, sober opinion about the future, the kind that hard-eyed government and business people like a Caesar or a Rockefeller paid good money for, is surely not driven simply by a fluctuating need to reduce anxiety. Finally, so disastrous a run of erroneous forecasts as to cause a complete turning away from the practice has never occurred. Nor has dissatisfaction with forecasts ever lasted for an entire age.

No doubt there are some valid elements to each of the suggested explanations and to others not noted. But history, regardless of the setting, suggests that it is precisely because one can "arrange" the future at least enough to make it worth trying that one sees so much concern with it.[1] While there are many aspects to this "arranging" of the future, the most important is prediction.

That a particular age is mostly "future-oriented" for certain reasons, and that an important aspect of that future orientation is prediction, tell us something about "why we need to know ahead of time." One can gain further insight by looking at what "foretales/prophecies" are, and how they are made.

It is interesting to consider the very terms themselves, and their evolution through time. There is, for example, an almost poetic correctness in English to the term *forecast*, as there is to its transformation from the older "tale" to the more modern "cast." One can almost see the fly-fishing line of thought flung out into the future and then brought slowly in on the reel, bringing with it what the cast has caught on the hook of time. One can almost see that casting about in the mind, that looking here and there, the building of that hypothetical future, its contemplation; here the accepting, there the rejecting. Alternatively, the term may well capture the sense of "casting" intended in metallurgy – a certain collection of elements bound together into a mutually reinforcing block of matter, which is the future. Finally, there is the movement to a greater sense of science in the changing from a "tale" about the future to a "cast." All of this is wonderfully, completely satisfactory.[2]

That said, what is this thing called "forecasting" that is so necessary, and in which we so regularly engage both individually and collectively? It may perhaps seem silly even to ask. Doesn't everyone know that "forecasting" is ... well ... "forecasting"? It is worthwhile, however, taking some time to mull over the question.

First, a forecast involves a statement about the unknown. The key word here is "unknown." Uncertainty may range from complete ignorance to reasonable confidence that the unknown is rather narrowly bounded. But without the uncertainty, we would know exactly what to expect and hence what to do. There would be no need to make a "forecast." In fact, the word would not likely exist.

Second, forecasting is characteristically oriented towards the future. Indeed that is how we have come to it. Exercises in archaeology and history aside, where researchers attempt to "predict" what happened in the past, "forecasting" usually implies orientation towards the future, normally a specific point in the future. Changing the time horizon changes the uncertainty. Thus for a forecast to be useful, and not mere whimsy, it must be "time-specific."[3]

Third, a forecast implies the existence of observations or information that underlie the particular statement about the unknown. Usually, whether directly or indirectly, the reliance is on historical information. In fact, it is very difficult to conceive of situations in which such dependence is not the case.[4]

Fourth, within a forecast we can usually identify some kind of underlying theory, simple or self-evident as it may be. Typically this implicit theory has as its most important characteristic an assumption of constancy. Perhaps the present situation is assumed to be identical to the future situation being forecast. Alternatively, the assumption of constancy may involve a constant rate of change in the phenomenon being forecast. In any event, a key requirement would seem to be some underlying assumption about a theory that explains the behaviour in question.

Generally speaking, these are the more important elements of "forecasting."[5] One might alternatively think about what a forecast is in terms of the doing of the act itself. By understanding how it is done, one may come to understand more about what it is and ultimately why it is necessary. Reflection suggests that in the most general of senses, forecasts can be made in one of only three ways. There are only three logical approaches to obtaining information that will be useful in forecasting that uncertain future. The Delphic oracle, or tea leaves, or the behaviour of animals before earthquakes, or more modern methods such as regression or time series analysis all find their taxonomic roots in one of these three families of approaches.

The first method is to question those involved in the phenomenon requiring forecasting. Information as to their opinions and/or intentions is thus obtained and used to make forecasts about its future. The second is to attempt to relate various other phenomena to the one requiring forecasting. Knowing this relation, having the necessary information on these "related" phenomena, and assuming that such relations will not change in the future enables one to forecast the future. The third approach is to analyse the past nature of the phenomenon itself. Using only its history, and assuming that the underlying process that generated past events will remain constant into the future, one can extend the patterns present in the data into the future to make a forecast.

There are other issues in the etymology of forecasting that would contribute to better understanding. For example, there is the role of detached reflection on the effect that a change in the time horizon over which one is "casting" has on the sense of what one is doing.

As noted earlier, one might alternatively abandon the etymological route entirely in favour of the historical, systematically examining forecasting through the ages. One would look at questions such as when it arose and in what context, what factors made it important in certain times or contributed to its relative obscurity at others. Indeed both of these suggestions are examined further below.

But we still have not reached the heart of why we feel this need to forecast. Based on what I have said, and at the level of common sense, perhaps the explanation really is simple. While the future is unknown or uncertain, it is nonetheless very important. As Theil (1966) suggests: "One does not know for certain whether or not it will rain or snow when returning home in the evening. Assuming that it is necessary to decide in the morning before leaving the house whether or not one should take a coat and boots [i.e. returning home later to get them (or wet in the evening) is assumed to be very inconvenient!], one is forced to make a prediction of the alternatives of rain or snow vis à vis no rain or snow at the end of the day in order to make a decision in the morning."

Situations such as this can occur on a larger scale and over a longer time horizon. Consider the government policy-maker who wants to know how things will look next year so that he can act now to change taxes or the money supply, or the sales manager who would like forecasts of future sales so that he can act now to improve sales if the forecast is bad. Over a longer time horizon, a prediction of the world's population in the year 2000 is crucial for determining what steps should be taken now to begin mining the sea for food.

Uncertainty is present in each of these situations. Without uncertainty the required actions would be self-evident. One would know exactly what to do. Because uncertainty exists, and excepting a belief in complete predestination, we must forecast to try to reduce both uncertainty and its consequences.

While such an explanation is appealing, the simplicity is deceptive. What is uncertainty? How exactly does the forecast get rid of that uncertainty? Does it get rid of all of it, or only enough to reduce uncertainty to a point beyond which further forecasting is unnecessary? What determines that level, that tradeoff?

While the role of forecasting in human activity has surely interested others, in our time those most concerned with it have been economists and social psychologists. Consider for a moment what they have to say on some of these issues.

SOME INTELLECTUAL TRADITIONS BEARING ON THE MOTIVATION FOR FORECASTING

The Economics Connection

While they may not realize it, having preferred to work with "perfect certainty" assumptions, modern economists have had important things to say about "forecasting." They tend to speak of "expectations," a word taken from statistics (the "expected" value of a random variable) that for most purposes they treat as synonymous with forecast, or prediction.

Examples include Fisher's explanation in the 1920s and 1930s of the distinction between nominal and real rates (which relies in part on "expected" inflation); Keynes's explanation in the 1930s of the speculative demand for money (which relies in part on "expected" interest rates) or his discussion of planned investment and saving; oligopoly theory's discussion by Cournot and later others of the "expected" reaction functions of rivals; the cobweb theorem's explanation of the price behaviour of suppliers (which assumes supply is a function of "expected" price); Friedman's permanent income hypothesis (which involves a rather specific sense of "expected" income); and finally the most recent introduction of "rational expectations" to macroeconomic theory by Lucas and others.

For economists, expectations develop out of a "rational" need to deal with the uncertain future. Whether or not to forecast, and how much of it to indulge in, are issues of the value of reducing uncertainty below what it would have been without forecasting, relative to the cost of doing so. Viewed in Marshallian marginal terms (e.g. Stigler 1961), economic theory suggests that one should forecast up to the point where marginal benefits equal marginal costs.[6]

Consider a simple example. Assume that nature manifests itself in one of only three ways ("states"), A, B, or C. These states have a probability of occurrence of 0.3, 0.4, and 0.3, respectively. Given that there are two possible "actions," X or Y, that one might choose, each of which will yield some "payoff" under each state of nature, one can construct a payoff matrix of the following form:

State of nature	Likelihood of occurrence	Actions	
		X	Y
A	0.3	10	20
B	0.4	30	15
C	0.3	20	40

Under uncertainty, one would certainly choose action Y, since the expected value of Y, which is $24 - 0.3(20) + 0.4(15) + 0.3(40)$ – is greater than the expected value of X, which is 21. With perfect information, i.e. knowing exactly when A, B, and C would occur, one could expect a payoff of 30: $0.3(20) + 0.4(30) + 0.3(40)$. Hence the expected value of perfect information in these circumstances is 6. This expected value – the cost of uncertainty – provides the incentive for expending resources to forecast.[7]

Many examples of why individuals ("firms" in much of the analysis) would wish to forecast can be found in the mathematical micro-economics literature, e.g. Muth (1961), Pindyck (1982), and Krasker (1984). For the most part they deal with the many aspects of profit maximization under uncertainty, all the while assuming this "rational" motivation for the making of predictions.

Chapter 5 adopts a similarly rational but somewhat different economic approach to the characterization of the demand for forecasting. It argues that firms, and especially their managers, demand forecasts to demonstrate "reasonable care" in the use of shareholders' money; to spread the responsibility for mistakes; and to organize firm-consistent thinking at budget time or in the negotiating of internal contracts.[8] Some of these explanations are clearly consistent with the older microeconomic theme of forecasting being motivated by a need to reduce uncertainty, i.e. by a "desire to have a small part of the future truth revealed ahead of time." Some border on other behavioural, non-rational motivations; these are not, however, in the mainstream of economics research on forecasting. For the most part this research is macroeconomic in nature and revolves around the recent rational expectations revolution in that area of the subject.[9]

The rational expectations argument in macroeconomics accepts much of what has been said to this point. In particular it argues that all economic agents use all information rationally available to them in a rational manner, rational being taken to mean economically efficient.[10] Several review articles, and at least three or four books, have appeared on this subject in the last few years. Shefferin (1983, 26) concludes: "It is difficult to find an area of economic thought that has not been affected." I agree. But, as is made clear in chapter 5, I am unhappy with the way in which such rational expectations have been characterized.

That there is a certain rationality to the need to forecast can surely not be doubted. That there is perfect rationality is a tautology. What is more, neither alternative tells us very much about why we get the actual forecasts we do – in their various forms, produced in various ways, and so on. For that, one needs a rational paradigm founded on a more traditional and institutional approach to theory, something that chapters 5 and 6 seek to provide; one also must turn to other, more behavioural reasons for forecasting, although rationality is obviously a behavioural explanation as well. Behavioural explanations are advanced principally by social psychologists. To the extent that they are more or less appropriate, they alter the emphasis from the economist's rationale to why it is that we forecast.

The Other Behavioural Sciences

That there are other, perhaps non-rational motives for forecasting is also clear. In chapter 5, for example, we will see that forecasts are often used as tools to motivate workers to greater efforts or rally them in times of difficulty. Consider the regularly inflated new car sales predictions made each year by the automobile companies. Certain other behavioural sciences, in particular social psychology, have looked at length into motives for forecasting. Again the literature is extensive.

It would seem, following Hogarth (1980), that social psychologists would agree with a number of the normative principles associated with rational choice behaviour in general. Forecasting is, as argued, the essential element. However, these experts, while they feel that people support such principles in the abstract, argue that actual behaviour in choice situations violates some of these principles, because of emotional state, the manner in which the situation is structured (by the decision-maker/forecaster), and limitations in natural ability to process available information.[11]

Examples of emotional factors would be regret for taking, or failing to take, an action; feeling less responsible for 'acts of God' (compared to "imprudent" behaviour) than is warranted by the actual statistical probabilities; and anxiety or fear about the consequences of actions, which severely distorts information perception and processing. The structure of a situation is subject to all kinds of difficulty, revolving around how one perceives so-called cues to causality such as temporal order, similarity, and predictive validity. Spurious correlation is always a real danger, as is mistaking correlation for causation or vice versa. Finally there is simply too much information available to individuals, especially in complex choice situations involving uncertainty.[12] People tend to simplify forecasting, making choices in circumstances such as these by using "simple rules of thumb" (heuristics) or with other decision aids.

These conclusions lead to all kinds of difficulties when it comes to forecasting, introducing into the process behaviour that is strictly non-rational when viewed ex post facto but that nevertheless grows out of the peculiarity that is the human character.

I have, for example, argued above that forecasting implies some reliance on historical information and a certain assumption of constancy. This requires that people "learn" from the past. The problem is that in many judgmental situations we cannot get all the data needed to deduce relationships. Moreover, we often seek data to confirm pre-existing ideas rather than to disprove them. In this context positive feedback usually gets weighed more heavily than negative. Thus our learning is deficient, biased, and wholly inappropriate. Further, and because of some of these characteristics, imagination comes to affect not only what is learned but what forecast develops from this learning and how it gets evaluated after the fact. Thus those of us with less creative imagination will learn something different from a given set of facts, make different predictions from that learning, and evaluate that performance differently from others with more creative imagination. So too will those of us with a better memory.

Hogarth (1980, 107) concludes that the "perception of events, their interpretation and extrapolation to future wants [i.e. prediction] thus depends on a limited, fallible, incomplete system which is held together by the meaning given to events in the environment, such meaning itself being a function of previous perception and experiences." We are a long way indeed from the economists' rational expector unless one adopts so broad, and self-serving, a definition that rationality becomes a tautology.

But surely this is overstating the findings of these social scientists. What their literature is saying is that there are circumstances in which forecasts will deviate more from rationality than otherwise. But economists also surely have a point: it is unlikely that economic agents everywhere and at all times will long survive in a climate of consistently and completely irrational expectations, no matter what the source of that irrationality. One thinks of our earlier example (see note 10) of those workers' stubborn persistence, or wrong perception, with respect to inflation expectations. There would almost surely be some movement towards rationality, the extent to which it remains bounded, that is unattainable or sub-optimal, being again a function of circumstances that generally lead to less than perfect rationality.

CONCLUSIONS AND AN OUTLINE

We are thus a bit closer to understanding why forecasting exists, why we seem almost to "need" to forecast. But in another way we have not made all that much progress.

"Foretelling/casting" has always been with us. Careful consideration of the terminology as well as the act itself suggests that it is an important part of our desires and efforts to control our destiny in an uncertain future. It may be more or less scientific or superstitious depending on the age and the sense one gives to the terms. But economists, social psychologists, and others who have studied the issue carefully agree that forecasting is a "rational" response, when done rationally, although it often has irrational aspects to it. Finally, it seems very age-dependent: in some periods it is important and socially well organized, in others less so. We live in a period where the former is the case.

That it is the case today is particularly true with respect to forecasting economic conditions – as well as weather and political conditions, which are not completely inseparable from economics, considering the role of weather in crop failure or that of governments in setting economic policy. Firms and governments all have quite substantial internal structures devoted to strategic planning.[13] They require economic forecasting, especially at the aggregate level of the nation or international and sub-national groupings. Thus if we are to understand the role of forecasting in human activity more generally, it is sensible to concentrate on aggregate economic forecasting.

This is not the only way to approach the subject. As noted above, a systematic historical study such as that of Landes to the measurement of time would also be extremely informative. Indeed some of this is attempted in chapters 3 and 4. But we can learn also from the study of how we in Canada organize forecasting, not so much at the level of the individual economic agent, who has been studied to death by the traditions already discussed, but rather at the aggregate levels.[14]

First, however, I shall review briefly the methods used to make aggregate economic forecasts in Canada (chapter 2). I have found, much to my surprise, that most people don't know how these forecasts are made.

Chapters 3 and 4 outline the modern history of aggregate economic forecasting in Canada; 5 and 6 describe the industry that has grown up in our time to satisfy the demand for this kind of prediction. Chapters 7 and 8 discuss the all-important question of accuracy and review the record of Canadian forecasters over time.

Chapter 9 contains some reflections on the public policy aspects of economic forecasting. In ancient Greece, who determined the fee that the Delphic oracle received? Who controlled the appointment of a new oracle when the old one died? Who guaranteed harm-free access to the Oracle, which indeed there was? In modern times, these and related questions involve considerations such as whether economic forecasters ought to be held liable for inaccurate predictions. Should they come under the truth-in-advertising laws? Should they be subject to regulation, to public-sector competition, or even to outright public ownership? Also considered in chapter 9 is the contribution that Canadian aggregate economic forecasting makes to policy-making. The discussion contains a thinly veiled plea for greater understanding of forecasting's true role in society.

Chapter 10 returns to review what has been uncovered about this curious and arcane subject. Perhaps we will have come to understand it better; perhaps we may come to agree with Hardy that we "don't altogether believe in forecasts, come to second thoughts on such." Let us find out which it will be.

CHAPTER TWO

Methods

"By the sun, moon, and stars ... "

Through time, the methods used for making aggregate economic forecasts have included almost everything conceivably of use, ranging from sunspots to tea leaves to elaborate mathematical models of the economic behaviour of nations. Books, indeed entire libraries, have been devoted to certain methods. One can cite immediately regression analysis in the modern era, and alchemy in the medieval. Thus it is presumptuous in a chapter such as this to attempt to discuss them all. Even omitting the non-modern approaches does not narrow the field appreciably: there are a great number of modern instruments that could be, and indeed are, brought into play.

These methods can be thought of in terms of three groups. One assumes that the appropriate way to make predictions is to survey people about their intended actions.[1] If they do not change their opinions in the time between being surveyed and acting, and if one has a representative survey, one can make a forecast of their future actions.

The other two groups of methods are ultimately causative in concept, but each interprets "causative" differently. The first group uses direct causative "bridges" to model behaviour and thus make predictions. Thus the argument behind forecasting consumption by Canadians in 1987 would go as follows. Theory and observation tell us that consumption is caused by (is a function of) income, wealth, personal taxes, and several other factors. By careful observation, and using appropriate statistical methods, we can estimate the nature of this relationship. Assuming that this estimated relationship will continue to hold over the next year, and assuming that we have forecasts of the values of the important "causing" variables such as income, then we can predict consumption.

The second group uses a broader sense of causation, arguing that there are a host of factors that "cause," for example, personal consumption. The best representation we have of their net effect is contained in the value for personal consumption itself.[2] Thus studying only past observations of personal consumption for regularities such as trends or cycles, and projecting these patterns into the future, will provide a forecast. "Eye-balling" or "back-of-the-enveloping" are more colloquial descriptions of this approach.

The time horizon over which one is forecasting is also an important element. In fact, for certain people in the profession horizon is at least as important as method.[3] Thus forecasting situations are sometimes classified as short-term (immediate), medium, or long-term. Such a division is perhaps natural, and we will adopt it to a limited extent in what follows. Unstated in such an approach is the belief that certain time horizons are easier to forecast than others. In particular it is usually believed that the long-term future is more difficult to predict than the short-term because there is far less change in the underlying "structure" determining events.[4] Hence it may require different approaches.

In fact, cultural, political, economic, and technological factors influencing the future are identical in the short and long run. Consequently, in principle at least, method is also invariant with respect to horizon. But in practice choice of method is often driven by other considerations, which lead almost inevitably to the use of certain approaches to forecasting over certain horizons. Considering that many long-term forecasts require one to predict further into the future than one has data from the past, it is not surprising that one finds survey approaches being used more frequently than regression.

The relative importance of those factors determining the future changes as one moves out over different forecasting horizons. In the very longest of the long run, technology will probably determine what the future will look like. Thus it is the trend, or rate, of technological innovation or diffusion that will require forecasting.[5] Methods for doing this, such as deterministic extrapolation or juries of expert opinion, are different from methods in shorter-run horizons, where the effect of international and domestic political, economic, meteorological, and a host of other directly causative variables would require attention. And in the very shortest of short runs it is likely that all else will remain fairly constant, and straightforward extrapolative approaches, using certain time series methods, can sensibly be used.

Thus one of the more important dimensions of forecasting is this question of time horizon. It orients the forecaster and influences his or her choice of instruments. However, it is less important, in my view, than the causative-non-causative distinction made earlier. Therefore, in what follows, the classification of methods follows principally the latter distinction rather than the former. Where appropriate, I treat longer-term considerations separately.

CAUSATIVE APPROACHES

Regression Analysis

Perhaps because we live in an age that seeks rigorously to explain the causes of things, regression is the king of the modern aggregate economic forecasting methods. As noted in chapter 3, it was not always thus: time-series analysis at one time enjoyed greater popularity. But at present regression analysis,[6] in both its simpler and more complex forms, is in evidence everywhere.

Regression analysis is, at base, a formal statistical approach to identifying relationships between two or more variables. The variable causing another variable is called independent; the one that is influenced by that same variable is dependent. An indication of relationship could be, and virtually always is, derived from some theory such as that consumption is caused in part by income. But it might also be due to simple observation about causal ordering.

If only one dependent variable is thought to be caused by only one independent variable, the regression is said to be univariate, or simple. If one dependent variable is caused by a collection of independent variables, then the regression is multiple (or multivariate). Where a family of dependent variables is caused by a collection of independent variables all acting interrelatedly, the situation is described as a system of regression equations, or a simultaneous equation system. Most large-scale economic models used for forecasting are based on such a system.[7]

As a consequence, the forecaster has to address several issues when using this method. The first concerns the general nature of the relation between dependent and independent variable(s). The second is the exact nature of such a relationship. These two issues taken together are said to be the problem of "estimating the parameters." Investigating this exactness, and indeed the relevance of the supposed relationship, is the third consideration. At last one is ready to forecast using the relationship.

To address some of these issues, professional practice suggests beginning by plotting variables, for example, in a pair-wise fashion. In the simplist, univariate case this will usually suffice to establish whether there is any relationship, and what its general nature is (principally whether it is linear or non-linear). In most instances the relationship, or some simple transformation of it, can be satisfactorily approximated by linear assumptions, whether it be univariate or multivariate.[8]

The next task involves estimating the exact nature of this relationship. Since no line (in the univariate case) and no plane or hyperplane (multivariate) can ever pass through absolutely every observed point in such a plot, some summary sense of "closeness of fit" has to be adopted. Most commonly used is the criterion that the relationship summarized by the regression equation must minimize the sum of the squared vertical distance to the x axis between the points and the line described by that equation. Abundant theoretical analysis supports this choice. But other criteria, such as minimizing the mean absolute distances, could also be adopted. To the extent that they are, they will summarize a somewhat different sense of cause and hence lead to different forecasts.

However, assuming that the usual criterion is used, estimates of the parameters that describe the line can be mathematically derived directly, as can the limits of confidence within which one can be reasonably certain that the true values of these parameter estimates lie.[9] This latter point is at once critical and subtle. The forecaster clearly recognizes that he/she has only a given set of data on the variables in question. Another sample under different circumstances would almost certainly yield different results. What is wanted is some sense, from this one given set of data, of what the range of estimates might be, given that the only, and hence best, estimate one has of the parameters is from this present sample.

But the setting of the limits of one's confidence is tricky. Convention suggests, for example, 95 per cent certainty, i.e. 1 chance of error in 20. But such odds are very much determined by the cost of making a wrong inference and, more crucially here, eventually a wrong forecast. Consider, for example, whether 95 per cent limits are appropriate if one is using such a model to predict whether the

Russians have just launched an intercontinental ballistic missile attack! Thus one's ideas about the required accuracy of forecasts come to play an important part in decisions about its acceptability.

To see this in another way, consider in particular whether the estimated confidence limits include zero. Alternatively one can ask whether the parameter estimates differ significantly from zero and whether they have the directional influence expected a priori. Does consumption, for example, go up when income goes up (i.e. is the sign of the income coefficient positive)? If not, but again as a function of the cost of being wrong in one's inference, or inaccurate in one's subsequent forecast of the dependent variable, there is no causal relationship to be exploited for predictive purposes.

This exercise of checking for the relevance of the hypothesized relationship is part of regression analysis diagnostics. That exercise at best is painstakingly carried out, at worst completely ignored. Usually it is preceded by careful checking to see whether the data used, and hence the resulting estimated model, conform to their assumed statistical character. If not, there is naturally a question of whether the inference one draws, and in consequence the forecasts one makes, are justified. Much of this diagnostic checking is done with regard to the estimated residuals from the model. In theory the true residuals for which these are estimates are assumed to be randomly distributed and average zero. If these assumptions don't hold for the estimated ones, it is evidence that the estimates of the parameters themselves may be in error.

Various possibilities exist. The residuals may be not random but rather serially correlated (the problem of "autocorrelation") with one another, as when a variable is left out or a non-linear relationship is thought linear. They may be systematically related to the size of the dependent or independent variable (heteroskedasticity), which is particularly prevalent when cross-sectional data are used to estimate regression equations.

Other statistical problems show up under the diagnostic microscope. One less directly of concern when forecasting is the existence of correlation between two or more of the independent variables. By assumption these influences must be independent of one another and additive in their impact on the dependent variable. If they are not, the estimated values for their respective parameters are incorrect. Alternatively, certain variables, or families of variables, may contain other variables within them. There then becomes a hierarchy of hypothesized relationships (nested hypotheses) that must be unravelled.

The litany of problems need not stop here. The data may, for example, be measured with error. In the wrong variable, such measurement error will cause problems. Alternatively, chunks of data may be missing because they weren't reported; or the definition of what is measured suddenly changes; or a strike or war makes the data unrepresentative for a time; or some of the variables can take on only two values (e.g. died, didn't die) while others that are causally related to them are more continuous; or not all of the causation working from the independent to the dependent variables happen all at once but has an effect only with time (or is distributed over time); and so on.

Ways of dealing with these problems have developed over time. Some are rather statistically sophisticated, others ruthlessly improvisational. Virtually every use of regression analysis is thus an exercise of judgment, which involves the delicate balancing of data dictates and statistical rigour against the costs of additional time and effort.

Particularly interesting in this regard for forecasting purposes is the problem of independent variable(s) value(s) precondition. If consumption in a given year is thought to be caused by income in this period $(C_t = \alpha + \beta Y_t + e_t)$, then in addition to the estimated model a forecast of consumption for next year will first require a forecast of income next year. Where is one to obtain this? And is the forecast of consumption then not at the direct mercy of the accuracy of the forecast of income?

Answers to these questions suggest that only if a) the forecasts of the independent variables(s) are much better (for example, more directly, or cheaply, available) than those of the dependent variable(s), and b) one is quite sure of the estimated model, ought regression analysis to be used to forecast. Otherwise it might well be better simply to use time series or survey approaches to predict the dependent variable directly, unless, of course, we can argue that the effects on the dependent variable(s) happen only with lags as, for example, in the case where this year's consumption is caused by last year's income $(C_t = \alpha + \beta Y_{t-1} + e_t)$. In these circumstances forecasts of the dependent variable(s) can be conditioned on known values of the independent ones. However, we are not always able to model behaviour this way. We are thus stuck with having to forecast a set of variables before using those forecasts to forecast another set, definitely not a reassuring situation! But such a practice is all too common and indeed explains much of the predictive failings, or limitations, of these causative approaches (especially in large-scale systems of such equations) in several important instances in the past decade or so.

Despite these and the many other potential difficulties noted, and still others not noted, regression analysis continues to enjoy a status akin to that of tea leaves or astrology in other times. Responsibly used, it is invaluable in aggregate economic forecasting. Badly, or unethically, done, it leads to forecasts that are completely wrong, misleading, and manipulative.

Simultaneous Equations

As has already been suggested, a system of such linear equations is ultimately the most complex way to characterize a nation's economy.[10] Models in principle, and in practice, run to hundreds, even thousands, of equations. When the structure of these models involves more than one equation, there is a mammoth task involved in conceiving of the system itself, collecting all the appropriate data, estimating all the equations (which may or may not be done using the approaches discussed above), carefully checking all the diagnostics after such estimation, and developing all the forecasts of the truly independent (exogenous) variables needed for forecasting. Indeed it grows so dramatically as one adds equations that almost all of this work is done by teams, often at the expense of the public purse (see chapters 3 and 4).

The major difficulty involves the simultaneity of relationships. Suppose one hypothesizes that the following system of two equations represents the economy: $C_t = \alpha + \beta Y_t + e_t$ and $C_t + I_t = Y_t$. Here the first equation, in which consumption is caused by income, is related to the second, where investment, assumed to be determined outside, or exogeneous, to the model (perhaps by direct government policy) and consumption combine to define income.[11] Assuming that one has estimated the behavioural relation and knows the value of the exogeneous variable, the system can be solved simultaneously for values of C and Y.[12]

Viewed at this small-scale level, the problems seem perhaps minor. But suppose we now expand this system to hundreds or thousands of equations, drawing in various sectors of the economy, modelling foreign trade, and so on. Think of the number of variables involved, of the co-ordination and conceptual problems associated with ensuring the internal consistency of all the interlinkages in a modern market economy, of just making sure the model will eventually solve. Then one has to estimate all of those equations one by one, checking diagnostics one by one, solving data-related problems one by one! As mentioned, slightly different, but still regression, approaches are usually required.[13] That does not make the work any easier.

Finally, when one has dealt with all these issues and verified that the model tracks the economy's past well, it is time to use it to forecast. The procedure is analogous to that discussed for the single regression equation discussed earlier. Forecasts of all the exogenous variables are collected and plugged into the model, buttons are pushed, and the computer is left to find the solution simultaneously consistent with values for all the variables. One can almost imagine it "trial and erroring" along, checking here and there. In reality, solution algorithms are used for dealing with these large matrix algebra problems.

One might suppose that when it is all done, something pretty terrific in the way of forecasts would have been generated. "After all, think of what we have done!" And for a while a lot of people did, not only the builders of the models themselves, who took justifiable pride in their accomplishments, but many other people as well. But the reader is able by now to understand that these models were bound to be in error when used strictly as forecasting instruments. The added complexity ensured nothing in this respect, not only because independent forecasts of the exogeneous variables would always be required to drive the models, but also because the many problems of conceiving and estimating the models themselves could never be eliminated. Judgment would always play a role. And judgment can, and always eventually does, lead to inaccurate forecasts.

However, these larger model systems are still much used for making economic forecasts. They are, among other things, wonderful tools for ensuring that forecasts are internally consistent and conform more or less with observed past, if not necessarily future, behaviour. As well, detailed investigation of the implications of one's larger-variable forecasts can be carried out. No better way is available to see the effect of a given forecast of interest rates on "that little corner of the economy way off over there." Moreover, model-builders have struggled with some of the problems, constructing deliberately smaller models that are more oriented to forecasting. And with time people who use them to forecast, and buy forecasts made using them, have become more aware of what they are getting from the exercise. We cannot expect much more, since all forecasts, no matter how large, elaborate, or elegant their statistical origins, will still come from basically judgmental procedures.

Input-Output Analysis

Another technique that is conceptually similar to, and sometimes used with, these larger system models (e.g. in the CANDIDE model of the Economic Council of Canada mentioned in chapter 4) is input-output (I-O) analysis. Originally developed by Leontief in the 1930s, and used heavily in centrally planned economies, it is a special form of general equilibrium analysis that breaks the economy up into sectors and estimates the flow of goods and services between them.

Consider, for example, the situation in which someone buys a television instead of taking his or her usual summer vacation at the lake. With a sufficiently minute breakdown of the economy, one could see what such a change implies in terms of changes in passenger transportation and hotel business. Certain people would be laid off, orders for new equipment cancelled. Construction would fall in these industries. However, in the television industry, more workers would be hired, plants built, and the like. These are known as the direct effects of the individual's decision. But there are second-order or indirect effects as well: discharged workers in the transportation and hotel industries will themselves change their behaviour, e.g. by buying less food and housing.[14] There is thus a rippling or indirect effect felt throughout the economy, which is principally a function of how interdependent the sectors are.

Input-output analysis permits us to measure both the direct and the total effects of such changes in economic activity.[15] These estimates are reported in the form of tables of input-output coefficients.[16] These give the information on what fraction of a dollar's output for a given industry must be forthcoming from all other industries which supply inputs to it, either at the first, or direct stage (given in the direct requirements table) or after all these rippling effects have taken place (found in the total requirements table).[17]

The principles involved and the calculations needed – but certainly not data collection, which is laborious and time consuming – are quite straightforward. So too is the use of input-output analysis as a forecasting tool.

With respect to the latter, there are two ways to employ it. One might forecast output levels using an econometric model and then employ the i-o tables to see what predictions of input requirements are implied. If these projections are consistent with economic and technical capabilities, the forecaster has a valid method for prediction. Such an approach has the benefit of identifying bottlenecks or obvious violations of constraints and common sense. In this case, final output predictions, or production process characteristics, will have to be changed. Alternatively, one might insert predictions of relevant inputs obtained elsewhere to calculate the implication in terms of final outputs.

There are, of course, problems with this method, as with any forecasting tool. These stem principally from the assumptions required of anyone wishing to use it for forecasting. They include assumptions that multi-product firms are in the industry of their major product; that input-output coefficients calculated for the industry as a whole apply to each firm; that all firms vary output together as final demand changes; that there is no change in the input-output coefficients between measurement times because of, for example, technological change; and finally that all changes of output, no matter how big or small, will always be in a fixed proportion to the input mix. The latter assumption means that no capital-labour substitution is permissible.

These problems, and several others not mentioned, are heroic in nature. But then so too are a number of assumptions needed to use regression analysis. Nonetheless, and again provided the forecaster is careful and willing to accept the required theoretical assumptions, input-output analysis is of value in making forecasts of both aggregate inputs and outputs.

TIME SERIES METHODOLOGY

Early Smoothing and Decomposition Approaches

For many, time series approaches are the most natural of the three families of forecasting methods. They were certainly the most important of the early modern methods. And while they have lost some pride of place, they still remain in use. They are, for example, at the heart of most common conceptions of the business cycle, seasonality, long waves in economic activity, and various other ways of structuring time.

As discussed above, all time series procedures generally have as a common conceptual base the attempt to characterize the history of the phenomenon in question in terms of patterns. These result from an unknown causing process that the user wishes to discover by inference from observing manifestations of it. One almost inevitably brings some preconception of the pattern, however broadly or narrowly restrictive, to the data. In the early modern period, these preconceptions were as often as not strongly influenced by technological constraints having to do with the processing of large amounts of data – just as was the case for regression analysis. With the advent, and advances, of computing capacity, other, more sophisticated approaches have been added. Now time series methods run together with causative approaches in their more extensive, multivariate manifestations.

Three or four of these earliest methods are worth noting, for they remain part of forecasting method in important ways. They are part of what is known as deterministic, as opposed to stochastic, time series analysis.[18] They thus conceptually ignore randomness in the process manifestations, while stochastic methods include such error possibility.

The first of these earlier methods is a family in its own right, sometimes referred to as smoothing. Grouped within it are simple naive models, equally straightforward averaging and functional representations, and finally such relatively elaborate approaches as exponential smoothing, which at present is enjoying a renaissance in economics – it has always remained an important tool in engineering analysis and prediction. Naive models include such possibilities as the argument that the next period's observation will be the same as this period's, or that it will be equal to this period's plus the change between this period and the previous period, or equal to an average of the two, three, four ... previous period's values, or to what it was last year in the same month, or ... [19] The list is potentially endless, limited only by one's imagination or the larceny in one's soul. These simple approaches are often used as benchmarks, i.e. relatively costless alternative approaches, against which to test the accuracy of more elaborate and costly forecasting methods. Given enough time and ingenuity, one can almost always come up a posteriori with one of these naive models, the forecasts of which will outperform the most expensive alternative. Hence the reference to larceny!

Perhaps the first and most developed of these approaches to emerge, one that in fact has some behavioural theory implicit in it and was relatively easy to calculate in pre-computer days, was exponential smoothing (not to be confused with the fitting of an exponentially increasing function in time, which we will meet in a moment). Exponential smoothing argues that next period's observation will be equal to some weighted average of previous period observations, with more weight in that average being given to more recent observations. In particular, the most recent will get the largest weight, the previous ones exponentially less, in principle back to the first observation, which would thus have an infinitely small weight. In practice, this latter conceptual problem is addressed with appropriate differencing techniques.[20] To estimate the appropriate model, various values for the weights are tried, the one-step-ahead forecasts are checked, and that value is chosen that minimizes the sum of the squared errors (the same criterion used in connection with regression analysis) between the actual data points and the best model's estimate of them. These estimates are thus often referred to as the smoothed values of the basic data. Exponential smoothing lies at the heart of, for example, Friedman's empirical work on the consumption function, and is also used extensively in production planning circles at the level of the firm.

The second of these earliest methods involved the fitting of simple functional forms in time to the data. Various models, again limited mostly by one's ingenuity, could be, and were, used. They included models in which the observed data were assumed to be a simple linear, or a more complicated polynominal, function in time. Exponential functions in time, and logistic curves or others that involve natural floors or ceilings in their formulations, were also used.[21] Such simple functional models remain the basis for making casual longer-range forecasts and are discussed more fully in this respect below.

The third method, a special type of the first family of averaging methods, came to enjoy particular favour in its own right. For years it was *the* way in which data were disassembled into components, in particular into trend, cycle, and season. It is known as classical time series decomposition and exists today, particularly for deseasonalizing data.

The method is quite straightforward. Any given data point involving subannual division (e.g. total beer sales in Canada in June 1985) is assumed to be the net result of the joint multiplicative influence of four factors – a trend (or longer-term influence), a cycle (hence the term "business cycle," which may vary for different industries and also be defined for the economy as a whole), a season, and finally an irregular component. Thus $B_t = T \times C \times S \times I$. To isolate the trend and cyclical components an ad hoc smoothing, often a moving average, procedure is calculated. In this case it would likely be a twelve-month moving average. That average value, being presumed relatively free of seasonal and irregular components, is thus an estimate of $T \times C$, and if the original data are divided by it, one is left with $S \times I$ (i.e. $TCSI/TC = SI$). The next step eliminates the irregular component by averaging the $S \times I$ values corresponding to the same month, thus providing the average seasonal factor. Dividing the original data by it would, it was argued, "deseasonalize" the data, leaving behind, or uncovering, the underlying trends in the data.

To forecast with the method, one would project the moving average (TC) using the other deterministic approaches discussed earlier, multiply that value(s) by the appropriate seasonal factor(s), S, and presto, forecast(s) for the appropriate period(s) ahead! The approach was (and still is in certain places) used extensively to deseasonalize all economic data and thus to make time series-based forecasts of the underlying trends in economic aggregates, such as real GNP.

These are the more important of the deterministic time series methods in use. As I said, they enjoyed much early favour, principally because of ease of calculation. Moreover, while they brought certain structural preconceptions to the data, these did not seem to offend against common sense. After all, didn't everyone know that most everything was affected by trend, cyclical, seasonal, and random or irregular components? Weren't the data clearly increasing exponentially over time? Didn't people use more of the most recent evidence in forecasting the future and less of the more distant past? And so on.

With time, though, computing capacity grew. As it did, time series methods, which required less structure and permitted error within their statistical formulations, could be entertained. And they were. But, as noted, deterministic approaches remain part of the methodological picture in forecasting.

Indicator Analysis

Before passing on to newer approaches, one additional early time series-related method must be mentioned. It is not univariate but rather the earliest example of a kind of deterministic bivariate time series approach. It is, of course, indicator analysis.

To this point I have argued that time series methods relate purely and simply to the evidence from the data itself. Hence the term "univariate." However, people soon became interested in the relation of aggregate economic series to one another, independent of any particular theory.[22] Did one series have a peak in its cycle before another? Did they exactly mirror one another? Did one lag behind the other? Was the same relationship true at the trough as at the peak? Was the observed pattern regular over time? These and other questions were asked. If one were able to isolate consistent relationships like this, one could, for example, use those early peaking or troughing variables to signal or indicate that average economic activity – as measured, for example, by real output or industrial production – was also about to peak or trough, thus indicating an oncoming recession or upturn.

Thousands of statistical series were examined in this light, first for the United States in the 1930s by Mitchell and Burns in response to a request from President Franklin Roosevelt for some kind of early warning system for the economy as it struggled up out of the Depression, and later for other countries, in particular Canada in the early and mid-1950s by Beckett and Daly. Certain series, such as real GNP, that seemed to characterize the economy's actual state were grouped together, called coincident indicators, and used to define the reference path or cycle of the economy. Others, for example, the number of housing starts in urban areas, that led this reference cycle were called leading indicators and sometimes integrated into one figure, the index of leading indicators; still others that lagged behind it were called lagging indicators. To qualify, series had to demonstrate regularity of definition and appearance, show timeliness in their signalling (e.g. giving sufficient warning, in the case of leading indicators, before the subsequent reference cycle turning-point), and meet certain other standards as well.

Refined over the years by subsequent study, the indicator approach remains alive as an instrument for forecasting major turning-points in the economy. In Canada several banks and Statistics Canada regularly publish leading indicator statistics. Statistics Canada's practice is particularly interesting, since the work developed out of a direct use of the newer stoachastic time series approaches developed in the late 1960s and throughout the 1970s, a subject to which we now turn.

Stochastic Approaches

The arrival of stochastic modelling of time series data has profoundly affected forecasting. The names most associated with this work, like the models of a late 1960s and early 1970s vintage, are those of Box and Jenkins. Stochastic approaches assume that each observed value of the series to be forecast has been generated by a stochastic process, i.e. is drawn randomly from a probability distribution. In the simplest example – a random walk – each successive change in the variable is drawn independently from some such probability distribution which has a zero mean.[23]

I have learned, as no doubt have others, that a brief discussion of this method is impossible! The conception is puzzling to some, the mathematical notation used at first a problem to virtually all. However, there are ways to provide a flavour at least. In multiple regression analysis, a given dependent variable may be a function of a series of independent variables. If one replaces those independent variables with lagged values of the dependent variable, one uses the term "autoregression" (AR in the jargon) to describe the resulting equation. Exponential smoothing is thus a kind of autoregression. Alternatively, one might imagine that a given value of the series was some weighted influence, not so much of its previous values but of the previous shocks or errors that have affected it.[24] Box and Jenkins used the term "moving average" (MA) to describe the equation so formed, a confusing usage relative to the more traditional one, to which it bears little relation. Finally, autoregressive and moving average models can be coupled together to form a general family of time series models called, not surprisingly, autoregressive-moving average (ARMA) processes.[25]

For statistical reasons, this family of models can be used only with stationary variables, those that do not walk away from their average value. Since most economic series are non-stationary, principally because things grow over time, something must be done statistically to make them stationary. The customary procedure is to difference the data, which is called integrating the series (though it bears little resemblance to the calculus term of the same name). If a series has been so integrated before the models are estimated, it is subsequently referred to as an ARIMA process.

While this may seem like a lot of statistical structure, it really isn't. Rather it is extremely general and yet quite parsimonious. Most economic series require no more than a few terms for adequate characterization. Knowledge about the likely structure is obtained by studying the manner in which given observations correlate with successive previous ones, i.e. by examining the autocorrelation function of the observations. Different processes will result in different autocorrelation patterns.[26] By studying those patterns, one can infer what process lies behind them.

Once identified, the exact values for the parameters are estimated using the usual minimized sum of squared deviations. Various diagnostics are carried out to ensure that the necessary statistical assumptions are met. As with regression analysis, they generally involve checking to make sure that the unexplained or residual part of each data point is randomly distributed about zero. The final step, as always, involves using the model to forecast. In this case, unlike in deterministic models, this step can involve statistical confidence limits, since there are probability distributions involved.

This "Box-Jenkins" analysis has revolutionized time series methodology. As we shall see in a moment, it has its problems, recognition of which has blunted the initial rush to embrace it. But we have not yet finished with this structure. To understand this, it is important to ask why it is necessary to stop at this univariate stage. Might it not be possible to study the cross-correlations between various statistical series to find out if there are autoregressive or moving average relationships being transferred (one must estimate a transfer function in this work) from one variable to another? Might not a given series be the result not only of an autoregressive process in its own right but also of a moving average process of some related series?

Indeed, these things are possible, as Box and Jenkins showed. The procedures are once again complicated but manageable with appropriate computing hardware.

What should strike the reader is that this sounds suspiciously like causation. Or at the very least, if there is significant cross-correlation between two series, i.e. Y_t is highly correlated with X_{t-1}, one is tempted to speculate that X may be causing Y.[27]

To close the circle, suppose that, using regression analysis and basing one's work on good economic theory, one finds a significant relationship between X and Y, thereby implying cause, while multivariate Box-Jenkins time series analysis methods, based on good statistical theory and applied to the same data, indicate no causality. What is one then to infer about the acceptability of the theory? This dilemma caused, and continues to cause, much heated discussion, for cases such as this began to show up in economics. Indeed, the whole question of causality, and the value of the econometrician's entire collection of analytical methods, has been much questioned of late as a consequence of this particular "worm," which continues to turn.[28]

This is, of course, cold comfort to the aggregate economic forecaster who must use the method. It is one of the reasons why there has been less than enthusiastic adoption of these Box-Jenkins techniques. There are other problems with it as well. Data requirements are substantial, interpretation of autocorrelation function patterns and diagnostics is somewhat judgmental (whether more so than with regression analysis is also the subject of debate), and the consequent predictions are of questionable character except in the relatively short run.[29] This latter result is particularly galling, given the amount of effort one puts in getting to that stage only to realize, indeed realizing all along, that the optimal forecast from the model very quickly becomes the mean of the observed series! Nevertheless the approach remains the most statistically sound of the time series methods currently in use, and as such it deserves consideration by the forecaster, where circumstances warrant.

Longer-Horizon Methods: Time Series

Finally a word on longer-horizon methods. Time series approaches are one of the two major families of methods most frequently used for long-term forecasting. Surveys are the other. For the most part the functional forms in time mentioned above are the most frequent. Countless examples exist; perhaps the most famous was the Club of Rome study by Meadows and others during the mid-1970s. It made extensive use of exponential growth curves to forecast population, oil consumption, and certain other variables. Not surprisingly, catastrophe was predicted to occur eventually.

This result was instructive not so much for the substance as for showing the care one needs to exercise when doing longer-term extrapolations. In particular one must recognize that variables may well have natural, or economic, upper bounds that cannot be violated. Thus if oil prices grew exponentially, sooner or later no one would use oil. Still another common mistake is to extrapolate further into the future than one has data from the past, predicting, for example, 20 years ahead on the basis of a curve fitted to 10 years of data from the past. This was essentially Kondratieff's mistake.

Various methods have been tried for getting around these problems in long-term forecasting. One such tool is morphological analysis, another cross-impact analysis. The former enjoys an old history, dating back at least to Ramon Llull, the mystic monk of the 13th century, who built his well-known forecasting wheel. Descartes and Leibniz commented on Llull as did Swift, satirically, in *Gulliver's Travels* (the calculating machine of the savant of Lilliput). What the method does is relate in a systematic fashion all possible combinations of occurrences in the future.

Consider as an example the problem of forecasting what the economy will be like in 15 years. There are a number of parameters of interest: prices, output, unemployment, interest rates, exchange rates, and the foreign trade balance. Assume that each can take on three possible states, high, stable, or falling. Attach probabilities to each set (e.g. high 0.5, stable 0.4, falling 0.1). Now have a computer print out all possible combinations along with their probability rating, arrived at, for example, by multiplying across the individual probabilities. One such combination might be falling prices, falling output, high unemployment, a deficit on foreign trade, i.e. a full-blown depression with probability of occurrence 0.027. Low-probability combinations can be grouped and their characteristics studied, as can high ones.

As a consequence, the technique is valuable for identifying gaps in one's conception of the future or for showing that the interaction of a collection of low-probability events can lead to a quite impossible general result. This is of particular value in technological forecasting. One aviation engineer used it to identify various possible configurations for jet engines that had not before been envisaged. But it is essentially a routine for identifying possible futures that requires "not the least help of genius" (Swift), except maybe in structuring the problem. As such, it deserves only passing notice.

SURVEYING

Introduction

Most aggregate phenomena depend on the total net outcome of individual decisions, whether taken by a few or a great many people, independently or through complex interactions, with a relatively high or low degree of control and reliability. Such events, actions, or developments range from a government budget to the outcome of an election, from the introduction of a new product to overall manufacturing and trade sales, from job vacancies in Toronto today to the prospects for total unemployment in Canada next year. Common sense suggests that in many such cases one promising way to predict what is likely to happen is to question the individuals directly concerned with the given phenomenon as to their opinions, plans, or intentions. This information can then be used to construct a forecast or to confirm, modify, or reject a forecast already made by other methods.[30] A survey of consumer or business buying plans offers a familiar example.

Not surprisingly, the idea that all that is needed to predict what people will do is to ask them is not only attractively but also deceptively simple. For one thing, the assumptions implicit in a prediction by survey are that the persons questioned are properly selected for the purpose at hand, which presumably means that they know their minds, that is, have relevant opinions, anticipations, or intentions; are able to verbalize their views or decisions accurately; and do not change their minds in any systematic or significant way between the time of the survey and the time of the event or action to be predicted. This is almost never exactly the case. And as a consequence, making predictions by means of a survey operational is fraught with danger.

One must be concerned with several questions, such as the choice of people to be interviewed, methods of interviewing, and questions to be asked. Let us begin with the choice of people to be surveyed.

Conceptually, two classes of people might be distinguished here – "experts" and "agents." Experts are those who possess pertinent information about the subject of the given survey or at least are more knowledgeable about it than others. Agents are those who take decisions and actions directly related to the events or variables surveyed. In practice, experts and agents may or may not be different individuals, depending on the objectives and conditions of the study. For example, if responsible business executives are asked about their company plans for new capital budget outlays in the next year, it is a survey of agents. If business economists advising the same corporation executives are asked about their forecasts of total national investment in plant and equipment during the same period, it's a survey of experts.

With these two distinctions in mind, let's briefly look at some general methodological issues. Following that, a few existing aggregate economic surveys of intentions and anticipations will be mentioned, as will some longer-horizon methods.

Issues in Surveying

Suppose that someone wishes to predict one or more variables that can be investigated by means of a survey. One can use an existing survey that collects the necessary information or conduct one's own survey. A firm might do a marketing survey by itself or by contract with a professional in the field if existing surveys do not collect the required information.

In general, it is clearly either impossible or impractical to solicit and collect responses from all individuals who can contribute useful information about the variables in question. Nor is it necessary. One can, as a rule, infer the true state of the variable in the population as a whole by surveying a suitably chosen sample of individuals.[31]

Common sense suggests that decisions on several things will have to be made as a consequence. Besides having to decide exactly what information is needed, when it is to be collected, what degree of accuracy is required, and how much is to be spent, one must choose the design of the sample survey – who constitutes the population and how will one select those members who are to be asked the questions. In addition, it is necessary to decide upon the size of the sample, i.e. how many responses should be secured. Finally, the instrument for interviewing people must be chosen; those who will conduct the survey must be trained; and the manner of presenting the results must be decided.

Nothing general can be said on how to decide what information is needed, when to collect it, and how much money to spend. These issues are highly situation-specific. It is useful, however, to discuss briefly whom will be asked and how and how the data might be analysed. Finally, some ideas about what could go wrong would no doubt be welcome.[32]

There are two basic kinds of questions in thinking about whom to sample. The first is how many, which is one of optimal sample size; the second is in what fashion they will be chosen, which is one of optimal sample design. The best sampling designs will usually be probability-based, with samples being drawn on a random basis, even though in practice many designs are adopted for convenience or other strictly cost-related reasons.

Perhaps the best known design is simple random sampling from an entire population. It presupposes that one can identify each person in the population from, for example, a list and that the population is relatively homogeneous, or else has a wide variety of characteristics. If systematic differences, perhaps in income, age, education, or sex, are present, the design has to be altered to reflect these different classes or strata; hence "stratified" sampling. A third design, cluster or area sampling, is a distant cousin of both random and stratified sampling. Here the population is divided into natural units (e.g. counties in Ontario), those units are then drawn at random, and everyone within them is contacted. Finally, there are all manner of non-probabilistic designs, ranging from the relatively unsophisticated, convenience approach – asking the person in the street – to more elaborate quota sampling.

Sample size generally follows from the design decision. Quite elaborate statistical theory that fills books on surveying guides us in how best to decide this. The calculations involve things like the cost of interviewing, the desired level of confidence in the results obtained (a function of what is lost from a wrong forecast), and beliefs about the variability of the population's characteristics. It is a discussion best left to those books!

Logically, the next question to be considered after deciding on whom to survey is how to gather the information. By far the most frequent method is direct questioning.[33] There are three major routes – mail, phone, and personal interviewing. Mail interviews are widely used, being versatile and inexpensive, though many people will not respond. Telephone interviewing, originally favoured for quick surveying but restricted because of availability of phones, among other things, has recently grown in favour because of the increasing costs of personal interviewing and the ability to computer dial. Most preferred of all, costs permitting, is personal interviewing. Clarification, proper recording, and follow-up are all easier with personal interviewing than with mail or phone contacts. These different modes are not mutually exclusive; they can often be combined effectively. Each has its place, and that place may well be modified through time as technology and other factors change.

Once data are obtained from a survey, there are at least three ways to use them from a forecasting perspective.[34] First, a survey may provide information on anticipations or intentions directly, in which case it is simply a matter of aggregating things. Second, a survey may provide information on population characteristics, particularly the average (mean or median) and the dispersion of behaviour (range or variance). These estimates can then be used to prepare predictions about those variables. Third, such estimates can also be used to confirm or reject forecasts obtained by other approaches.

The second method is perhaps the least obvious.[35] Consider the simple example of wanting to predict the average monthly consumption of home heating oil by Canadian households. To do so we design a sample, select respondents, and find out not how much they intend to consume but how much they do consume, i.e. their estimate. From that exercise, and using that estimate, we can predict current Canadian consumption. Moreover, as many researchers acknowledge, that estimate may also be a better predictor of future consumption than asking for the forecasts of the same variable directly.[36] As a result, while a prediction may be conceptually different from an estimate, for many practical forecasting purposes it is useful to think of the two terms as synonymous.

There are many problems with surveying. The sample may not be representative; perhaps respondents can't be reached; there may be a discrepancy between what the respondent meant and what is recorded; interviewers may cheat. Careful craftsmanship will reduce the chances of error. It can never eliminate them completely.

Existing Canadian Aggregate Economic Forecasting Surveys

Two existing aggregate economic forecasting surveys are of particular note in Canada, the first, the Survey of Business Investment Intentions, the second, the Survey of Consumer Attitudes and Buying Plans.[37] The former is carried out by a department of the federal government, the latter by the Conference Board of Canada. As chapter 3 reveals, they both enjoy a long history.

Each year the investment intentions survey asks about 300 of Canada's largest companies (representing all sectors) for specific plans relating to the upcoming period, usually annually over a five-year horizon. Information is collected also on actual current investment spending. That way detailed information, by sector and for the economy as a whole, is available on what companies expect to invest and how accurate those expectations have been.

As we shall see below in chapter 7, the survey stands up to scrutiny quite well. Certainly errors are possible. Unforeseen delivery or construction delays, for example, will cause inaccuracy, especially in utilities or transportation and communication. But, on balance, such surveys are of value in predicting investment spending, especially for manufacturing.

The consumer attitudes and buying plan survey, which is a monthly exercise, gathers information of two types, thoughts about the general state of the economy and buying plans. Answers to questions such as "Do you expect to buy or build a house for your own year-round use during the next twelve months?" are used to form two indices, one of attitudes, the other of buying plans. Again problems can develop. For example, respondents may not be able to indicate exactly their opinions or to attach probabilities to what they intend to buy.

Much contention surrounds the use of these measures of consumer sentiment for forecasting consumption behaviour. In the late 1950s and early 1960s it was one of the more important topics in economics. Several studies were done at that time, and since, on whether such indices add anything to the explanatory or predictive power of more traditional causative models of consumer behaviour which stress income, interest rates, and other variables. Although his findings can be questioned, Angevine (1974), using Canadian data, concluded they did. The literature suggests that, by itself, the survey will not result in very accurate predictions of actual consumer behaviour. But the results are of important judgmental value, especially in periods of highly volatile consumption expenditures. Aggregate economic forecasters continue to pay some attention to them.

Longer-Horizon Methods: Surveys

As noted in the time series discussion earlier, surveys are the other major way to make forecasts over the long term. The practice of asking people of supposed "intuitive powers" for their predictions of the future is as old as man himself. Indeed, in the case of the prophets and others, these opinions often were, and are, forthcoming without being requested! Another age's "wise old men" are today's "experts," particularly as most long-term prediction today involves technology and its likely evolution.

Ideally, one would prefer the opinion of one person, that particular "genius" whose "vision" sees through the mist clearest. However, when the genius of the genius is in question, as it normally is, the tendency is to rely on a survey or poll of such geniuses.[38] For important psychological reasons, such polls are known to have a conservative bias in their predictions. Techniques such as brainstorming or role playing have been introduced to circumvent this. One in particular, the Delphi method, does not have these experts meeting face to face. Rather each is polled individually. The results for the group are reported to each participant, and he or she is asked if first estimates are now to be revised. This iterative process can be repeated, if necessary, until a consensus is reached. Usually only one such iteration is involved.

One could give countless examples of how these methods have been used to make long-term forecasts. They were (are) the very heart and soul of the so-called futures approach to forecasting, which enjoyed a brief period of success in the 1970s but has since nearly vanished. The particular product of this school was often a "scenario," describing what that future world would be like. "In the Canadian Arctic Islands by 2000, $1\frac{1}{3}$ billion barrels of oil will have been produced, a prototype nuclear-powered submarine will have operated successfully, and a fleet of 10, each with a capacity of 2 million barrels of crude oil, will be under construction." A scenario was often barely distinguishable from either the even longer-term predictions contained in the science fiction literature of writers such as Arthur Clarke or an older product such as the detailed predictions given by St John the Apostle in Revelation. The method nevertheless contributed for a time, however briefly, to the way people in Canada forecast the future.

CONCLUSIONS

This brings to a close the consideration of most of the important ways in which aggregate economic forecasts are made in Canada.[39] There are other approaches, such as general equilibrium models or the developing tendency for certain variables to let the market itself tell us what is forecast for the future. With respect to the latter one thinks of currency, commodity, or stock markets with their futures prices for currencies or commodities on the one hand, options on future indices and interest rates on the other hand. Other approaches, developed by scientists and operations research people, could have been noted: spectral analysis, linear programming, and queuing theory. Spreadsheet programs were not considered because they are not (yet) in the mainstream of aggregate economic forecasting, at least in any way comparable to what has been discussed.

What does deserve comment is how one makes the appropriate choice of instrument, given so many ways of going about it. This very complex question cannot be answered by any set of practical guidelines. In looking at the various methods, I have tried to suggest where they might be appropriate, what the problems might be. Several factors will influence which methods could be used in given circumstances: time horizon, accuracy, and the amount of information available are some. One cannot analyse historical data if none is available. Yet another consideration is the cost of the particular forecasting approach relative to its expected benefit.

These factors have to be weighed constantly. There are always trade-offs to be made both within and across techniques. Because one regularly encounters various different situations, knowing which approach to use evolves with experience. A feeling develops for which method gives the best results in given circumstances. It is precisely this realization that continues to make forecasting an art despite the attempts of successive generations of Canadians to reduce (or elevate?) it to a science – the subject of the next two chapters.

CHAPTER THREE

History 1945–64

" ... Can ye charm away warts?"

Apart from a few scattered pieces, little is available on the earliest days of aggregate economic forecasting in Canada.[1] Certainly such forecasts have been made regularly. Complete records of forecasts dating from the 1950s exist privately, for example, within such corporate institutions as Sun Life, the Toronto Dominion Bank, and Bell Canada. But no systematic attempt has been made to consider the origins of this forecasting, the important figures and their intellectual inspirations, and how the industry evolved, or why. Because these kinds of forecasts are such an important part of economic life, it is strange that business and economic historians have tended to ignore them. Lest Canadians be thought particularly negligent, little work on the history of this most important economic activity has appeared elsewhere. As is noted rather soon, the modern forecasting industry is young by historical standards. Perhaps this is one reason for its having been ignored to date. I will make an effort here, and in the following chapter, to remedy this failing.

Before proceeding to do so, we must note several methodological aspects. The first issue concerns the group of economic agents to which the history is restricted; the second, my method of gathering historical data.

The first issue revolves around an attempt to define a forecasting "industry," the history of which can then be told. The appropriate label – industry or other – is not easy to choose either conceptually or empirically. Most texts in industrial organization (Scherer 1980), the discipline in economics most frequently concerned with the issue, as well as virtually all industry studies (Kudrle 1975), advance several alternate concepts of "industry." This has led Nightingale (1978, 31) to observe: "The term 'industry' ... has been in a state of confusion ever since the 1930's ... Contemporary microeconomic theory assigns an unambiguous meaning to 'industry' only in the case of perfect competition and perfect monopoly. Outside these theoretical extremes there is no theoretical concept to which the term 'industry' can usefully be applied."

However, most economists agree that something like a forecasting industry does exist. This sense of "industry" conforms roughly to the ideas of oligopolistic interdependence and production substitution stressed in most theoretical definitions.[2] But, as with other industries, its exact boundaries are unclear.

In Canada organizations such as the Conference Board, Data Resources (DRI), Wharton Economic Canada (formerly Chase Econometrics), and Informetrica are clearly seen to be "in." So too are those government departments, banks, investment houses, individual firms, and private consultants known to make economic forecasts and to which economic agents frequently turn for such services.[3] These agents would include the Royal Bank, Wood Gundy, the Economic Council, and Singer and Associates.

Most of these agents occupy the core of the industry. Moving outwards, one begins to grope a bit for its limits. Organizations and individuals that routinely predict longer-term economic events, sometimes called "futurists," produce a product quite identical technically to DRI's longer-term forecasts or those of groups such as Shell. They thus have a history to be told. However, inasmuch as they are clearly perceived to lie at the frontiers of the industry, only indirect reference is made to them here.

Still further removed lie advertising and market research agencies, as well as brokerage houses doing financial research. These institutions are less directly a part of the industry than the organizations mentioned earlier. However, because they make some forecasts, are important to such a large segment of economic activity, and were in earlier times perhaps the main suppliers of publicly available aggregate economic "forecasts," the present history includes some discussion of their role. But it concentrates on those institutions that are at present clearly closer to core membership in the industry.

The second important methodological issue relates to the nature of the historical sources used here. Methods used to study the evolution of other industries – watch and clock making, air transport, steel, and cement – can provide considerable direction as to both possible sources and the appropriate structuring of the historical reporting. Unfortunately, there are virtually no published sources to draw on, whether earlier histories or, more important, actual data about the industry. This absence of data is particularly bothersome. In contrast to what might be available on, for example, steel pro-

duction, data on business services (which aggregate economic forecasting is considered to be, for national income reporting purposes)
are extremely thin and historically incomplete, regardless of country.
With respect to structuring of the historical reporting, earlier approaches point to changes in factors associated with structure, conduct and performance as the major determinants of the observed
record. In that sense it is most helpful.

Except where expressly noted, virtually all of what follows is based
on oral history. Moreover, it is principally anecdotal. It is derived
from interviews with approximately 200 organizations and individuals. Each interviewee was asked about his or her own professional
history, that of forecasting in their organizations, and of the industry
as they knew of its evolution. Reliance on such data gathering is
hazardous, particularly because of missed major actors and selective
memory. A recent broadening of accepted practice, particularly in
economics, however, sanctions this procedure (McCloskey 1982). One
can therefore be somewhat less tentative about what follows. In any
event, there was no other choice. But the work is probably more
interpretive than it might otherwise have been.[4]

One final point before setting out. Any history is necessarily selective in respect to the period it covers. And while it is sometimes
difficult to define such a period, time usually provides significant
events for dating purposes. This history is no different. It is modern:
post-second World War. This suggests that the industry is very young.
In its present form it clearly is.[5]

THE PRELUDE: PRE-1945

Forecasting is as old a profession as the oldest. Indeed, for some, it
has perhaps resembled the other rather more closely than is com-
fortable! That forecasting as an industry antedates gold mining or
iron smelting can be unquestioned. Shamans appeared as foretellers
in all the earliest civilizations – and with a highly organized business.

Later the industry flourished, particularly in certain places and
periods. The Oracle at Delphi is well known – an early example of
a near-monopoly of the prediction business. Another important centre,
flourishing later, was Alexandria. One might also consider the Old
Testament prophets.

Forecasting of this early type can be found throughout the Roman
period. Supported by "science" appropriate to the period, it was
used extensively by Romans of all walks of life to predict crop failure,
personal destinies, or worldwide catastrophes. Other examples of
predictions can be found for this period. The Chinese book of "di-

vination," the *I Ching*, is of particular note, as is the book of Revelation in the New Testament, a collection of predictions by St John the Apostle about Armageddon and its aftermath, unrivalled since for its lyrical richness.

This kind of predicting of future events continued well through the Middle Ages up to the Renaissance. The monk Ramon Llull, and Nostradamus, are perhaps the best remembered forecasters of this period. Important as well were the Alchemists. But with the coming of the Renaissance and the growth of "science," the old association of forecasting/prediction/prophesying/divining with religion or the black arts gradually began to die away. Merlin and all the mystics and seers of earlier times slowly gave way to the likes of Francis Bacon. The continued presence of religiously based predictions of "doom," the regular consultation by some of astrological charts, the presence in science fiction of groups able to foretell the future, even the practice of flipping coins, all indicate that this early "superstition" has not died out totally.

While a most interesting subject for historical reflection, this tradition does not concern us, except as a distant predecessor of today's activity.[6] The secularized economic/commercial forecasting industry of today probably has its roots in the Physiocrats and certain late-nineteenth-century French economists. But it is only with the twentieth century, particularly the late 1920s and 1930s, that the industry in its present form began to develop.

Crawford (1955) reports "that by the late 1920s, techniques were available whereby most sales forecasters could prepare reasonable estimates of future sales."[7] Cockfield, Brown and Company, a Canadian advertising firm, opened a commercial research department in 1928, the first of its kind in Canada, which did work throughout the 1930s on tariff briefs, sales potential for specific industries, and other issues that involved aggregate economic forecasting as it would be recognized today.[8] The Canadian Institute of Planners, principally an urban planning group, also developed in the 1920s.

Work was also being carried on in other countries in fields that laid the structural groundwork for the later development of the industry proper. Efforts such as Kuznets's on national income accounting and Leontief's on input-output analysis and those of early (US) National Bureau of Economic Research people such as Mitchell and Burns on indicators became available and began to find their way into Canada. For example, the Dominion Bureau of Statistics and the Rowell-Sirois Commission had estimated some aspects of the Canadian national income accounts and were generally aware of developments elsewhere.

But much of this activity was relatively new. Certainly programs to deal with the Depression and the dawning awareness of the thrust of Keynes's (1936) work were beginning to suggest a much greater need not only to know more about the economy but also to predict where it might be headed. Like Keynes's work, much of this research was a phenomenon of the middle to late 1930s. The Second World War started just as it was beginning to develop a wider audience. The greater organization and control of an economy at war required more elaborate systems for defining, reporting, and predicting economic activity, but there is some question as to whether the war speeded up this process, or whether the forecasting industry would have developed sooner had the war not intervened. The war definitely changed the momentum of development. But relative to what occurred in the decade immediately after the war, there was little organized aggregate economic forecasting in existence before 1945.[9]

In summary, the roots of modern Canadian forecasting developed in the 1930s. They grew out of the Depression, the work of Kuznets and Leontief, of Mitchell and Burns, and of Keynes. Because of the intervention of the Second World War, these contributions did not begin to be used to predict peacetime economic activity in an extensive way until the mid-1940s.

THE "FIRST GREAT LEAP FORWARD": 1945–57

As the war wound down, concern began to develop about a postwar recession. In addition there emerged a desire not to repeat the reparations debacle of the First World War or the experience of the Depression, a new sense of confidence brought about by the intervention of government at all levels of the economy during the war, a strong inclination to take up work set aside five or six years earlier, and some new methods and machines growing out of the war effort. All these factors conspired to bring about an outpouring of forecasting activity during the years after the war.

In keeping with the key role in explaining business cycles that Keynes assigned to investment, the behaviour of which would thus, it was felt, make or break the expected post-war recession, one of the first forecasting initiatives was the survey of investment intentions designed in 1944 by Urquhart and others at the Department of Reconstruction and first carried out in 1945.[10] It was also a logical outgrowth of the war effort's organizational apparatus.

At the same time a simple forecasting model, which drew on the developing national accounts work of Goldberg, was also being designed in what would now be recognized as a typical Keynesian framework, again by Urquhart and with the direct help of Macklin and the influence of Bryce. The work was finished by mid-1946 and remained one of the principal ways of organizing and presenting forecasts until well into the 1960s.

Attempts at public-sector forecasting also began quite early in the post-war period, taking principally the form of one-day conferences of a small group of government and private-sector economists organized by individuals such as Firestone. As well, since the government forecasting community was quite small, regular meetings of all concerned were held to discuss issues and co-ordinate activities. Not unnaturally, prediction of activity in other sectors of post-war reconstruction, in particular labour markets for demobilized soldiers, and housing, drew the attention of the federal public service. Efforts were made to develop a labour force intentions survey similar to the type used to survey investment intentions. They were not terribly successful.[11]

Equally important, as economies returned to peacetime structures, was information abut international trade and finance. Concern over traditional agricultural exports led Ware and others at the Department of Agriculture to embark on a large research program to study agricultural markets. Others in the Bank of Canada, and in the private sector at such places as Sun Life, began to work towards constructing flow-of-funds accounts, using them eventually to predict balance of payments, capital flows, and the like.

Yet another field of research opened up – econometric modelling. It was to have the most important impact on the forecasting industry of all these new endeavours. Work began in 1947. Pursued by Brown and several others (Daly in particular), with Klein from the United States contributing during the summer that year on a consultative basis, a first model was built during 1947 in the Department of Reconstruction and Supply.[12] It was intended from the beginning for use as a short-term forecasting tool.

The model has, for once, been reported elsewhere, particularly in a highly readable history of macroeconomic modelling by Bodkin, Klein, and Marwah (1985) and by T. Brown (1970) himself. Suffice to say "the model tended to underpredict consumption demand [and hence real national product] in the immediate post war period, but the subsequent inflationary pressures were reasonably well-captured, once full-employment constraints were introduced into the model."[13]

Thus throughout the federal government a great deal of activity was under way quite quickly in the post-war period. Because of the early influence of the Industry, Trade and Commerce (ITC) group and the continued impact of C.D. Howe, the minister, this department provided control and co-ordination, being virtually the only one to produce formal forecasting documents throughout this entire period.

This narrative suggests a kind of continuity to the development. Certainly many of the principal actors were present throughout. But the work moved in fits and starts, primarily because of the lack of data. Researchers often had to take time to develop data before they could move on. The econometric modelling group, for example, had to construct its own real GNP series. A debate about the need to and in what form to adjust Canadian data seasonally substantially slowed work through this period.

Clearly seasonal adjustment was important to a country like Canada. Once data could be properly seasonally adjusted, the recognition time relating to basic changes in economic activity was drastically reduced, and much more rapid, and potentially effective, policy changes could be implemented. Subsequently, machine-capacity advances began to play a role, especially later in the period, when computers began to cut calculating time and cost dramatically. Again it was the researchers themselves who helped develop the hardware and software they needed.[14]

These data and machine limitations caused difficulty in the case of the work done at ITC by Daly, Beckett, and later Schwartz on developing Canadian indicators. Moore had published (in 1950) an updated version of Burns and Mitchell's US work mentioned in chapter 2. Because of data limitations and the need to analyse large numbers of series, the Canadian study took rather longer to get under way and complete. But by 1957 Canada had its own series of indicators – a clear breakthrough in identifying peaks and troughs in the business cycle, as well as in its prediction.[15]

Of interest is the way in which these new methods were received and used at the time. Machlin reports that public service managers, in the person of Bryce, MacKintosh, Howe, and others, were for the most part economists themselves, had relatively close ties from the war with those doing the actual work, and thus were not hard to convince. This fact, as well as the small size of the public service and the more or less regular meetings to discuss and co-ordinate thinking, helped to develop collective acceptance of the new technology.[16]

To this point it has been implied that only the public sector was involved in the work. This impression is by and large correct. Private organizations such as Bell Telephone, Sun Life, and the Bank of Nova Scotia were among the few to set up economics departments in this period. Individuals such as Keay and Carter, Popkin, and Rogers played important roles in this respect. For the most part, these departments were statistical gathering and reporting groups. Perhaps the major exceptions were some of the financial institutions such as Sun Life, which played an important role on the analytical side, particularly in regard to the flow-of-funds developmental work of the early 1950s mentioned earlier, and the private-sector market research and advertising agencies (Neilson, International Surveys, and others being set up in this period), which, along with universities, served to carry the bulk of the research into consumption.[17]

Again, as a consequence of small numbers, private-sector individuals working in the area tended to develop forums for meeting regularly to discuss forecasts. Smith, for example, was active in the development (1955) of MONECO, a group of Montreal-based forecasters whose activities were patterned on those of the New York Downtown Economics Club.[18] As well, they met regularly with the relatively small numbers of public-sector forecasters, for example, at those conferences organized by Firestone. Moreover, as in recent times, individual forecasters moved between sectors, working for a while in the public and the private sectors.

But the developmental work occurred principally in the public sector. In a sense this is the Canadian way in the face of technological onslaught. In this instance it was perhaps even justifiable. Because of the almost perfect "public good" characteristics of information about forecasting technology, in particular the virtual impossibility of keeping private any returns to innovation, it is perhaps sensible to expect that this would have happened. Computer software registration problems are a more recent manifestation of the same phenomenon. It needn't have been so, as the example of the United States indicates, more of the work having been done there in near-government institutions such as the National Bureau of Economic Research, Brookings, and the universities. But coming hand in hand, as it did, with the development of the national accounts data – a clear public good – and taking place in a period immediately after a war in which people had become used to the government taking a lead in these kinds of activities, there was no doubt a strong incentive on the part of a recovering private sector, with other more immediate operational resurrection on its mind, to let government handle this new analytical work.

Canada tended to adopt American approaches and methods – a manifestation of the public good aspects of forecasting, to say nothing of an older and broader Canadian approach to technological transfer. And, as in other fields, both before and since, Canada in the process of adopting American technology, came to provide leadership in some areas, such as seasonal adjustment.

THE MIDDLE YEARS: 1958–64

By the mid-1950s this furious activity seemed to have run its course. The election of John Diefenbaker, whose distrust of backroom, eastern Canadian cabals quickly put paid to the close private-public-sector forecasting community interaction; the publication of the Gordon Commission's findings, with the first ever publicly available, long-term predictions for the Canadian economy; and the release of the Canadian indicator study all point to 1957 as the appropriate end to the era of the "first great leap forward."

The election and its immediate aftermath were of particular importance with respect to forecasting because of the "Diefenbaker Affair." On assuming office, the incoming government discovered forecasts of an economic downturn made in the previous year by its predecessor. Brandishing the forecasts in the House, Diefenbaker accused the former government of having been warned about the recession and done nothing to avoid it. Thus his government was not to blame for the recession that was indeed taking place. Perhaps the major legacy of the affair was that for years, until well into the 1970s, no detailed government forecasts were made available publicly. To this day, certain departments of the Canadian federal government remain excessively "gun-shy" about their forecasts because of the experience.

But many of those involved in the first great leap forward recall the years 1945–57 warmly. They were "heady times indeed," what with post-war conversion and reconstruction, new conceptual and methodological paradigms, and the need to develop whole new data sources. And for a decade, until the next great leap forward in the late 1960s, the situation was far less explosive than in the previous one. That is, a hiatus of sorts appeared to set in.

The natural course of research leads had been exhausted and a recession occurred in the late 1950s. This latter event caused questioning of the new approaches. This is not to suggest that forecasters were not active during the next ten years, for as we will see they were. Rather, the world was relatively stable, and the methods and data at hand were reasonably adequate for aggregate economic prediction. Nor is it to suggest that advances were not being made steadily in computer technology, one of the major causes of advances of a subsequent period. It was simply a quieter time, in which the newer technologies developed in the late 1940s and the 1950s were gradually diffused throughout the larger community.

There were several attempts made to "go commercial." Not all were successful. The Canadian Economic Consulting Association, for example, was established by Hood and others but later folded. Perhaps the most important of those that succeeded was Beckett and Associates, which began operations in the early 1960s. By 1966 it had about 50 clients and a subscription list to a monthly newsletter of about 200. Originally intended to capitalize on the national indicator work, for which it is perhaps most recalled, it quickly spread out to provide a range of forecasting services based on all of the new technologies: national accounts forecasting, firm-specific multiple regression demand estimation, input/output analysis, trade studies, and later stock market analysis.[19]

Many private organizations such as the banks were content to "buy in" forecasting services in this way rather than developing their own. It is not completely clear why. It has been suggested, by Beckett among others, that they were unwilling to invest in the staff overhead positions that the work would have required. Again, there were exceptions, in particular at Sun Life and Bell. The latter was always subject to rate regulation and thus required more firm-related aggregate forecasts. As noted above, it maintained a sizeable statistical and forecasting operation from early in the post-war period. Certainly some of the banks (e.g. Toronto Dominion and Nova Scotia) had departments of economic analysis. But these were small operations that really began to develop only in the mid-1960s. No doubt there was still considerable caution and uncertainty about the commercial value of the work.

One important innovation that did gain acceptance during this period was the survey of consumer attitudes and buying intentions. As noted above, soon after the approach appeared in the United States during the 1950s, the private sector seriously considered introducing such a survey to Canada. But it was not until 1960 that Maclean-Hunter was finally able to deliver. Borrowing heavily from the US experience, that firm maintained the survey until 1972 when it moved to the *Financial Post*. In 1975 it was shifted to the Conference Board, its present home.

Events elsewhere were, however, beginning to generate a new momentum for change. The beginning of the American space program and the introduction of transistors greatly accelerated the work on computers. These advances permitted the manipulation of much larger amounts of data. This in turn allowed use of mathematics of a much higher order, generally known to social scientists for some time but inaccessible for applied work because of prohibitive calculation costs. Awareness of the breadth of the potential applications of this now possible technology to economics, finance, marketing, and other subjects began to spread during the early 1960s, especially after the introduction of the IBM 360 in 1964. Particularly recognized in the United States, it led Fama, Fisher, Lorie, Tobin, and others into financial markets research; Bass, Montgomery, Wells, and others into psychological consumer research; and economists such as Adams, Eckstein, Goldberger, and Klein deeper into large-scale econometric modelling.

By the end of the period, Canadians were gradually becoming aware of the nature and thrust of this work. The relatively young Economic Council of Canada was calling for a public forecasting body to capitalize on these new methods. It found the idea difficult to sell. Attempts by others such as the Private Planning Association to become involved also foundered. As in the earlier period, indifference to the potential value of the work and/or fear of unrecoverable investment stemming from public good considerations no doubt played a role.

However, the work of individual Canadian econometricians from the earlier period such as Brown and May was going forward, and others were also at work. Bodkin, Klein, and Marwah (1985) note three efforts in particular. The first relates to the variants of Brown's early models, which had reached model IX by late 1959, the last in this series he was to build directly. It consisted of eight sectors and 48 equations in all. Like its predecessors, it was used principally for short-term forecasting. Brown was to go on to build others, particularly one (1965) for the Royal Commission on Health Services, but the remaining work on the original Trade and Commerce models continued with May until Finance took over maintenance and development of this series in 1964. Kuiper concluded the work in 1970 with model XVI.

The second model was built by Caves and Holton in 1959. While never used for longer-term forecasting (it was intended to help study Canadian long-term economic growth), it represents one of the earliest examples of non-government modelling being entirely university built. Yet another early model that was an offshoot of university work, in this case a dissertation, was Bakony's 1959 model, later versions of which helped focus the Economic Council of Canada's thinking on models during its first years and helped lead naturally to larger efforts in the early 1970s.

Third and finally, "perhaps the most significant early econometric model of the Canadian economy was that constructed by Rudolf Rhomberg (1964), which broke new ground on the subject of the determination of the rate of foreign exchange in a floating regime, and as well, had an interesting discussion of the comparative efficiency of both monetary and fiscal policy under a floating rate, as contrasted with a fixed rate, regime."[20] While never directly used for forecasting purposes, it had an important indirect influence on subsequent forecasting in Canada through its extensive study of the appropriate values for fiscal and monetary policy multipliers.

Near the end of the period these new approaches seemed to take hold in a more important way than elsewhere in the Research Department of the Bank of Canada. While more appropriately a subject for the next chapter, Freeman, Post, and Stewart (with the help of Helliwell) had begun to organize the bank's analytical work around the concept of a large-scale econometric model. Using data from 1952–3 to 1965, they were, by 1967, to complete RDX1, the first in a family of research development experimental (RDX) models that were to follow in the late 1960s and early 1970s. But as is evident, and like the work of Rhomberg and others, it came relatively late in the period. For the most part, those middle years in the forecasting industry were ones of relative calm, implementation, consolidation, and base-building.

CONCLUSION

As the foregoing section implies, the end of an era in the history of aggregate forecasting in Canada was at hand. On the horizon stood one of much greater technical complexity than anything known before. As we shall see, what began with borrowed technology and bailing wire was soon to blossom into an important industry by service-sector standards.

These early days have been recalled here. We have seen that the natural precursors of the 1940s work were developed in the late 1930s, but application to normal activities was not felt until later because of the war. After 1945 there was an explosion of activity on many fronts – surveying, econometric modelling, indicators, deseasonalizing, and data and calculating/computing development, to name the most important. This wave of developmental activity lasted for about a decade and was followed by a period of five to ten years of relative quiet as these technologies found their place in ordinary, daily commercial life.

Nostalgia develops as one comes to understand this period in the industry's history. As has been noted, Beckett, Brown, Daly, Firestone, May, Popkin, Urquhart, and others who made important contributions write and speak of it in terms used by pioneers everywhere. Because of the small numbers involved, they were naturally drawn together by their normal activities, to say nothing of the important royal commissions in this period, such as the Gordon.

They made major strides towards implementing replacements not only for the superstitious in forecasting but also for that sense of helplessness and inevitability before the dictates of the business cycle that had been the accepted personal and collective economic lot for a century or more. Many other factors affected this process. But these individuals defined what data had to be collected, collected it, shaped and reported it, and used it to model economic activity to such an extent that they could predict economic activity far better than ever before. Their work permitted others to alter policy measures such as taxes and the money supply to improve economic life. Indeed so basic was some of their work that it can be found in the general vocabulary and thoughts of the average citizen, much in the way that the work of Freud and other major psychologists has worked its way into that vocabulary as well.

With the important groundwork in place, a sense of awareness of some of it in the commercial community, and the new machine advances beginning to come on stream, the next burst of methodological activity was not far off.

CHAPTER FOUR

History 1964–87

"... you can know at once."

Spurred perhaps by the growing sense of the potential power and control suggested by the new methods discussed at the end of chapter 3 and by the 1960s "cultural revolution," a desire began to develop early to mid-decade for regulatory and government intervention to correct "abuses" in society. Automobiles, worker safety and the environment were among the areas affected. This intervention required more data, more analytics, and, inevitably, more forecasting. As well, problems were beginning to surface with respect to the international monetary system, which were accelerated by the Vietnam War. By the late 1960s the continued momentum generated by all these factors finally seemed to become manifest. And at this point the next period of accelerated activity in the industry, or the "second great leap forward," begins.

For reasons that will become evident, I have decided to divide the years 1964 to date into three relatively distinct periods, namely 1964–73, 1974–8, and 1979 to the present. Perhaps historical perspective 20 or 30 years hence will see the appropriate choice differently.

THE ECONOMETRIC REVOLUTION: 1964–73

The first period can be seen in retrospect as the developmental phase of the second great leap forward. It was a time of revolution in econometric method. The coincidence of supply and demand shifts noted earlier brought forth a virtual explosion of research activity on all the aggregate economic activities of concern to forecasting.[1] It is worth briefly sketching the outlines of this activity before considering several aspects of the period in greater detail.[2]

Consider, for example, that the Bank of Canada's RDX model work blossomed in this period; the CANDIDE interdepartmental project of the federal government under the leadership of the Economic Council of Canada was carried out; the University of Toronto's Policy Institute brought out TRACE and QFM; the Department of Energy, Mines and Resources began preliminary energy modelling; and the Department of Agriculture embarked on its FARM model work. As well, the people at Statistics Canada began to develop on-line computerized data services and longer-term systems modelling, and the Department of National Defence started into the Hitch/McNamara planning revolution. At the same time research in the consumer and capital markets was being fundamentally advanced in its own fashion. Multivariate methods such as factor analysis were developed and used for the first time to reduce the large masses of data on consumer behaviour to meaningful concepts. As well, the development of Canadian financial data bases and applied research on the nature of efficient markets were altering thinking about capital markets. In 1970 the Hudson Institute in the United States began what was to be a three year, multi-country, "futures-oriented" study that looked at energy, the environment, and other issues of concern. It included Canada and would have some influence on federal government circles in the early 1970s.

As this outline suggests, much of this work was carried out within the federal government, just as it had been in the first leap forward. However the motivation in this instance was perhaps slightly different. Certainly the universities played a much larger role. But virtually all the work was done in public organizations, principally because of the substantial, non-capturable, front-end costs that the building of the large-scale models involved. In the earlier period post-war reconstruction concerns perhaps distracted potential contributions as much as the costs. No doubt the relatively limited number of people who were familiar with the new technologies at the early stages in both periods meant that efforts would be concentrated in a few isolated places in any event. However, this still does not necessarily explain why the work was done publicly.[3]

This public-sector involvement was evident at all times, in the "capital-building" years (1964–7) and the "take-off" years (1967–73). In certain instances this public-sector work was a joint effort. For example, the Bank of Canada, the Economic Council, and the National Energy Board (NEB) co-operated on the development of data bases; training courses at the Council were attended by people from the Bank, the NEB, and federal government departments.

But again, as in the immediate post-war period, the early work tended to be focused in one place, in this instance the Bank of

Canada's research department. In the first leap forward, the Department of Industry, Trade and Commerce (ITC) had seemed well in control. However, its virtual monopoly on federal government forecasting began to break up, principally with the arrival of John Diefenbaker's government. Bureaucrats in other departments may have spotted a potential power vacuum and stepped in, or perhaps there was a conscious attempt to place more analytical and predictive capacity closer to the tools of fiscal and monetary policy. Whatever the exact reasons, by the mid-1960s there had been a shift of considerable responsibilities in this regard from ITC to both the Department of Finance and the Bank. But any of the three still might have been expected to be the seat of development, the Economic Council a possible fourth. However, the Bank emerged early as the focal point.

There are various reasons for this. On the surface Finance, with Hood's econometric experience, might have been expected to have been the focus. And indeed work was carried on in the department over this period, especially by Kuiper, who produced the final version, model XVI, in the Brown-May tradition, in early 1970. But while the model would have been up to the task, "records of actual use for economic forecasting are extremely scanty."[4] Several possible explanations for this can be given. The "Diefenbaker Affair" is one. Second, Finance was a large department with diffuse responsibilities. Third and finally, Hood himself was less concerned with econometric work at this point and Kuiper had left the department in 1970. Thus econometric modelling at Finance went into a decade-long hiatus, reappearing only in the early 1980s.[5] Also, ITC was viewed with some suspicion because of its earlier pre-eminence and in any event was kept busy simply maintaining the investment surveying and indicators work.

The Bank of Canada was a smaller, more focused organization, as a rule less directly in the public eye. Freeman and Stewart at the Bank viewed this early modelling work as the appropriate managerial tool around which to reorganize and upgrade the Bank's research capabilities. It had the double advantage of forcing a link between the old-line industry/sector analysis sub-groups and making much more explicit the assumptions all were bringing to the exercise.

As noted in chapter 3, a skeletal version of RDX1 was available by 1967, the full model being published in 1969. It was a model of 101 equations (50 of which were behavioural) and benefited principally from the contributions of Helliwell, Officer, and Shapiro.[6] But it quickly became obsolete, primarily because a much larger model, especially on the policy instrument side, was seen to be needed. Work was thus begun on its successor, RDX2, which would come to have several versions, e.g. RDX2/Yellow (1971), RDX2/Blue (1973), RDX2/Green (1974), and RDX2/Red (1976), and be used during most of the 1970s.[7]

Academic consultants were brought in to do much of this early work. The expertise was not available in-house; bringing in academics made the selling of the work to senior management easier, since an image of the work as experimental or research-oriented, and necessary to the upgrading of in-house capacity, could be more easily developed and maintained; and there was time pressure involved. It may well also have been the Bank's way of patching up relations with economists in general! The decision was to prove critical. These consultants were to pass back their ongoing work to graduate students, thereby considerably widening the educational value from the public good work. Helliwell, Officer, and Sparks were to make particularly noteworthy contributions in this regard. Not incidentally this approach helped to create a large pool of labour skilled in the new technologies, which was to gradually take over at the Bank, Finance, and elsewhere in public and private organizations because of inevitable attrition.

There is little point in describing the model(s) these experts were to build, for details are available elsewhere.[8] Suffice to say that the earliest version contained 258 equations, the later ones up to 516. In its various guises RDX2 was used for a large number of policy simulations and experiments, and for forecasting.

Many of those involved speak of the excitement of the work, the excellence of the computing facilities made available, and so on. It was at first necessary to use the University of Montreal's (U of M) computer, the only one large enough. Several of the major figures of this period (Stewart, McCracken, and others) speak with fond recollection of shipping boxes of cards by bus, and weekend all-night blitzes. This situation was remedied rather quickly, as much for fear of the safety of those involved as for convenience! Hardware resources thus gradually evolved from U of M to the government (CDPSB) and still later to COMPUTEL and SDL.

The conclusion of much of the early thrust of the RDX2 work at the Bank, about 1973, helps to date the developmental period. Consultants began to withdraw from active involvement, giving way to those who had come to the Bank during the development work and stayed on. As will be shown, others left to apply their new skills elsewhere.

While the most important, the Bank's was by no means the "only game in town." Two other model projects also began in this period and led to others, while themselves remaining in existence to the present.

The first project was begun in 1966 by Sawyer and others at the University of Toronto. Ante-dating by one year the formation of the university's Institute of Policy Analysis, with which it was to become inextricably linked, it was to become well known principally because of the work of Wilson and, later, Jump.[9] Their first model (Toronto Annual Canadian Econometric – TRACE) was based on annual data and had about 180 equations when up and functioning, which it was by the summer of 1969, when it produced its initial set of forecasts. It was used primarily for medium-term (five-to-ten-year) projection.

Recognizing that the Bank's RDX2 was a quarterly model, and finding client demand for such a service, the University of Toronto group decided in 1969–70 to build a quarterly forecasting model (QFM, principally the work of Jump and Winder) to support TRACE. Forecasts from both these models were produced by the institute during the early 1970s, regularly from QFM, intermittently from TRACE. For a time in the mid-1970s the group would become closely allied with DRI's Canadian operations, through reciprocal marketing rights to QFM, modelling influences, and Wilson and Jump's personal and professional relations, and with Klein's PROJECT LINK work in the United States. With respect to the latter, TRACE was the Canadian model involved and as a consequence was part of some interesting simulation work to study the reaction of the Canadian economy to external shocks.[10]

The institute's modelling work would continue into the late 1970s and early 1980s. By that time QFM and TRACE would both come to be supplanted by another model, FOCUS, and the institute would be less directly involved in commercial forecasting. While perhaps not quite so large-scale as the Bank's efforts, the institute's projects were trend-setting. Their special contribution was the development of the first quarterly econometric forecast to be made publicly available.

Moreover, while the university was a public-sector institution, some of the money for the work came from private sources, which was also unique. Backed by several large Canadian companies (petroleum, banks, insurance), the work did, however, suffer somewhat from doubts on the part of these private-sector clients as to whether the new technology would prove commercially valuable, especially since some of the early forecasts were inaccurate in certain respects. No doubt there was also a considerable clashing of the old and new here as well. The bringers of the new technology were perceived as young, intellectual, certain of the truth, and not necessarily diplomatic. Those already in place, older, more experienced with complex reality, less dogmatic, were, needless to say, sceptical and offended. The inevitable result was bad feeling, wavering support, and wounds that carry down to the present. But with time the work came to be accepted as making a substantial contribution to aggregate economic forecasting in Canada.

The second project was, of course, the Canadian Disaggregated Inter-Departmental Econometric model (CANDIDE), which was later to become known world-wide for, among other things, the degree of its sectoral detail. As has been noted above, the Economic Council, and particularly one of its earliest heads, Arthur Smith, had for some time recognized the need for public-sector modelling. Responding to steady pressure from this source and to the evident activity and importance of the work at the Bank and Toronto, and following consultant's reports in 1970 by Bodkin and Denton as well as Matuszewski, the federal government made an interdepartmental decision to build a model under the auspices of the Economic Council. A team of model-builders led by McCracken was assembled in-house and started work on CANDIDE 1.0 in the fall of 1970.

Starting later than the Bank, with no managerial motives in mind, and a much broader constituency of interest groups to satisfy, the council used a small, in-house group, whereas the Bank had earlier followed the outside consultant's route. A comparison of a list of the personnel involved, and the nature of the models that emerged, suggests virtually independent efforts. So too would a certain bureaucratic interest in having a product different from the Bank's! However, co-operation between the two groups was actually quite close. In all years of the CANDIDE project there were a number of meetings with people from the Bank, both at the working technical level and in various steering groups; there was continuous exchange of papers as CANDIDE developed; and all papers behind RDX1 and RDX2 were reviewed by the CANDIDE people to ensure that old ground was not being reworked.

Work proceeded at a furious pace, and the model was completed by early 1972. It was made publicly available in the council's ninth annual review of that year and in a series of project papers published in 1973. Further work was carried out in the 1970s and 1980s under a series of project managers, including Bodkin, Waslander, and Preston. Today CANDIDE continues to be the cornerstone of the council's modelling efforts.

Because there is a fair degree of similarity between the various versions of the model, and because it is well documented elsewhere, I will note only that CANDIDE was (is) a large, medium-term, annual model, with substantial disaggregation thanks to imbedded input-output sub-models. Model 1.1, for example, had 2,049 equations; 616 behavioural and 427 input-output identities; and 453 exogenous variables for policy instrument parameters relating to tax, money supply, and demographic data.[11] The model has played an important part in the medium-term conditional projections that have appeared in several of the council's annual reviews (e.g. 1972 and 1979) and has provided a host of other services, simulation-related and involving basic research.

These were then the principal mainstream projects ongoing during the second great leap forward. One important additional initiative, albeit derivative, also deserves mention. By 1970 both the Bank and Statistics Canada were maintaining large databases in machine-readable form. The resulting savings in time and cost were sizeable and are one of the distinguishing differences between the Canadian and US environments during this period. The Economic Council helped considerably to encourage and aid in the development of these databases.

Throughout these years the private sector continued to use the tools developed in earlier times. Beckett and Associates, the largest private-sector forecasting firm, is an interesting case in point. It might easily, or so it seems with hindsight, have maintained its prominent position in the process, becoming the giant of the industry. Indeed it would likely have made the start-up of several commercial houses in the period just ahead unnecessary had it decided to invest in the new technology at an early stage.

Several reasons are given for its not entering into this developmental fray. One was clearly sunk human capital and a sense of personal insecurity with the new technology. But more important, there were serious conceptual questions, especially on the part of Beckett, as to how successful the models would be in capturing structural shifts and policy considerations. As well, the firm's strategy had changed in the direction of stockmarket and more microeconomic prediction. Further, it was felt that any new aggregate forecasters who might enter the industry were as likely as not to increase the total market for all suppliers, thus proving of benefit to Beckett and Associates in any event. Discussions were held with some of the Toronto modellers mentioned above but came to naught. Beckett decided not to get involved. The result was that new firms with new faces soon began to appear. Instead of expanding the market for all, they tended to take away from traditional markets, and Beckett and Associates slowly faded from the centre of the stage.

Several additional developments were also noted above, in particular the longer-run work of the systems analysts and futurists as well as work in the consumer and financial sectors. Each of these developments were in a sense off-phase in Canada as compared to the work in economics. That is, application of the American work to the Canadian situation was started much later in this period than, for example, economic modelling work. Thus, for example, important work on Canadian financial markets by Brennan, Schwartz, and others, and on Canadian consumer behaviour, by Tigert, Weiss, and others, was not to come until the mid-1970s. While research had certainly begun to appear on, for example, database preparation by Rorke and Morgan in the financial area, the main thrust was perhaps five years behind that of aggregate econometrics.

The same might well be said for the "futures" or "systems modelling" efforts that began to emerge at this point. Much disparaged by mainstream, short-term, economics-based forecasters as the product either of an "over-active imagination on the part of the pot-smoking, blue-skying, counter-culture of the sixties" or else "of engineers who didn't understand economics," these two threads to longer-term forecasting nevertheless enjoyed considerable popularity briefly, especially in certain federal government circles such as the Privy Council. For reasons noted below, they vanished almost as quickly as they seemed to develop. However, the methodological aspects required far less "development" than that of the econometric models.[12] In any event, the real impact of futures and systems modelling was to come in the relatively narrow period from 1973 to 1978–9.

By about 1973 this developmental phase seemed to have run its course in Canada. Again, considerable discussion is possible as to whether the implementation phase that followed would have been quite so explosive had not the first oil shock, dramatically higher inflation, increased governmental activity, and floating exchange rates sent policymakers scrambling for whatever tools could help make forecasts in a suddenly very different world. Certainly, the conclusion of the front-end developmental work left many in the research groups with little to pursue in this regard but much to do in the dissemination of the new methods they had developed, again a pattern that had an earlier post-war equivalent. Thus implementation might have been expected in any event. But it would not perhaps have been as dramatic as that which actually transpired.[13]

IMPLEMENTATION: 1974–8

Various examples can be given of this "rush to implement" during the period 1974–8. As noted, the Bank of Canada and the Economic Council went active with their models very early in this period, the interdepartmental nature of the CANDIDE project gradually winding down; a new private Canadian forecasting company, INFORMETRICA, started up; DATA RESOURCES, an American company, took over some of the University of Toronto's model work and went commercial with a Canadian subsidiary; and the Conference Board of Canada more strongly entered the forecasting field with a model of its own. Within government, the federal Department of Transport started its modelling; the Department of Regional Economic Expansion's ill-fated attempt to regionalize CANDIDE took place; the Supply part of the federal government's Department of Supply and Services began its relatively complex operations-research modelling of the supply side of government; and a whole long-term/futures "school" blossomed in such departments as Environment and the Solicitor General's and in the Privy Council Office. Institutes multiplied. Among others, the Hudson Institute opened a Canadian office in 1974; GAMMA, a multi-university, Montreal-based futures group, began operations in 1974; and the Fraser Institute was started up in 1975.[14]

It was also a time of fundamental change in private-sector forecasting. Organization after organization began to integrate the new methods into their planning activities, especially during the later part of this period. Consider the following sample of comments from those involved. "It was a one-man show until five years ago when it expanded dramatically" (a large transportation company). "Pre-1976 we forecast real demand simply by extrapolation" (a hydro utility). "When I joined in the early seventies they were still in the quill pen era. They had no data, no modelling capability" (a large bank). "In 1975 we were asked to prepare out first forecast" (another utility company). "Nothing was done before 1975. Everything was on a 'wing and a prayer' basis" (a provincial government). "Before 1978 we just gathered information" (a major oil company).

Regulated companies such as Bell Canada and the utilities, especially hydro companies, tended to be the first off the mark, principally in response to government regulatory commissions which began to demand solid statistical evidence developed in the "new manner" to back up requests for rate increases. But others were well in by the late 1970s. Departments were restructured, subscriptions to the new commercial services purchased; in many instances organization-specific methodological work began in-house.[15]

For each one of these organizations there is a story, but proceeding in this fashion would be out of the question. Fortunately there are some common threads. In many instances it was groups of former public-sector developmental people who spun off into the commercial implementation of what they had helped to create. This was yet another repetition of earlier, post-war events. For example, Mc-Cracken, on contract to the Economic Council to build CANDIDE, formed Informetrica once the major part of the work was finished; Wilson and others at the University of Toronto informally joined DRI; Maxwell of the Bank went to the Conference Board; and Drouhin established Hudson in Canada after leaving the US study.

Another thread is that as part of a polite but mad scramble for market share, there was a pronounced effort made to differentiate respective products. Hudson pursued the commercial futures market, while Gamma looked to the more institutionalized/government one. Informetrica concentrated on econometrics for the federal and provincial government market as well as crown corporations, associations, and the like, while the Conference Board worked to become a full-service commercial/government organization, and DRI the main commercial supplier. The Fraser Institute deliberately decided not to enter the aggregate economic forecasting market at all – a strategy that the C.D. Howe Institute and the Institute for Research on Public Policy (IRPP), both of which came into activity in this period, also adopted.[16]

Other threads have been alluded to above. For example, there was a pronounced increase in the presence and use of computers, a dramatic upgrading of the educational level and analytical abilities of those entering staff positions, and a strongly perceived need for any kind of planning help in a suddenly different and potentially threatening world of inflation, oil shocks, regulation, and flexible exchange rates. Regardless of organization type, sector, or other distinguishing characteristics, virtually every case was affected by these factors. Demand- and supply-related factors conspired everywhere to require and permit an active and extensive commercial aggregate economic forecasting industry to develop in the short space of about five years.

Hand in hand with this commercialization came application of modern finance theory and analytical tools to the stock market and capital structure. Efficient market hypotheses, capital asset pricing models, and other "new" concepts, plus data only recently made available and the computer capacity to support all of this, brought an equally important revolution in the way people analysed and thus predicted stock market behaviour and the impact of financial instrument choices. The kind of analytical thought done in the research department of a large brokerage firm was thus as fundamentally different from what it had been only several years earlier as was that in economic research and planning departments. The same was true for consumer research.

However, much of what seemed so new was really a continuation of the old. Those who remained in, or came to, the public sector continued the work begun there. For example, new versions of CANDIDE and RDX2 became available. As well, those who had earlier built models for the public sector now built again for the private sector. McCracken, with his TIM model, at 2,600 equations larger than, but in many ways similar to, CANDIDE, and Maxwell of the Bank, with AERIC at the Conference Board, were perhaps the two most important. The linkage of the University of Toronto group to DRI, with a new model resulting, has already been noted. But whether "old" or "new," this technology was being used in the late 1970s by a broad spectrum of economic agents to make forecasts.

DOWN TO THE PRESENT: 1979–87

It is difficult to date exactly when this rush to implement ended. Some observers would argue that the continuity of some of the industry's activities suggests that implementation has never stopped. But most note a clear braking on activity, a hiatus, from the end of 1978.

There are many reasons one can advance to explain this shift. The new methods have become more familiar, been absorbed into planning structures, been developed into the everyday. As they have done so, recognition of their limitations has also begun to emerge: estimation problems, the critical dependence on good and timely data, the need to adjust ("bump") the models to capture "structural shifts" not modellable in any other way, the fact that the forecasting problem has really only been "displaced" to exogenous variables, in particular those of policy, and the cumbersome aspects of using the big models and of periodically re-estimating them. Perhaps the most damaging has been the demonstration that the models are not necessarily better predicting tools than other methods. It has been alleged that they have indeed failed in this respect in several notable circumstances, particularly in 1974–5 and 1982–3.

At the same time substantial theoretical disarray has been present both in macroeconomics and econometrics. Debates of the early and mid-1970s over causality sparked by the new time series method as well as the rational expectations revolution in macro theory have spread into the wider community of the economics profession. They have contributed to a certain theoretical hesitancy, a slowing down in the rate of theoretical advances in applied method, and a sober reassessment everywhere about what we really know about aggregate economic activity and how to model it correctly. These factors, and others, have led also to a shift in emphasis both in theory and in policy from short-term intervention to longer-term structural considerations. Models designed to aid fine-tuning of monetary and fiscal policy seem somehow passé or irrelevant to discussions of the Japanese challenge or industrial policy.

Development has also been strongly influenced throughout this period by budget constraints within governments, particularly those beginning in 1977 in Ottawa. This has led to less money being available for purely methodological work. The entire futures branch of the industry especially has suffered, as policy-makers have chosen to protect first capabilities relating to the immediate future and, of course, from the general tendency everywhere to shorten time horizons as inflation concerns grew in the late 1970s. In addition, economic performance generally was poor, especially during 1981–3. Business service industries usually suffer particularly badly in such circumstances. Economic forecasting has not been immune.

These factors help explain the considerable change of mood since 1978. This is not to suggest that all activity has ceased.[17] Modelling efforts, for example, have gone forward. Repeated attempts to build good labour market models have been made, notably by the federal Department of Employment and Immigration, but have generally failed. Regional models, at the federal and provincial levels, have been attempted. Most have foundered because of poor regional data and inadequate linkage. The Department of Finance has finally developed an aggregate model (QFS); Statistics Canada also has one of its own, as well as a new leading indicator series. The Bank of Canada built two new models, RDXF for forecasting and SAM for quicker analytical turnaround; as mentioned, the University of Toronto group also has a new model (FOCUS). Perhaps to be expected, energy modelling has blossomed everywhere, but principally at the University of British Columbia, with the MACE model. Others at EMR, Gulf Canada, the National Energy Board, and the Alberta universities have also been active.

Finally, the forecasting companies themselves have been developing their own new aggregate, sectoral, and regional models. The Conference Board, for example, in 1982 introduced a new medium-term forecasting aggregate model (MTFM). It, and Informetrica, have functioning regional models. As well, they and the others have made determined efforts to make the models more "user friendly."

Perhaps the event of most significance to the industry was the entry in 1980 of Chase Econometrics, a service of the Canadian subsidiary of the American bank similar to that provided by the bank in the United States. Staffed at the outset by DeBever and certain others of a more recent Bank of Canada period (i.e. those involved with RDXF – yet again a repeat of earlier patterns), it made inroads in the industry with an aggressive pricing policy, a simplified model and accessibility, and a generally developing sense of good service. Its lineage did not hurt, the reputation of Chase Econometrics being well known in Canada. As well, the corporate ownership of DRI has changed, as has that of Chase itself with the merger in the United States of Chase and Wharton. But these activities have as yet had little effect on the industry in Canada.

While all these developments are noteworthy, and many individuals, older in the field as well as new to it, have made important contributions, they are nonetheless extensions or refinements of what has gone before. They are part of the "wearing in," of the "everyday after the initial blush." Various pieces of evidence support this sense of refinement relative to the past. For example, several comparative model seminars have been organized by the Department of Finance since 1978, principally in 1979, 1982, and 1984. As well, histories of modelling activity have begun to appear, notably those of Bodkin, Klein, and Marwah (1985), Daub (1985), and O'Reilly (1985). Both types of activity are often signs of maturity and stability. As such, they make the post-1978 period different in important ways from the earlier phases of development and implementation.

CONCLUSIONS

Thus one arrives at the present from a historical journey that had its beginning in the earliest mists of time but effectively dates from the 1940s. We have seen in this chapter that the period since the mid-1960s has been in many ways an almost carbon copy of the earlier cycle of methodological revolution followed by implementation, and then reflection.

In this instance the revolution was econometric: large systems of equations representing the aggregate economy were estimated with high-speed computers and then used to examine the economic behaviour of various groups in the country, to simulate the response of the economy to various shocks, and to make predictions. As with the first developmental cycle in the 1940s and 1950s, there is historical lore about the period, shared by members of the various teams that built these models, at the Bank of Canada, the Economic Council, the University of Toronto, and other groups. Flush with the enormously expanded computing capacity that became available, they built ever-larger models until they began to realize that size was no guarantee of anything, least of all predictive accuracy. At this point model size stabilized or was even reduced.

But surely this is a common course of events in periods of rapid technological advance. Indeed the history of aggregate economic forecasting in Canada is what might be expected in such a knowledge-based industry. That is, it is marked by flux. There are periods of methodological advance, followed by adoption, followed by advance. In this instance, as in many others, these cycles would seem to have been driven principally by technological developments, here in computers and econometrics. Sociological changes, such as theoretical insights, education, and a demand for government, also played a role. Unquestionably the public good nature of the basic product of the industry, namely information, has had a good deal to do with it as well. Coincident with this activity has been a fluctuation in the collective professional psychology in economics between periods of discovery, certainty of truth, and excitement and ones of consolidation, hesitation, and disappointment.

Together they have all contributed to the development of an aggregate economic forecasting industry that, as we shall see in detail, consists of a mixed bag of participants but principally of a core of four commercial firms. Around them cluster other organizations such as banks and governments, which also perform generalized aggregate forecasting, as well as market research/advertising agencies, brokerage houses, and other groups and individuals such as utilities, resource companies, and futurists that are more sector- and time-specific but aggregate in character.

We seem to be at the end of one of these cycles. There is a sense, not only with the professionals but with the public at large, that increased analytical complexity does not seem to have delivered on its earlier promise.[18] Added to this is the confusion arising from the cross-currents of macroeconomic theory uncertainty, the impact of microcomputers and spreadsheet programs, the increasingly efficient financial and other futures markets (where hard data, i.e. actuals, count for more than soft, i.e. forecasts), and the shift in focus from short-term stabilization to longer-term industrial policy concerns, whether inspired by technological revolution, Japanese success, or other considerations. These all point to a world of considerable hesitation and concern.

This attitude need not be the prevalent one. As we shall see later, in chapters 7 and 8, careful consideration of the accuracy record, with respect to short-term and long-term prediction, indicates that the industry has at least held its own, if not improved relative to earlier periods, in the highly volatile 1970s and 1980s. Moreover the Canadian record is no worse than elsewhere in the world. Indeed Canadian industry has led in selected technological developments. Thus Canadians are entitled to pride of achievement. Also, such confusion and concern are often taken elsewhere to be a sign of maturity, which is unquestionably the case here. No doubt the industry will be considerably different in five or ten years. But that has happened before, and it has survived.

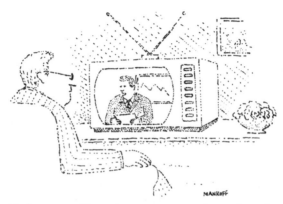

"On Wall Street today, news of lower interest rates sent the stock market up, but then the expectation that these rates would be inflationary sent the market down, until the realization that lower rates might stimulate the sluggish economy pushed the market up, before it ultimately went down on fears that an overheated economy would lead to a reimposition of higher interest rates."

CHAPTER FIVE

Demand and Supply

"Now, what is the harvest fortnight to be?"

Aggregate economic forecasting in Canada is thus relatively young as industries go. Nevertheless it has an interesting and dynamic history, especially since the Second World War. It behooves us to look more closely at the industry for a number of reasons. To begin, let us briefly review what comprises the industry at present.

As discussed hereafter the industry consists first of the majors, which I shall mention in alphabetical order. The Conference Board of Canada, located in Ottawa, is perhaps the oldest continuing forecasting operation in the industry.[1] It is a non-profit organization supported primarily by private-sector subscription and offers a broad selection of services, some of which (e.g. conferences) are only distantly related to forecasting. Its principal forecaster/modeller has been Maxwell (another ex-Bank of Canada man, RDX2), although Stokes, Gusen, and recently London have also been important contributors.

Data Resources of Canada is, like Wharton Economic Canada, a subsidiary, in this case of the US company of the same name, itself a subsidiary of the large US publishing company McGraw-Hill. Located in Toronto, it began operations in the mid-1970s, drawing part of its influence from the work of Eckstein and others in the US parent but principally from the University of Toronto Policy Institute's modelling work, that of Wilson in particular. Together with Empey, the two made important contributions to DRI's fortunes, which depend for the most part on a private-sector clientele, although certain governments are represented as well.

Informetrica is a privately owned Canadian organization. Located in Ottawa, it was also founded in the mid-1970s, by McCracken (responsible for the early CANDIDE models of the Economic Council, who has remained the major factor in Informetrica's forecasting work; Jarvis, Ruddick, and Jacobson also have made contributions. Its clients are drawn from various sectors but include a larger proportion of governments than the rest.

Finally, there is Wharton Economic Canada, formerly Chase Econometrics, the most recent entrant to the industry, and the smallest. It is a wholly-owned subsidiary of Wharton Consulting and Economic Information Services (WEFA-CEIS) in the US which is itself owned by WEF Assoc. AG, a Swiss company. Located in Toronto, the firm services a country-wide clientele drawn from a fairly broad representation of government and business.

In the loose group of contributing members that are also perceived to be part of the industry, there are a number the forecasts of which are regularly made public. These include, by way of example, the Royal and Toronto Dominion banks. As well, there are various individuals and/or organizations whose forecasts frequently, but not regularly, appear publicly. In this group one could cite, for example, the people at the Bank of Commerce and at Pitfield McKay, Messrs Grant, MacNess, and Gampel, and a few others, including the *Financial Post*. Finally there are companies with a strong history of in-house independent forecasting that never publish forecasts.[2] Perhaps the most important of these is Bell Canada. To this group of private-sector members one must add government and near-government organizations, the most important of which are the Department of Finance, which sometimes releases forecasts in budgets; the Bank of Canada, which seldom releases any; and the Economic Council of Canada, which usually publishes them in its annual reports.[3]

In summary, the industry has a concentrated group of four majors at the core, and other members scattered throughout various organizations. Forecasts may or may not be made public, or only irregularly so.

There are a number of reasons for looking in detail at the industry that has developed. For example, do the issues raised in chapter 1 stand the harshness of empirical light? In this context one might document the nature of the demand for forecasts, investigating whether the motivation for forecasting is "rational" or not. Nearly all the work done recently on how classical models would change if rational expectations were introduced represents rational expectations in a time series theoretic, system-consistent fashion and in that manner can be said to explain the expectations, e.g. Fair (1979a and b), Taylor (1979). This approach is equivalent to assuming that the quantity of steel produced consistent with general equilibrium is by definition rational and that the way to explain the observed quantity is to use a multivariate time series model involving all other variables in whatever model of general equilibrium one happens to have at hand.

While it is clearly a permissible, indeed the ultimately generalizable, approach, it is not the manner in which economics has traditionally explained steel or any other major product. Rather economics has used a "micro" paradigm to study the consumer, the firm, and the industry, aggregating up from these basic units to an understanding of macro behaviour.[4]

Using this traditional approach to explaining rational expectations, one might argue that the demand or supply of expectations was based on rational criteria much in the way that the actions of economic agents have always been assumed by micro theorists to be rational. This would immediately suggest that traditional economic analytics could be applied to explain expectations just as it explains haircuts or steel. Further, the extent to which one could explain expectations in this way would be as good a test of the plausibility of the rationality assumption as the extent to which our economics-based explanation of any actions of economic agents was a test of the assumption of rationality more generally found in economic theory.[5]

Accepting such an argument leads to the traditional industrial-organization literature with respect to other industries. It is possible to cite, among others, the early work of Bain (1959) on general industry studies, Caves (1962) on air transportation, Kudrle (1975) on international tractors, and Brock (1982) on telecommunications. These studies analyse an industry by looking at the nature of the demand for the product and/or service, the characteristics of its supply, the resulting structure of the industry, how that industry "conducts" itself (or "behaves"), and its performance. In this chapter we will concentrate on demand and supply, in the next on structure, conduct, and performance (S-C-P).

Use of the S-C-P paradigm has inevitably given rise to consideration of public policy. I will proceed likewise, inasmuch as we are interested in discovering whether governmental intervention may be required. Questions involving truth in promotion, excess profits, collusion, and so on are every bit as appropriate to forecasting as they are to banking, steel, or any other industry. We will, however, put these aside until we know the industry better, that is, until chapter 9.

THE NATURE OF DEMAND

Introduction

The first subject to be considered as regards the Canadian aggregate economic forecasting industry is the nature of the demand for its product(s).[6] As we have seen in chapter 1, several intellectual traditions inform the theoretical issue, most notably economics, and social psychology. For present purposes, and because of what I have argued in the previous section, it is preferable to concentrate on economic explanations. Before explicitly characterizing the issue in economic terms, we shall examine it first in another less formal, but equally informative, manner – namely, how users organize their forecasting and what they see as its benefits.

Organization

Because there are many different forms of economic organization, one might expect equally varied forms of economic forecasting. However, because the information must ultimately reach those who need it for their particular decision-making, and because such decision-making points are common to many different kinds of organizations (e.g. vice-president of corporate planning, chief economist, deputy minister/minister), there tends to be a limited number of ways in which forecasting is organized.

Briefly, aggregate economic forecasts are demanded regularly by senior management, usually quarterly but certainly annually with updates, in detail as they relate to the organization's activities (international, domestic, industry, and region being the most important), and over varying planning horizons – frequently of one year in length for budgeting, five years for longer-term planning, and sometimes even further ahead, especially for strategic-choice situations.

These forecasts then enter the organizational decision-making planning calculus in one of two ways: either via the black box or in a specific, programmatically linked way. The latter is characteristic, for example, of regulated companies that must document planning at each step for purposes of commission hearings; the former is probably more the rule. It was quite surprising to discover that many of those who demanded forecasts had no real idea how they were used in making decisions. They were "somehow simply a necessary background to decision making.[7]

Further, except as regards the total amount of information demanded, there would seem to be no necessary link between the way the forecasts are used and the amount of forecasting demanded. That is, some organizations with very large demands use them in a black box fashion, while others tie them thoroughly to organization-specific planning. Demand, it would seem, is driven by considerations other than the system by which the forecasts are integrated into the organization's decision-making procedures.

One such general factor may be the recent growth of the number of forecasts publicly available to decision-makers in organizations. Information theory has long recognized the public good nature of forecasts. As we have seen, evident externalities explain why much of the early developmental work was carried out in public institutions. Because of the increased public availability of forecasts in recent times, organizations have reduced their private purchases, and thus the organization of forecasting has become even more diffuse.

Another factor that has seriously influenced demand for aggregate economic forecasts in recent times and hence how the function comes to be structured within an organization is the development of futures markets as they relate to certain important economic phenomena such as interest and exchange rates. Certainly there is considerable question as to the ability of present futures rates to predict accurately the appropriate future spot rate (Baille, Lippens, and McMahon (1983). Moreover, it is clearly not possible to use such markets to predict all actions. Consider that the construction period of a mine may well be longer than the longest available output-price futures contract horizon. In such circumstances hedging is still imperfect. But with these qualifications, and because hedging and forecasting fulfil similar functions, the growth in the number and coverage of cost-effective futures markets, along with financial theory work and education concerning efficient markets, has helped to push much of what would previously have been forecast out on to the futures market, thereby reducing the organization's demand for aggregate economic forecasts in its traditional form and increasing its indirect integration into decision-making processes.

Other economic factors, such as the increasing education of managers to the value of forecasting information and the role that the information revolution has played in the centralization v. decentralization of the organization as a whole, and hence also the forecasting function, have been at play as well. Some suggest that in the political sphere it is now possible to short-circuit the forecasting function by improved methods of lobbying (i.e. to negate the need to predict by determining the decision!).

One could continue citing such general demand-inspired factors and their impact on how the forecasting function is organized.[8] However, more specific benefits from economic forecasting are probably the major motivators of its demand. It is worthwhile considering some of these in detail.

Benefits

Lack of knowledge about exactly how these forecasts are used in decision-making might suggest that demand is largely "bureaucratically" driven in the way that magazine subscriptions might be. As will be discussed below, this leads directly to the hypothesis that demand is cyclically determined. But when more probing questions are asked, other benefits or motives surface. To be sure, "increasing productivity or profits" is always among the first. But how does forecasting contribute to this aim? Perhaps, as in traditional inventory theory, it helps to smooth fluctuations in effective demand for output.

Reflection reveals other, more important, concerns. The first is what might be called "avoidance of the big mistake." Whenever a decision on something of critical concern to the organization must be made, be it to build a harbour, prison, airport, or mine or to launch a new product line, stock offering, or government budget, aggregate economic forecasting is called forward. "If it helps us save the cost of one wrong, bad or ill-timed move, it will have paid for itself many times over." The important words here are "helps," for as noted it is one of a series of factors contributing to the decision, and "paid for itself many times over," which suggests a very high benefit/cost ratio.

But this comment may reflect more than the speakers care to admit. It also suggests that dependence on forecasting, especially in circumstances such as this, may be a convenient way of spreading the responsibility of senior management.[9] Such a delegating of responsibility is not necessarily restricted to the confines of the organization. Forecasting also plays an important public relations and marketing role. It is one of the means by which the demanding organizations indicate to their own public (e.g. a bank to its depositors, a brokerage firm to its clients, a government to its citizens), and the world at large, that they are actively and responsibly involved in the "ongoing current of business activity."[10]

One such public manifestation of responsibility via forecasting is clearly mandated. As discussed in chapter 4, one of the major characteristics of the 1970s was the sizeable increase in the amount of government-regulated activity. This resulted in a rapid growth in forecasting demand: regulatory bodies required evidence that rate requests were based on "solid economic opinion" (again the "reasonable care" criterion). This reasoning also extended to government budgeting, leading, for example, to the publication of economic forecasts with successive budgets from 1977 onwards.[11]

Viewed in a more charitable way, and certainly as an offshoot of recent agency theory work, the forecast represents a "common benchmark" around which everyone in the organization can group. It provides the basis on which "internal contracts" between managers and workers, managers and owners, and others are agreed on and on which they will be judged. In this way it becomes an organizational tool helping to ensure consistent thinking about the future.[12] In many circumstances its uses are even more explicitly exploited to help "rally the troops to greater efforts."

These are some of the more specific benefits from economic forecasting that motivate demand. Let us turn next to an attempt at a more formal representation.

Measures of Demand

The actual modelling of the demand for certain services such as haircuts is relatively straightforward. However, the demand for information, of which an aggregate economic forecast is a part, is quite another thing. Measurement of the dependent variable, usually quantity, is particularly difficult. A measure such as the number of variables forecast multiplied by the number of times they were forecast might suggest itself. Even were it possible to develop such a series, other problems would remain. For example, it is unlikely that all demanders place equal weight on each variable in the way that such an approach assumes.

And what of the main independent variable, relative price? It is argued (Rathmell 1974) that one of the characteristics of demand for business services is that price is not an important factor, an observation of many, already noted above. Yet others feel that they are aware of exactly how much they pay for such services, complain in a certain sense about costs relative to the benefits, and indeed cancel subscriptions or close down their forecasting departments in response to downturns in business, as they did during the last big recession in the early 1980s. This evidence certainly suggests sensitivity to relative price.

There are therefore measurement problems and contradictory hypotheses concerning the fundamental economic equation of demand. Alternative hypotheses advanced above also need to be considered: demand may be generally highly sensitive to cyclical activity, or to strikes/oil shocks/increased government regulation; futures markets or the increased availability of forecasts in the public domain may have reduced the demand for forecasts; a better educated management may have raised the level of demand for forecasts; and so on.

Ultimately the attempt to estimate a model of demand founders

TABLE 1
Correlation Analysis of Selected Firm Data

	Correlation coefficient (R) of					
Source of data and variables	Real subscription fee	Average forecasting error[b]	Real GNP	Days lost to strikes	Number of MBA grads	Real government spending
Confidential Firm						
No. of clients	−0.19	−0.58	0.41	−0.19	0.52	0.46
Total real revenue	0.14	−0.51	0.69	−0.40	0.84	0.76
Conference Board[a]						
No. of clients[c]	−0.35	0.95	0.07	−0.71	0.75	0.95
Total real revenue	0.42	0.51	0.20	−0.90	0.99	0.88

[a] Available for the period 1980–4 (inclusive) only.
[b] For a sample of forecasters (as reported in Daub [1981] and updated) predicting real GNP.
[c] Estimated implicitly as membership revenue divided by the subscription fee.

not on these considerations but on the absence of enough data. To understand this it is necessary to recall that the majors are very young commercial ventures; two are wholly owned subsidiaries, one a private company (hence no public data are available on three of the four); and no Standard Industrial Category (SIC) group statistics on "the forecasting industry" exist.[13] Thus it is impossible to secure enough data on quality, whether time series, cross-sectional, or pooled, with which to estimate a model.[14]

Other data on demand that require less rigorous statistical assumptions are, however, available. First, some firm data from one of the four majors were made available on a confidential basis.[15] Second, there are some publicly available data from the Conference Board's annual reports since 1981. Third, there are data obtained during the direct interviewing referred to in chapter 3 that, depending on how one handles the issue of what is supply and what demand, give some indication of the nature of the demand for forecasting services. Fourth, there are SIC data on "services to business management," in particular on "other business services." This category includes forecasting houses and is thus a very broad proxy. Finally, there is some anecdotal evidence with data. Each is presented briefly in turn.

The confidential firm data (Table 1) suggest that with respect to two possible quantity proxies, namely the number of clients and total real revenue, the majority of the possible explanatory demand-related variables have decent correlations with signs, as expected. Thus, for example, as the size of a generalized forecasting error goes up, demand falls; as real government spending, real GNP, and the number of MBA graduates (a possible proxy for increased demand due to managerial sophistication) grow, so does the demand for forecasting. The relative price results are confusing with respect to sign, small in any event. Perhaps the most curious result is that as days lost to strikes (a possible proxy for increased uncertainty) rise, the demand for forecasts falls. One would have expected the reverse.

This result is, however, confirmed by the Conference Board data, which also yield a strong negative correlation with days lost to strikes.[16] The explanation may well be simply that as the days lost to strikes decrease, the volume of business rises, and hence the demand for forecasts rises much in the way that the transaction demand for money is related to real growth. Confirmed as well is the strong relation between real government spending and education and the demand for forecasts. In other respects the Conference Board data results are either confusing, insignificant, or perverse. With respect to the latter it would seem that as the forecasting error rises, so does the demand for forecasts! This is likely a result of the small number of observations available.

The third piece of evidence on demand is the cross-sectional data obtained from the personal interviews and subsequent correspondence. As Table 2 indicates, these data are grouped by public and by private sector, with several subgroups within the latter. They relate estimated total expenditures on forecasting to net total budget, in the case of the public-sector data, and to the size of the organization's sales and assets, in the case of the private-sector data.

From the public-sector sample it is estimated that during the year 1982–3 the federal government spent approximately $15 million on forecasting, an average of 0.09 per cent (1/10 of 1 per cent) of the total budget net of transfers.[17] Further it would appear that there is some slight evidence of a correlation between the size of a department's net total budget and the amount it spends on forecasting, thereby providing indirect but weak evidence for the major mistake avoidance motive.

The private-sector sample indicates that the organizations in the sample spent an estimated total of $18 million on forecasting, an estimated overall average of 0.04 per cent (1/20th of 1 per cent) of their total sales, 0.006 per cent (about 1/110th of 1 per cent) of their assets. While sales are most certainly not equivalent to net budget transfers, the latter likely being closer to total expenses, public-sector

TABLE 2
Evidence on the Nature of Total Expenditures on Forecasting 1982–3[a]

| | Public-sector sample | Private-sector sample | | | | | | | | | |
| | Net budget transfers | Banks and insurance | | Regulated company | | Brokerage | Other | | Total | |
		Sales	Assets	Sales	Assets	Sales	Sales	Assets	Sales	Assets
Total forecasting expenditures as an average fraction (percentage)	0.09 (1/10 of 1%)	0.02	0.003	0.02	0.007	0.30	0.01	0.01	0.04	0.006
Correlation coefficient with total forecasting expenditures	0.81	0.900	0.911	0.834	0.227	−0.487	0.486	0.902	0.577	0.508

[a]Obtained from a sample of 7 federal government departments in the public sector, 25 organizations in the private sector.

organizations probably spent more on forecasts than the private sector. This is a piece of evidence broadly consistent with the ideas of reasonable care and the public good/lead role of governments advanced above. Within the private sector, brokerage houses spent a considerably higher proportion of sales on forecasting than the rest, followed by the regulated companies and banks or insurance firms, all of which exceed those in the "other" category (a broad cross-section of industries such as steel, automobiles, oil, gas, and transportation). Those who need to demonstrate reasonable care most directly seem likely to spend the most. The correlation evidence suggests that for the private-sector sample as a whole there is a positive but not extremely strong relation between the amount of money spent on forecasting and both sales and assets, with banks and insurance companies exhibiting the strongest such tie-in.

The fourth piece of evidence is from SIC data on "services to business management," in particular, "other business services." This subcategory accounts for 16 per cent of gross domestic product (GDP) ascribed to "services to business management" (in 1971), itself 2.4 per cent of total GDP (i.e. "other business services" being thus 0.4 per cent of total GDP). A correlation analysis of the same type as that conducted above indicates that during the period 1974–81, the constant dollar (1971) GDP of this "other business services" SIC category was strongly negatively related to relative real prices and strongly positively related to real GNP, real government spending, and the numbers of MBA graduates.[18] These results are as expected and encouraging. So too was the result that the sector's GDP rose slightly as forecast error fell. Once again the days lost to strikes variable has a negative correlation. If one uses real total revenue for this "other business services" group instead of its GDP, the size and signs of the appropriate correlation coefficients remain the same, except for the forecasting error variable, the size of which increases substantially.

Finally there is some anecdotal evidence. Briefly, and by way of example, it was taken as a good sign by several of those interviewed that the forecasting department in a certain bank had as much budget per one million dollars in assets as other staff departments, or as forecasting departments in other similar institutions. Alternatively, the fact that a budget has not been cut when another department's had, or when business turned bad, was taken as indirect evidence of a demand for forecasting.

These are then five pieces of evidence on the nature of demand. The data are approximate and frankly weak. The intention is primarily to indicate what kind of analysis is needed as more data become available. Let us now pass to a consideration of supply.

HERMAN

Obviously, you weren't at the meeting this morning.

THE CHARACTER OF SUPPLY

Introduction

The nature of supply in the forecasting industry is relatively straight-forward as compared to that of demand. Superficially it would seem to be characterized by ease of entry, sizeable human capital invest-ment, and discontinuous production, characteristics typical of service industries. And indeed, to a certain extent, it is. But as we will see, there are complications. As with demand, the data concerning supply are weak. It was once again impossible to proceed in the usual way. Rather, as above, data were obtained on a confidential basis, indi-rectly and during interviews. Given this limitation, let us consider in turn the nature of inputs and costs, the question of technologies, and certain measures of supply.

The Nature of Inputs and Costs

Being a service industry, particularly being based on information, forecasting's major input is people. While estimates vary somewhat, about 50–80 per cent of total costs are for people. The remaining

20–50 per cent is spread across computing and other "machinery," subscriptions, travel, printing, and certain miscellaneous expenses such as rent and depreciation.

Thus, to explain forecasting supply it is necessary to explain labour supply and demand. There are two major markets involved, one for professionals, the other for white-collar clerks and typists. For the latter, there is nothing to distinguish the industry's demand, or the nature of the supply it faces, from the more general market for such services. No union or other contract issues have had any particular effect on forecasting suppliers, most of which are rather small.

The professionals, the key to the operations and the single largest cost item, are typical of business service professionals more generally.[19] Essentially they sell their human capital, are in most cases highly mobile, require no specific professional accreditation, and make their way principally as labour-service entrepreneurs. This is true regardless of which supplier is under discussion. Because of this, and because of the nature of the technology associated with forecast production, education, technological innovation with respect to the preparation and delivery of forecasts, and alternative labour market opportunities, especially in education or more purely policy-related fields, are the major factors influencing the professional labour situation in the industry.

Because of the eclectic nature of this professional labour, institutional arrangements concerning its employment vary greatly. In some instances there is a single owner who employs professional labour in the usual way; in others it is a partnership with juniors, much as a law practice; in still others all work for a large corporation with nothing other than indirect share ownership. All such labour is potentially highly mobile, and the value of the product is tied to the reputation of key individuals. Thus there is always a fear of leaving or splitting up and a constant search for new, and good, people.[20] This labour characteristic, and the transportability of the technology, are one of the important supply characteristics of forecasting.

Because total costs are so strongly determined by labour costs, they will vary considerably with the quality of that input. The forecast of real GNP made by a single-person operation with a small amount of human capital involved is thus different from that of a multiple-person operation that brings to bear collectively much more human capital. Also, because labour is the key input, total costs will generally vary quite directly with demand.

However, there are two added elements of importance. There are quite substantial front-end costs that must be incurred in the form, for example, of the construction of an econometric model. Because of a certain resemblance to natural monopoly situations, these costs are extraordinary to the usual business service front-end overhead charges, represent a fairly sizeable barrier to entry, and help explain in part the somewhat oligopolistic nature of the industry discussed later in detail. As an aside we should note that there is considerable discussion in the industry about the ability to finance this asset. In many instances financial institutions will not recognize these models as an asset requiring long-term financing. Such an approach thus contributes to the practice of cloning, if not outright copying, models developed with public money. This is yet another manifestation of, and exactly what would be expected from, the public good, externality characteristics of forecasting information.

Added to this cost is another more typical of business services generally, namely the sense of discrete cost arrival, especially with respect to plant and computer cost. That is, both the facilities and the hardware costs tend to be discrete, are required at a certain level for start-up, serve to a certain level of demand, and then must be increased in block fashion. Little about facilities choice is unique to forecasting and the importance of computers will vary with their role in the forecasting method used. But the computer is the one input most directly influenced by potential technological change. Because such change has been so profound in the last 20 years, the very nature of forecasting supply has shifted. Fortunately computing costs have fallen. To that extent total costs for a given-quality product have also dropped. However, other uses or products have been developed, and so computing costs remain significant, albeit less critically than in the early 1970s.[21]

So the nature of inputs suggests that the production function, and hence total costs, may be somewhat stepwise, with important front-end costs. As noted, this ought to imply a certain pressure for economies of scale everywhere, the stepwise arrival of an important input cost a reduced number of eligible production optima (i.e. in terms of scale) if economies of scale don't for some reason hold over all ranges of output.

However, economies of scale everywhere are not the rule; there is no one single all-encompassing private forecasting house, principally because front-end costs are less important than the human capital costs, where scale economies are not to be expected. There are other reasons why scale economies don't necessarily dictate a single firm. The Canadian market for forecasts is quite small relative to exploitable economies. Also, as has been noted, competing institutions such as futures markets are at work setting limits to certain forecasting product markets.

However, because of the discrete arrival of the two other important cost elements, and the tendency for human capital to specialize and spin off, the size of forecast suppliers does tend to be fairly similar. Indeed a sense of optimum scale does prevail. As measured by number of employers, it is bi-modal, being either smaller (1–7) or larger (20–25). Almost every forecasting supplier will be of either one size or the other, regardless of the size of the larger organization within which it may reside. Few are greater or lie between.

There is a parallel here to other business services suppliers such as accountants, management consultants, and lawyers. All have an important profesional human capital cost structure and for the most part exhibit the same sense of optimum size for similar reasons, i.e. smaller or larger but not one, naturally monopolistic firm or many in that middle-size region, where the discrete arrival of other major costs such as computers or plant would be poorly exploited.

Technologies Employed

It has been suggested that all manner of methods can be found. Ultimately they are derivatives of the three approaches to making forecasts that make up the taxonomy discussed in chapter 2. The major suppliers are distinguished by their extensive use of associative methods, in particular econometric methods. As well, some surveying is used by the Conference Board and others (note the board's "Survey of Consumers Attitudes and Buying Intentions"). However, far less extrapolating, in the form, for example, of Box-Jenkins or other more sophisticated time series–theoretic approaches, is used than one might expect. As well, spreadsheet programs for personal computers are beginning to make major inroads, inasmuch as they facilitate relatively quick simulation exercises.

Several other distinctions are worth noting. Many suppliers continue to distinguish themselves as "analytical" (econometric) or "consensual" ("gut-feel," reading and talking, but not doing any explicit analysis). As I stressed in chapter 2 there is a lot of "gut-feel" in analysis and certainly implicit analysis in arriving at a "gut-feel" forecast!

In the past virtually all forecasts were annual in nature, usually for one year ahead, at most two. Prepared in the latter part of the previous year, or early in the year to which they applied, they were heavily tied in an annual budgeting cycle with its relatively short-span considerations. From time to time one would find a 10-year forecast being done, especially for large capital investment.

This older product is still found in the mainstream – the "bread and butter" forecast. But much greater emphasis is being given to both shorter-term (e.g. quarterly, over horizons from one to six quarters) and medium-term (usually five-year) forecasts. In both instances this supply-related change comes as a reaction to alterations in demand. In the former, greater short-term instability due to inflation and oil shocks, and hence a need to know sooner, or in more short-term detail, is cited as an important determinant.[22] In the latter, a shift in both macroeconomic and management theory from fine-tuning to structural issues has moved horizons further out.

This is not to suggest that the forecasting horizon extends unbounded. Indeed, within the last 20 years the industry has undergone a quite radical transformation on the long end from "future-oriented" concern for the next century (e.g. Global 2000) to today's reduced emphasis on the long term. Strong inflation and then economic downturn have, of course, altered the discount rates of economic agents. Thus while certain suppliers such as Informetrica maintain considerable long-term detail, emphasis has shifted to the medium term.

Economic events at large have had two other important consequences. Since 1945 the shift from real considerations to price and then back to real factors during the latest downturn has altered the focus of suppliers from real to price and back to real variables. Recent instability has also led suppliers to an increased provision of several possible futures – interval, or scenario forecasting – even over the short term.

Thus circumstances in both demand and supply have affected the techniques of supplying forecasts. Perhaps the most important aspects of the change in supply have already been noted here, that is the evolution in econometric, macroeconomic, and sampling theory and the change in computing capabilities. Supply will always be dictated by theoretical possibilities with respect to techniques; there will always be dramatic tension between the complexity and speed of various techniques. In that respect the industry's supply, and hence its costs, will likely remain primarily determined by the nature and cost of its human capital.

Measures of Supply

Because of the many difficulties noted, no rigorous supply modelling has been attempted. Rather the same kind of evidence as was presented earlier with respect to demand is considered here as well, i.e. selected summary measures from several sources.

The confidentially available data (Table 3) indicate that total labour costs were on average about 55 per cent of total cost ($R = 0.95$) during the period in question, the second largest expense item being computing (17 per cent of the total). A plot of total costs indicates that they are continuously linearally related to the number of clients ($R = 0.59$); that of total costs divided by the number of clients u-shaped. This evidence suggests that start-up costs are quite important. It also means that there may be some sense of optimal size present: if the number of clients serves as an adequate proxy for output, the AC curve is u-shaped. Data on the number of employees help to confirm this: the total number has stablized in the 20–40 range after several years of operation. There does not, however, seem to be strong evidence of a stepwise total cost function. The individual data indicate that the portion of computing costs jumped in certain years but that the firm compensated by reducing other costs.

The Conference Board annual report data indicate that total salaries were on average about 50 per cent of total costs ($R = 0.99$), "other" costs in total the remaining 50 per cent. Again, total costs were linearly related to the estimated number of clients ($R = 0.88$), with no important breaks. Evidence on the number of employees indicates a relatively stable number over the five years and confirmed fairly high start-up costs.

Table 3 also reports on an examination of the detailed income statistics of the sic category "other business service" organizations for the period 1974–82. It indicates that salaries and wages were on average 47 per cent of total expenses net of cost of goods sold, all other expenses being 53 per cent (data on computing costs could not be broken out). The respective correlation coefficients (0.99, 0.99), as well as the standard deviations, confirm that, for the larger service industry group of which forecasting is a part, labour costs are the major element of supply.

With respect to the data obtained from the interviews, Table 4 indicates that for the public organizations in question, estimated labour costs for forecasting were about 75 per cent of, and highly correlated with, their estimated total forecasting costs, other costs about 25 per cent (with 1/10 of 1 per cent of their total number of employees involved in forecasting). This compares to the private sector, where about 80 per cent of costs, again with high correlation, were for people, 20 per cent for other expenses (with roughly the same proportion of people being involved in forecasting). The frac-

TABLE 3
Measures of Supply for Two Forecasting Organizations and the SIC Industry Group "Other Business Services" 1974–84

	Labour costs		Computer costs		"Other" costs		Total costs
	% of total expenses[a]	Correlation with no. of clients	% of total expenses[a]	Correlation with no. of clients	% of total expenses[a]	Correlation with no. of clients	Correlation with no. of clients
Confidential firm	54% (0.95)	0.50	17% (0.39)	0.90	29% (0.94)	0.48	0.59
Conference Board (1980–4)	51% (0.99)	0.92	(–)	–	49% (0.92)	0.67	0.88
Other business services (1974–81)[b]	47% (0.99)	–	(–)	–	53% (0.99)	–	–

[a]The figure in brackets is the correlation coefficient.
[b]Data on computer costs could not be separated out.

TABLE 4
Additional Evidence on the Nature of Supply from a Sample of Public and Private Organizations 1982–3

	Public organizations	Private				Total public and private
		Banks/insurance	Regulated	Brokerage	Other	
Total labour costs (as % of total costs)[a]	77% (0.98)	78% (0.98)	84% (0.99)	78% (1.00)	75% (0.99)	78% (0.97)
Number of forecasting employees[a]						
As % of total distribution (≤ 7, 7–20, ≥ 20)	0.14% (−0.13) 0.16, 0.16, 0.67	0.12% (0.96) 0.57, 0.00, 0.43	0.13% (0.96) 0.00, 0.25, 0.75	0.13 (0.24) 1.00, 0.00, 0.00	0.06 (0.77) 0.75, 0.12, 0.12	0.12 (0.38) 0.50, 0.10, 0.40
Other costs (as % of total costs)	23%	22%	16%	22%	25%	22%

[a]The figure in brackets is the correlation coefficient.

tion of people and the percentage of total costs accounted for by labour expenses involved in forecasting were noticeably higher in the regulated and banking/brokerage organizations relative to the other companies in the sample, once again providing indirect support for the force of the reasonable care hypothesis advanced above (as indeed does the evidence from the public-sector sample, where the fraction of people employed in large forecasting departments is quite large). Finally, the distribution of the number of employees devoted to forecasting loosely supports the earlier contention concerning optimal size: 50 per cent of the organizations in the total sample had seven or fewer people working in forecasting, 40 per cent more than twenty, with only 10 per cent reporting a number between these two sizes.

SUMMARY

As suggested at the beginning of this chapter, aggregate economic forecasting has evolved to a point where it is worthwhile considering it in some detail. By so doing one can hope to shed some light on theoretical issues of interest, as well as investigate whether public policy with respect to the industry may be required. To aid in this analysis, the classical industrial organization paradigm of structure, conduct, and performance (s-c-p) has been adopted.

The present chapter has considered the nature of the demand and supply of aggregate economic forecasts. Fully acknowledging the weakness of the evidence, it reaches the following conclusions. In theory, the demand for forecasting is motivated by a number of different intellectual traditions. Careful study of its uses today reveals several important underlying factors: relative price, business activity, and education, all of which influence specific motives, including a desire to avoid making large investment mistakes, a need to demonstrate reasonable care in the use of public or private monies, and a desire to spread management risk or to marshal an organization to common environmental assumptions and goals.

The actual modelling of the demand for forecasting is complicated by several factors, the most damaging of which is an absence of sufficient data. What data are available suggest that demand is probably strongly positively related to the level of overall business activity, especially to government spending. As expected, whether measured directly or implicitly via the size of the forecasting error, relative price would seem to be a factor, as is the education level of those who use the forecasts. Increased uncertainty, at least as represented here, does not seem to play a role.

With respect to supply, the principal input is human capital. Returns to it account for a major portion of total costs; estimates range from 50 to 80 per cent. Because the remainder is largely computer or plant-related, it might be supposed that total costs tend to be stepwise, with fairly high front-end costs. The small amount of evidence available confirms that front-end costs are likely quite important but does not support the stepwise arrival argument. There does seem to be a fairly consistent sense of optimal size, firms being either small or large, with few in between. Nor, for reasons discussed above, is there one naturally monopolistic firm.

All kinds of technologies are used, the predominant one being a large-scale econometric model. Forecasting horizons have tended to both lengthen and shorten in recent times, medium-term forecasting becoming relatively more important as compared to either the shorter or extreme longer term. Because of data problems similar to those encountered with demand, supply modelling of the preferred type, using production functions and cost curves, is not possible here. However, summary data from three different types of sources tend to support the assertions made above about the nature of supply in the forecasting industry.

CHAPTER SIX

Structure, Conduct, Performance

"Then take this ... 'Tis a crown-piece."

THE STRUCTURE OF THE INDUSTRY

Introduction

It is interesting to examine next what industrial structure emerges from the nature of demand and supply. Such a consideration leads naturally also to an investigation of conduct, and ultimately performance, in the industry. Both can be used to assess further whether the characterization of structure is valid. Besides this more analytical reason for looking at structure, examination of the industry in these terms is valuable for purely descriptive purposes. In both of these respects it is customary to consider various additional issues about structure, particularly the size distribution of firms, the nature of ownership (private/public, foreign, interlocking), and the question of growth, whether by entry, exit, or merger.

The forecasting industry is part of the tertiary sector, which in Canada accounts for about 45 per cent of GNP. More particularly, as noted above, it is part of the "services to business management," three-digit SIC, industry group. Green (1980) notes that this business services sector as a whole typically has a very low concentration ratio, being essentially monopolistically competitive because of actual or perceived quality differences between suppliers and some entry restrictions, usually resulting from certification, licensing, or other similar requirements.[1] While Green does not explicitly comment on the issue, it can be implied that the degree of foreign, public, or interlocking ownership or control can also be expected to be low relative to the economy as a whole. It is worthwhile considering whether these general conclusions apply to the forecasting industry.

Size Distribution of Firms

The distribution of firms by size is usually expressed in terms of the percentage of total assets, sales, employees, or value added accounted for by the four or eight largest firms. Such concentration ratios are determined principally by issues already noted in connection with demand and supply, particularly the size of the market, economies of scale, mergers, and the nature of input competition.

Two difficulties present themselves in this regard with respect to aggregate economic forecasting. The first is the problem of an appropriate definition of the industry; the second, an absence of data on assets, sales, employees, and value added. The first is especially perplexing in estimating the relative size of the "non-majors," the second in being able to assemble hard data on even an approximate concentration ratio.

Because of these difficulties one is thrown back somewhat on causal empiricism, collective impressions, and informed estimates. As described above, the industry consists of four major core producers, the Conference Board of Canada, Data Resources, Informetrica, and Wharton Economic Canada, and a collection of non-majors, which may buy from the majors but have also traditionally produced some of their own forecasts. While it is difficult to document exactly, my contention here is that the industry is basically an oligopoly of the four majors.

Several pieces of evidence point in this direction: the frequency with which the four are cited by the media; the comprehensive nature of their client bases, touching as they do virtually all areas of business and government; and the fact that most economic actors concerned with economic forecasting consider them of central importance. Evidence below on pricing, service, and other behaviour also yields strong confirmation of this conclusion. To be sure, there is no explicit trade association or government regulatory board that would help indirectly to support such a conclusion. But this is not always found in oligopolies. Moreover, because of the special importance of the four firms in question, the industry is certainly not monopolistically competitive as that designation is used. For these reasons, and after much reflection, I have come to think of the industry in terms of oligopoly, which in some ways parallels the situation in the steel industry, where there are three or four major core producers and a group of specialty firms arrayed around the fringes.

Because of the simple absence of, and/or insufficiently detailed, data, it is impossible to know exactly the relative importance of the four. It is likely that Wharton Canada, the newcomer, has the least billings, employees, and so on, the Conference Board and DRI the most, with Informetrica closer to the latter two than to Wharton Canada. But even so general a statement is open to question, for each arrays itself differently with respect to product mix. Depending on one's definitions, of revenues in particular, relative importance may change somewhat. Such a characterization is therefore only approximately correct.[2]

Such an industry structure is perhaps typical for Canada. As with manufacturing, Canadian forecasting is probably considerably more concentrated than in the United States. To be sure, DRI and WEFA–CEIS (Wharton Consulting) are probably relatively more important there than others, but they in no way represent as important a force as do the four majors in Canada.[3] Alternatively, Canada's is less concentrated than a number of other aggregate forecasting industries elsewhere in the world.

These international comparisons, and earlier comments on supply and demand, suggest several reasons for the degree of concentration. Of equal importance are the size of the potential market, principally domestically but also internationally; the nature of the technology relating to scale issues and restricted technologies; and the degree of direct import competition. Thus it is argued that the Canadian market for aggregate economic forecasts is relatively small because of population; the traditional character of Canada's industrial structure (which restricts the number of potential clients and causes many of the natural resource producers that export to be more interested in forecasts of other countries); dependence on the United States, forecasts of the US economy being thus more important; and certain other factors noted above relating to demand, such as traditional management education patterns and poor anti-collusion enforcement. As well, because there is relatively little interest outside Canada in forecasts of the Canadian market, little exporting of forecasts is possible.

One aspect of the Canadian market that influences the size distribution of forecasting firms is its distinctive regional nature. A large part of the manufacturing and financial sectors, population, and government is concentrated in Ontario and Quebec, with the major natural resource sectors being located elsewhere. The latter are more concerned with the external markets, the former relatively more with Canada. One would thus expect Canadian aggregate economic forecasters to be concentrated in Ontario and Quebec, as indeed they are all, serving the rest of Canada directly from these locations.

The nature of the technology needed to produce aggregate economic forecasts is also an important determinant. The specificity of human capital, the block arrival of certain costs, and the relatively restricted choice of technologies all indicate that there should likely be a restricted number of major producers in the industry but no natural monopoly. Finally, there is little import competition to speak of, principally because foreign producers such as DRI and Chase have entered the market directly, "buying out" Canadians who possessed the technology relevant to the Canadian market.[4] This too is typical of the Canadian economy and suggests that both the tariff, in this case on printed materials, and government subsidies to help build the public good models and data bases may once again have influenced industrial structure as they have more generally.

US Influences

Pursuing this latter point for a moment, US influence in general is important to Canada. About a third of Canadian business in 1973 was foreign owned or controlled, primarily by US interests; over 50 per cent in manufacturing, mining, and smelting, and petroleum and natural gas. One would expect this percentage to be lower in the service sector for reasons discussed above, such as certification or licence requirements. Generally speaking this is true with respect to "services to business management," which include lawyers, accountants, and advertising agencies; while certain large American firms are present, the bulk of the industry in question is basically Canadian owned and controlled.

With respect to the forecasting industry, two of the four majors, Wharton Canada and DRI, are wholly owned subsidiaries of large American companies. If the estimates given in the previous sector are approximately correct, the degree of foreign ownership or control is about average for Canadian industry more generally. Comparisons to situations elsewhere internationally indicate that both DRI and WEFA-CEIS are present in quite a number of countries. In many of these countries, though, domestic forecasting organizations are the most important actors in the industry.[5]

This degree of foreign ownership is, however, deceptive, for the influence of the American forecasting organizations is a good deal more pervasive than the figures suggest. For example, all of the majors use the main American forecasting houses for predictions of key American exogenous (to the Canadian models) variables. Indeed DRI and Wharton Canada's operations would fail to accept directly such forecasts, indeed performance goals and other directives as well, at their hazard. The Conference Board and Informetrica, both of which have to date used WEFA-CEIS for these American forecasts, would do so only under extraordinary circumstances. As well, there are many personal links between organizations on both sides of the border. Finally, as I have argued elsewhere (Daub 1984b), these "intellectual linkages" have in the past led, much as they have with Canadian research and development more generally, to the Americans influencing in a major way the problems, concepts, and techniques that the Canadian forecasting industry takes to be important. Perhaps the major exception would be in data management.

However, it is necessary to balance this observation with the conclusion that in general such ownership and influence, while important, does not imply that the American can, or would even wish to, determine what is forecast for aggregate economic activity in Canada. Indeed an understanding of the history of the Canadian industry and the way it functions makes the notion somehow preposterous. The models of the majors are, after all, completely Canadian. But because of these links, and those in the two economies more generally, they exert important indirect influence.

Changes in Structure

The history of aggregate economic forecasting since the mid-1970s, and the data on total revenue, obtained, as before, from both a confidential source and the Conference Board's annual reports, indicate fairly steady but not spectacular growth. This growth has come about by internal expansion on the part of existing firms and the entry of Chase in the early 1980s.

As anyone can make a forecast, it might be supposed that entry is free. As we have seen, in reality certain barriers are present. The two most important are the large human and non-human capital requirements needed to construct a model of sufficient importance not only to forecast a relatively broad number of variables (i.e. to attract a substantial client base) but also to establish a sufficient reputation for quality, and the fact that the market is not large enough to support many firms. Economies of scale thus require an entrant to displace an existing firm, not necessarily an easy task. Because it brought capital, a certain econometric reputation, and de Bever's Canadian modelling skills, Chase was thus able to enter successfully. The anecdotal evidence that it displaced the other three firms with repect to several clients is quite strong.

Internal growth has been achieved not only through greater sales of aggregate forecasts but also through product diversification into such areas as consulting, regional model building, data services, computer time sharing, software preparation, and training. Indeed, purely aggregate economic forecasting, while still the flagship product, has become considerably less important to performance in recent times. These firms might thus perhaps be viewed better as simply large data suppliers that use forecasts as a convenient vehicle to summarize, access, and hence sell their data services. No doubt this explanation applies more to some firms than others.

Much of this diversification has been necessary because of the increased public availability of aggregate economic forecasts. The source of these forecasts has in part been the majors themselves, which used their obvious interest to the media as a form of indirect advertising, or those organizations in the associated fringe, such as the Royal Bank, that began to release publicly once private forecasts, again for their own presumably strategic reasons. But they have also come increasingly from government-related activities, in particular budgets (e.g. the federal Department of Finance), regulatory hearings, and the express activities of certain government organizations such as Statistics Canada, which has published some aggregate economic forecasts in recent years. Thus while public ownership is not directly a factor, its indirect influence is felt. Some of the implications of this for the industry are explored in detail later in chapter 9.

THE CONDUCT OF THE INDUSTRY

Introduction

In the conduct or behaviour that follows from these structural characteristics, several classes of actions are noteworthy – pricing, promotion, product differentiation, and tactical considerations, having primarily to do with collusion and deliberate attempts to close out competitors or potential entrants. These are classical concerns stemming from suspected oliogopoly and, depending on their presence or absence, serve to confirm or deny its existence.

Pricing

Pricing practices in the forecasting industry vary somewhat but generally are based on an annual subscription fee plus a variable charge for additional services such as simulation, data access, and additional modelling. This fixed subscription fee may be uniform to all clients or scaled depending, for example, on client size. In these respects pricing policies in the industry differ somewhat from those in other business service areas such as law, accounting, and real estate, where uniform pricing also applies but tends to be fixed fee regulated by a larger trade organization. Service-related pricing policies are often cost-plus in nature, and this is also true in forecasting, though there are certain competitive-based characteristics to consider as well.

The foregoing may suggest that the industry is somewhat different from other service industries where price is usually not as significant a factor as service or reputation and from oligopolies more generally, where price is too dangerous a strategic variable. There is much debate about these two propositions within the industry. With respect to the former, some argue that price is irrelevant, since "the annual fee really is peanuts to a large corporation; the big difference is people and service." Others feel that it is relatively important, especially as data and techniques are perceived to be common to all suppliers. Price was clearly a tactical weapon in at least one instance, namely the entry of Chase in 1980. It equally remains one in the minds of the majors, each of which refers to various ways the product mix is chosen, and priced, to ensure if not exactly head-to-head competition, at least the tempting of a rival's client to try a slightly different forecasting product.

But each of the majors inevitably begins and ends discussions on competitive variables with non-price elements. Service, reputation, and breadth of product line are the ones most frequently mentioned. Moreover, announced subscription prices tend to change rather infrequently. One of the majors, for example, has made only three such nominal price changes for its major product in about 10 years of operation. As well, the Conference Board is a declared non-profit supplier, which makes it difficult to analyse its pricing behaviour in conventional terms, or relative to the others. Thus it is likely that price competition is not a major factor in the industry. The benefit/ cost ratio to the buyer is too large, service and reputation are proportionately too important, and the risks from an all-out price war are too great for it to be otherwise.

As noted, however, pricing games are still played! Several of the pricing models from the theoretical oligopoly literature are present. Perhaps the most evident is the price discrimination model based on tie-ins, which the industrial organization literature associates with computer punch cards and safety razor blades. Here the forecast is the computer or razor, access to data and simulation are the punch cards or blades. Heavier users of the latter pay proportionately more, so that the forecasts act almost as loss-leaders, the bulk of final revenue coming from the other activities. There does not appear to be any clear price leadership at work, although some degree of umbrella pricing is reported.

While competitive bidding for clients is not the rule, in the odd instances where it has developed price has been one of the factors considered. Some also suggest that the kinked demand curve is an element in explaining pricing in the industry. Price increases on subscriptions are not necessarily matched. As well, buyers may be tempted in such instances to switch to in-house supply. Price decreases are more likely to be matched either directly or by changing prices on other elements of the mix to offset indirectly any shift in customers. Thus major price changes on subscriptions are infrequent.[6]

Clearly, to the extent that the Conference Board chooses to change its subscription fee for different sizes of clients, or alter its fees for additional simulations relative to straight subscriptions, or change the pricing of its forecasting-related fees relative to its conference pricing practices, it will probably change the demand for DRI's various products. But what is being argued is that price is less a factor than other variables in the marketing mix. What is likely to have a much greater effect on a competitor's revenues is a change in one of the major's reputation for service or the quality of its product. The latter might develop from several well-publicized inaccurate forecasts, or alternatively from the acquisition of a particularly well-respected economist.

Product Differentiation

Thus product differentiation is perhaps the major competitive variable in the industry. There are various dimensions to this discussion, which depend in part on the appropriate definition of the industry's product. Viewed in its broadest sense, the product includes not only forecasts of various sorts but also computer simulation, access to data, and consulting services. If one restricts the discussion to forecasts per se, there are still many potential ways to differentiate the product. For example, a firm could develop a quarterly national model when competitors have only annual models; go medium term if others are only short term; provide sectoral or regional detail if others are only aggregate; publish monthly updates if others do so only quarterly; provide special sectoral forecasts of, for example, oil or automobiles; or build a smaller model when others are larger. The possibilities, if not endless, are nonetheless extensive. Many of the above tactics have been used.

Such attempts to differentiate are natural. So too are attempts to broaden the product definition. Competition can then go forward on aspects of the broadened product. Thus one may deliver forecasts twice yearly to a gathering of professional economists from all of one's clients, or yearly and publicly to the client's directly in different regions of the country, or individually by mail or in person. One can package simulation or data access privileges in the same way banks vary the number of cheques as a function of the nature of one's account. Again the possibilities are quite extensive.

While it is quite difficult to generalize about the respective product strategies of the four majors, some patterns are evident both to the objective observer and to those in the industry. The Conference Board might be thought of as being the full-line supplier, having quarterly, medium-term, and regional models, a survey of consumer intentions, and so on. It also has a broad range of clients across the country. Informetrica has the most extensive sectoral data, but in an annualized format with predictions out to the year 2000. It has fewer clients, which are also geographically more concentrated. DRI, located in Toronto, publishes monthly revisions to its forecasts which are available over a range of horizons. It has special sectoral models and a range of data access options and serves a fairly broad client base, primarily in the private sector. Wharton Canada's model is much smaller; its public profile much lower; its self-perceived image one of the new guys on the block, of running faster. In the words of one interviewee who mixed commercial metaphors shamelessly but whose characterization is not without merit: "Informetrica is the Cadillac of the business, the Board – Chevrolet, DRI – Ford, and Wharton Canada maybe Avis."[7]

In addition to the natural aversion to pricing wars there are two other reasons for this product differentiation activity, which stem from the nature of the product itself. First, a forecast of, for example, real GNP is essentially a homogeneous product. Real GNP after all is real GNP, much as #2 spring wheat is #2 spring wheat. Second, such a forecast has many of the characteristics of a public good. It is quite impossible to trademark, copyright, or otherwise make private the returns to a simple forecast of real GNP. Without the direct aid of a price war, which profits no one, it is therefore necessary, if one is to capture returns, to tie other forecasts in, to vary the sense of product by including data access, and more generally to do anything else one can imagine to differentiate the basic product.

Promotion

In the presence of strategic restrictions on price competition, and such an obvious emphasis on product competition (as well as an absence of any trade or professional association to restrict same), one might be forgiven for expecting a deluge of promotional competition. The situation would seem not unlike that of autos, beer, or the brokerage business. And yet one encounters no billboards extolling the virtues of the Conference Board's latest forecasts or cute slogans about DRI's data accessibility ("Try DRI's CPI"?). Instead promotion is carried out primarily by word of mouth, supplemented by direct mail campaigns to, and personal solicitations of, selected groups of potential clients. Regular forecasting conferences are also in part a promotional vehicle. But perhaps the most important route is the free advertising afforded by personal interviews with the media about the firm's latest forecast.

This latter vehicle is double-edged: the public good aspects of the forecast mean that once it is released, returns to the forecast cannot be recouped. However, the strategy behind the approach is clear. Only enough forecasting information to attract the media is provided. This then establishes a certain public reputation. Clients are thereby motivated to purchase additional products, including other forecasts, data simulation, and consulting.

The economics of this trade-off are impossible to establish. Indeed they are often obscured in discussions by reference to an obligation to provide society with some benefit free of charge, a public service motivation that is unquestionably genuine but not the whole story. But if the survivorship principle is any judge, it is a practice as continuously old as the industry, which suggests it must be cost-effective. The industry is now mature enough for it to have died out had the loss to public release exceeded the value of the free publicity.

The economics of the situation unquestionably dictate this promotional strategy. The cost of more conventional vehicles, such as television or targeted magazines, relative to the potential client base or to the maximum price that could be charged, makes these options uneconomic in the extreme. As well, there is undoubtedly a certain sociological aspect having to do with the professional nature of the business. Most of the majors feel that an excessive or aggressive promoting of one's wares would if anything reduce one's reputation rather than enhance it. As a consequence, promotional practices are typical of those usually found in service industries, with one exception unique to forecasting – namely the deliberate use of free advertising which the media regularly provide as part of the public's continued interest in the firm's main products – and perhaps one or two other industries.

Other Tactical Considerations

Several important practices that do not conveniently fit under the usual price-product-promotion rubric remain to be considered. The most important are "place," collusion/predation/exclusion, and research and development.

With respect to the first, marketing theory speaks of 4Ps, the fourth being "place," that is "where" the product is sold or alternatively its channels of distribution. This dimension is of little consequence here: most of the majors market directly to professional business economists in their client firms. Indeed for one of the majors the number of such economists to be found in an organization is an important key to potential clients. Practices such as the Conference Board's regular forecasting conferences can be viewed as an attempt to market directly to decision-makers, but even in this instance the continuing aspects of the business directly involve the client's economist(s). The economist(s) may act as a private-label retailer of the majors' basic products. Thus the product reaches market by a different channel of distribution.

Collusion, predation, and exclusion are practices often associated with oligopoly. Short of actual prosecution, evidence on the existence of such practices is inevitably anecdotal (and thus a function of the source's integrity) or educated hunch. In the former department there are stories told of attempts by one of the majors, using threats of a price war directed at his clients, to buy out a distant local supplier; of efforts to arrange exclusive cross-marketing arrangements with a US house to the detriment of competitors; and so on. There is also allusion to mutual "back-scratching," for example, always sending a client whose need one cannot meet to the same competitor. It is impossible to establish conclusively that such practices took [take] place on a regular and general basis. It would be surprising if normal activity to foreclose potential competitors or to buy or close out weak existing ones does not take place. However, flagrant activity of the Eddy Match case variety does not exist.

Nor is there likely overt collusion to fix prices or divide markets, whether on a product or location basis. Obviously none of the majors would admit that it did. But after much interviewing and reflection, my impression is that it does not. Consider, for example, that several recent purchasers of forecasting services stated that when making their initial choice they had talked with several of the majors and found all of them actively soliciting the business. Moreover they had heard back from those who lost out urging reconsideration. Other pieces of such indirect evidence confirm this impression of an absence of overt collusion.

Tacit collusion, however, is something else. It is difficult to define tacit collusion more generally, or in this instance the distinction between it and a kind of professional ethic of not raiding the competition's clients or of having an unofficial understanding that a certain product (or type of client, or location) generally belongs to the competition while others come accordingly "to us." But my impression is that there is something like this practice at work in the industry. Comments made above about each of the majors concerning product differentiation, location, and preferences for certain types of clients all confirm it. There may be perfectly good reasons for it. Informetrica has close links to the Economic Council and generally throughout the federal government because of its principal actor's CANDIDE work; DRI is involved with the Toronto business community and the Ontario government because of the early associations of DRI with the University of Toronto; and so on.

Such areas of special interest are by and large "generally understood" and respected. Certainly no trade association or industry-sanctioning body similar to the Canadian Bar Association or the Canadian Medical Association exists to facilitate such overt or tacit collusion. Alternatively there is perhaps more public knowledge about competitors than is customary in most service industries. A competitor may be cited or interviewed by the media. Depending on the circumstances, a good deal can be learned about its thinking and strategic emphasis from such an interview. As well, principals "come across one another" probably more frequently, at professional meetings, directly through sitting on the same panels, and so on, than do the principals in the steel or auto industry. Thus there is a good deal of opportunity for monitoring the competition. And while overt collusion has not developed and it is professed that there is "no love lost between the majors," it should come as no surprise that an understanding of sorts about respective price product, promotion, location, and other strategic considerations has developed.

In research and development to support product differentiation, there has been some additional competition. Countless examples can be cited: the move by the Conference Board to develop a medium-term model, of Informetrica to develop a regional model, of DRI and others to build energy models; of Wharton Canada and all the others to develop personal computer forecasting software; of all the majors to tinker continually with the econometric aspects of their basic models, to develop new and better data sources, or to refit the entire model in the face of historical data revisions by STATSCAN. All require considerable research and development effort.

Not all of this work is in reaction to methodological developments elsewhere. Some independent work is in fact carried on. But for the most part, because of the public good argument advanced above, the industry relies heavily on basic research carried out in universities or outside Canada, principally in the United States, for fundamental changes. These outside sources tend to define the areas of current concern and to determine the momentum of technological change. It is argued below in chapter 9 that this practice explains not only why a certain mismatch between supply and demand has developed at certain points in the industry's history but also why the industry goes through periods of furious technological activity followed by ones of relative quiet. Further to this latter point, there is always a kind of tension between the rate at which the researchers in the universities would like the basic research to be adopted and its commercial viability as perceived by the industry. But these observations are no different from those relating to R&D in Canada more generally; they share many of the same explanations and suggest many of the same remedies.

THE PERFORMANCE OF THE INDUSTRY

Introduction

The final step in most industry studies is an examination of actual performance. Although conduct or behaviour is also part of performance, custom has distinguished it from performance, in particular from issues of profitability and efficiency. I have followed this approach here. As well, public policy concerns follow directly from a completed discussion of performance. Liability for error, regulation, and public ownership are among the important public policy concerns one can raise with respect to the industry. These various elements of performance are considered in chapter 9.

Profitability

In addition to a simple desire to know, the principal motivation for studying an industry's profit history is to confirm or deny one's hypothesis about its structure. Continued abnormally high profits in the face of observed high concentration confirm, at least in a simplistic way, suspected oligopoly or monopoly. Hence there have been a host of studies over the years both in individual industries and on economies as a whole attempting to link various measures of profitability to various measures of concentration. They have met with various degrees of success!

The present study is thus not unique in its difficulties with profitability. It will be recalled that an argument for oligopoly has been made. Thus the data should suggest abnormally high profits. Unfortunately the data are not substantially up to the task, for reasons noted earlier. Two of the four firms are wholly owned subsidiaries, another is a private company, and the fourth is a declared non-profit organization. It is also argued by many who have studied service industries that many of the professional service groups, such as doctors, lawyers, and management consultants, choose deliberately to take some of their profits in the form of tax-deductible expenses such as cars, office furniture, and prestigous buildings. For all these reasons, any discussion of the profitability of the Canadian aggregate economic forecasting industry is bound to be indicative at best.

There are several types of evidence one can cite. Data used above in respect to demand and supply can be considered. They come from a confidential firm, the Conference Board's annual reports, STATSCAN data on "other business services" and "services to business management" in total, and anecdotal sources (three or four pieces of information).

With respect to the confidential firm, one can compute the several different ratios customarily considered. These include rate of return on equity (π/E), rate of return on assets $([\pi + R]/A)$, price-cost margin $(P-C)$, and profits earned on sales (π/TR). They do not include the more recently suggested Tobin q statistic (market value divided by replacement cost), since this would require a market value measure such as stock price, obviously not available in this industry.

Table 5 indicates that for the firm in question the rate of return on equity over the given period was about 20 per cent, that on assets about 15 per cent, and that on total sales about 6.0 per cent. As well, the margin of price over average total cost was about 8 per cent of average costs.[8] The rate of return on equity and sales is quite similar to that reported for "other business services" or indeed to "services to business management."

Given the degree of imprecision attached to the estimates, the results for the Conference Board tend to confirm those obtained for the confidential firm. Certainly the percentages are lower. But inasmuch as the Board is professedly non-profit, one would expect them to be so, as they are generally, except for the price/(retained) earnings ratio, there being no shareholders in the traditional sense.[9]

TABLE 5
Selected Indicators of Performance

	Ratios[a]							
	π/E	$[\pi + R]/A$	$P - C$	π/TR	FA/E	LTD/E	R/TC	CA/CL
Confidential firm[b]	22%	14%	8%	6.0%	28%	23%	1.8%	0.93
Conference Board (1980–4)[b]	36	8	8	4.4	94	22	0.4	1.02
National Statistics (1974–84)[c]								
Other business services	26	—	—	10.3	51	22	2.4	1.20
Services to business mgt.	21	—	—	8.3	49	19	2.2	1.20
Total services	16	—	—	6.3	113	54	3.6	1.00
All businesses	13	—	—	5.9	84	66	6.8	1.10

[a] π/E = average pre-tax profit/average equity; $[\pi + R]/A$ = rate of return on assets; π/TR = profit earned from total sales; $P - C$ = interest as a portion of total costs; CA/CL = the quick ratio (current assets/current liabilities).
[b] Estimated from financial statements available to the study.
[c] STATSCAN 61-207.

Finally the calculations on data from "other business services" and "services to business management" indicate that the appropriate rates of return are generally higher for these groups than for the total services sector, or for business in general.

Each of these pieces of evidence suggests that the industry makes abnormally high profits relative to business in general, a result consistent with its suggested oligopoly-like structure. However, they also indicate that the industry is no different from other business services, such as advertising agencies, engineering and scientific consultants, accountants, architects, lawyers, and computer service firms.

The anecdotal evidence on profitability is mixed. One interviewee from a major commented, "You'll never get rich in this business"; another, that his was "the most profitable of all operations in the larger company." A casual application of the survivorship principle suggests that since the majors have continued in business for some period now, indeed through a major recession, without exit, the industry must surely be profitable. It is difficult to know whether these anecdotal observations about the Canadian industry are typical. There is some comparative anecdotal evidence for the United States. For example, it is rumoured that when DRI in the United States was sold to McGraw-Hill, profits after the sale were not as high as they were before, even though DRI still made money. Also, reports accompanying the attempted sale of Wharton Econometrics to the French in 1983 indicated that Wharton had lost money since 1980.[10] More recently, in an article concerning the rumoured sale of Chase Econometrics, also to McGraw-Hill, it was suggested that DRI in the United States "had suffered set backs recently."[11]

Thus the anecdotal evidence is both confusing and difficult to interpret. Because of the absence of a similarly detailed study of the industry in other countries, it is difficult to know exactly what the actual measures of profitability obtained here indicate about structure. They certainly point to concentration but might also be due, for example, to tariff protection. The absence of a trade association or sanctioning body is no conclusive proof that concentration is not the explanation. In the "other business services," some groups such as lawyers and accountants have sanctioning bodies, which probably explains their higher profits. But they are more monopolistically competitive than the forecasting industry. Besides, others in this group, such as advertising or market research agencies, do not have such bodies and are also profitable and concentrated. Thus in the forecasting industry higher accounting profits probably reflect market power stemming from increased concentration.[12]

Efficiency

Whether or not the forecasting industry is "efficient" in the various senses of that term is difficult to evaluate, as it is for most any service industry. Nonetheless there are pieces of evidence one can cite.

Table 5 indicates that the ratio of long-term debt to equity for both the confidential firm and the Conference Board is about the same as for the rest of the business service sector. So is the ratio of interest charges to sales revenue. That the debt/equity ratios are no different suggests, at least implicitly, that the forecasting industry uses capital in its various forms at least as efficiently as other similar kinds of businesses. The same may be said for the relationship of assets to liabilities, especially the quick ratio, which, while a bit low relative to business services, is nonetheless virtually identical to services in total. Table 5 confirms that people are the most important asset of the industry, indeed of the entire business services group: the fixed asset to equity ratios are much lower than for services in total or business in general.

It is also possible to look at other labour-related measures. For example, the ratio of clients to number of employees has remained relatively stable or increased slightly for both the firms in question during the past few years. One suspects that the same is true for the other majors. Earlier evidence on the bi-modal nature of size by number of employees which the forecasting suppliers have come to adopt also points to optimal size having developed. Without comparative figures on the us industry, or other Canadian service industries of this type, it is difficult to judge if this indicates efficiency. But reasoning from the survivorship principle we might at least tentatively conclude that it does.

The continued attempts at technological improvement indicate some efforts towards dynamic efficiency. Again there are no good statistics on the ratio of research and development expenditures to sales to document this. Moreover the argument is complicated by the public good aspects of forecasting technology. But casual empiricism suggests that the industry is regularly at work re-estimating equations, developing new models, introducing new software packages, and otherwise behaving in ways that indicate an ongoing struggle to be more efficient.[13] There is no clear-cut evidence of a difference between a wholly owned subsidiary such as DRI and Informetrica, although there have been some suggestions that the us subsidiaries may import more technology from the United States than Informetrica, which does more of its own work.

Thus the evidence that can be marshaled suggests that forecasting is at least as efficient as similar business service industries, and compares favourably with other business in most other respects as well. Because of the absence of a similar study to this, it is impossible to know how it compares with the US industry. One suspects that it is on a par.

SUMMARY

In summary, it is argued here that the industrial structure that emerges in Canada from the interplay of the demand and supply of aggregate economic forecasts can be thought of as an oligopoly of four firms. That structure is the result of a relatively limited domestic, and virtually no export, market for its major product, the nature of the technology needed to generate an acceptable-quality product, and little direct import competition of the traditional kind. There is, however, a strong indirect influence exerted by the US forecasting industry, even if the estimated direct ownership or control is about average for Canadian industry more generally. The industry is concentrated in central Canada for obvious reasons and has grown throughout its relatively brief history both by internal expansion due to diversification and by entry. Publicly available product has always been a factor in the industry and, while not directly so at present in a major way, does provide a potential limit to private-sector activity in the industry.

We have also considered various aspects pertaining to the industry's performance. An investigation of conduct relating to pricing, promotion, product differentiation, and other behaviour reveals a very rich array of strategic practices in many ways typical of rational competition in an oligopolistic setting. Price changes are as usual gingerly considered; attempts at product differentiation supported by some research and development are the norm; and so on. Promotion is, however, somewhat different, being essentially indirect and at others', principally the general media purchaser's, expense. A type of unspoken agreement seems to have developed that may be a function of service industry ethics, rough strategic equilibrium, or some other factor.

Finally, the industry's profit and efficiency were considered. Again because of the nature of the data, one must exercise caution. But the several pieces of evidence cited seem to indicate that the aggregate economic forecasting industry makes abnormally high profits relative to business in general. However, it is no different in this respect from other business services. Because of the absence of comparable studies for other countries, it is difficult to know whether these higher profits are due to concentration or to other factors such as tariff protection. One suspects, however, that they reflect market power stemming from increased concentration. By and large the evidence suggests that the industry is at least as efficient as similar business service industries, comparing favourably with other business in most respects as well. It is impossible to know how it compares to the US forecasting industry. It is likely that the two are quite similar in this, as in most other, respects.

It will be recalled that at the outset of chapter 5 several reasons were given for wanting to look more closely at the industry. The first involved a desire to document whether certain hypotheses about behaviour were more or less correct. One can now reasonably conclude that the evidence presented in chapter 5 on the actual nature of demand supports hypotheses about it advanced earlier in chapter 1.

One hypothesis, that of rational expectations, was of particular interest. Viewed in its entirety, the evidence in chapters 5 and 6 strongly supports the conclusion that forecasts are rationally determined. Further it suggests that the output of the industry is equivalent to the rationally determined expectation. In economics, we easily accept the argument that the number of haircuts or the quantity of steel supplied is rationally determined, and one has every right to expect the same with respect to forecasts.

Thus, in doing a rationally enhanced, long-term simulation for policy purposes, it would be incorrect under this argument to use directly forecasts implicitly provided, whether approximated by multivariate time series theoretic or other econometric means. Much more appropriate would be a series of forecasts provided by forecasting firms directly.[14]

There is one other important implication. It is a derivative of the foregoing but deserves special emphasis. Traditional aggregate economic forecasting is only one of a series of possible instruments for dealing with the future. As relative price is changed, deliberately or by events, one can expect its demand and supply to change. Further, when there are serious questions about its intellectual place ("safety" or "value" is an equivalent concept in the context of other products and services), its presence is altered. This latter point is important with respect to the increasing adoption of efficient markets/rational expectations arguments in theory, and hence to practices that "let the market forecast for us." Because of this, we have come to demand less and less of traditional forecasting. It is unlikely that such forecasting will disappear completely, because the efficient markets hypothesis subsumes efficient forecasting and because human nature somehow requires traditional forecasting. But the role of traditional economic forecasting has changed significantly because of these shifts in demand and supply for it and potential substitutes.

CHAPTER SEVEN

Accuracy

"You are not certain, of course?"

As a consequence of the final section of the previous chapter, the reader might be forgiven his or her wonder at suddenly coming on a chapter or two that propose to consider the accuracy of Canadian aggregate economic forecasts. Was it not, after all, concluded that the industry was both profitable and efficient? Surely this implies satisfaction with its product – and their accuracy.

To be sure this requires the added assumption that the "revealed truth" motive for demanding the forecasts is important. But that was never disputed earlier, only the contention that it was the only motive. However, accuracy of the forecast will always be an important issue. Thus one inference from the past success of the industry must surely be that consumers find these forecasts acceptably accurate.

So why do we have the judgment of Bacon or Hardy? Why do we see headlines today like "What Good Are Forecasters Anyway?" How can it be that the industry prospers but its customers complain incessantly about one of the product's major characteristics? What is it about this infernal question of accuracy that is so infuriating, but not so much as to keep us from coming back for more? These and other important similar questions are one of the reasons for systematically considering the entire issue of the "accuracy" of forecasts independently. What can the term possibly mean? How is it measured? What has been the actual record?

Another reason for pursuing the subject lies with my observation over time that most people use accuracy as a proxy for other concepts, two in particular, that really concern them. The first is as an approximation for benefits from forecasting, against which they dutifully, if subjectively, set off costs to determine the value of the exercise. The second is as a convenient measure that summarizes a host of things that they are upset about but can't articulate. I have given the example elsewhere (Daub 1984b) of how dissatisfaction with economics, especially with the relative absence of clear macroeconomic policy direction (stemming from the confused state of macroeconomic and econometric theory and practice), often surfaces as criticism of the accuracy of aggregate economic forecasts which supposedly derive from that theory. Whatever the motive, and surely another is purely the interest in seeing what the record has been, there is thus justification for considering the accuracy of Canadian aggregate economic forecasts.

Before doing so, we must note one problem, which is known in the philosophy of science as the prediction dilemma. It "has evinced great concern ... [about] the feasibility of social prediction."[1] Nagel (1961) puts it this way: "Even when sociological predictions of future social events are the conclusions of competent inquiries, these conclusions can be made invalid if they come to the attention of the people at whom they are directed and if, in the light of the knowledge of this prediction, these people alter the patterns of their behavior upon whose study the original conclusion were based."[2]

Two possibilities exist, self-fulfilling and self-defeating predictions. The argument goes as follows. If I predict a recession for next year, and everyone believes me, they will increase savings, spend less, invest less, build up inventories, and thereby cause the very recession predicted" (self-fulfilling). Alternatively, if I predict a recession for next year, and the government believes me, it will increase the money supply and cut taxes to offset the expected recession, thereby making my prediction self-defeating. If one, therefore, wishes to comment after the fact on the accuracy of the forecast, one would presumably have to know how much of this self-altering activity, whether self-fulfilling or self-defeating, came into play. In general no one can know this, and therein lies the methodological problem.

Several responses to this prediction dilemma have been proposed by Henshel (1978) and others. First, there is the possibility of making "compensated" predictions. That is, forecasters would take the self-altering behaviour of their predictions into account. Economics would seem to have adopted this approach as part of its rational expectations assumption. Second, one could issue either "sealed" or "real-time" predictions. These would be ones that were not publicized or were so complex as to be unable to alter behaviour in the time available for making decisions. Third, it may well be that history has its own momentum, unalterable in substantive ways by any prediction. Fourth, no one forecaster enjoys sufficient prestige to have his or her forecasts self-altered in this way.

I would argue that the fourth response is the most directly relevant to our discussion here. Counter-examples can, of course, be given, but they almost inevitably relate to things like stock or commodity market predictions. I know of no documented instance in which a single forecaster, government or private, has been able to talk down an inflation, that is, predict falling prices and have them fall solely because of that, or in any other important way alter major national economic aggregates. The reasons are, I think, straightforward. People know that past and present forces have, to a certain extent, their own way of altering the future, and that no one has sufficient foresight and/or power to foresee exactly, or make come true, that future. In short, people don't completely believe forecasters! And for these reasons one is able to ignore this prediction dilemma and go ahead with measuring accuracy, however defined, but not including compensation for self-alteration.

Then why do people buy forecasts they don't believe? There is an answer, though. I gave it earlier. They may be behaving rationally, in that their ignorance is less if they do. Or they have other reasons for which they need the forecasts, i.e. other than for changing their own behaviour. Recall that they may want to motivate others, spread risk, and so on. None of these requires them to believe completely, or at all for that matter, in the prestige of the forecaster to the extent of self-altering the forecast. And even if one person, or for that matter a group of persons, did, not all economic agents would. Here I cite my own observations of the perspicacious character of humankind as proof! One could use a more appropriate term from economic theory like "bounded rationality" to argue similarly. As a consequence, one is entitled to consider the accuracy of aggregate economic forecasts directly without worrying about the prediction dilemma. That is not to say that the notion of what constitutes accuracy is much clearer yet. Let us next consider what the term might conceivably mean in the present context.

WHAT CONSTITUTES "ACCURACY"?

Introduction

It is probably fair to say that accuracy is whatever one wishes it to be. I always respond to any question about how accurate Canadian forecasters are with the rather flippant request: "If you tell me what you mean by accurate, I'll tell you whether they are, or not." This is not to condemn the quest as futile but rather to suggest that the whole business is rather more complicated than it might seem.

"... I was an economic analyst for a major bank, but I was only 17% right in my forecasts and they demanded at least 23% accuracy ... so, uh ..."

Consider the typical aggregate economic forecaster such as Informetrica, the forecasts of which you might wish to assess/judge. First you must decide whether you wish to base the judgment on one variable or a collection. If the latter, is there a hierarchy of importance in the errors? How do you plan to weight them in some overall assessment? Then you must decide if it will be just one year you'll choose, or an average over several years. If the former, the year you choose might be atypical. If the latter, what average are you talking about? And what about the variance? And how do you decide if it's large enough to constitute "inaccuracy"? Might you not be more interested in the record at turning points in the economy? Or whether forecasts in some years are more or less accurate than others? Should it not all bear some relationship to how well other forecasters are doing? Or how well you could have done using other methods? Or what you lose from being wrong? One could go on for quite some time like this.

To help structure the research, and ensure some uniformity of results, it has become customary to consider two classes of measures of accuracy. The first group, absolute measures, considers any deviation from the actual value to constitute inaccuracy; the second, relative measures, compares the absolute accuracy measures to some outside criteria in order to introduce some perspective to the evaluation.

Absolute Measures

At the simplest level the deviation of a single prediction from the actual constitutes error under the assumption that exactly predicting the actual is the object. There are several problems, however. First, there is almost always measurement error present in economic variables. Data are constantly being revised. Which revision does one use — the first, the latest, the last? If one waits for the last, it may well be 30 or 40 years before the final historical revision is made! With time, the practice of using the first estimates has developed. Because of unavoidable delays in obtaining the data for complete revisions, the early estimates are the only ones available on which to base subsequent forecasts. Also, to use the completely revised figures would amount to making the forecaster responsible for estimating future revisions in the data.[3]

Second, the year in question might be atypical in some respect, either for some real reasons, or because the forecaster's crystal ball was abnormally cloudy or clear that year. Would it not be "better," that is, more representative, to add a few more years into the reckoning before coming to a judgment?

Most of us would likely say "yes;" thereby falling into a "big pit." How many years? How will we capture the representative/typical error? An average? What average — the mean, median, mode? Ought we to weight some years more heavily than others in that average? Perhaps the most recent? Or one that for some reason completely external to our work was considered more atypical than the rest? And is not the variance of errors as important as their average? We might, for example, want the really big errors to count more in that average than the others, so why not argue, following our earlier discussions of the basis for regression and time series estimation, that it is average, or sum, of the squared errors that counts? And interesting as the average might be, are not the signs of the individual errors also important to know? That is, how many times did the forecaster underestimate the actual, how many times overestimate it? In that respect, if the variable in question went through a cycle, or several such cycles, over the years in question, did the forecaster make the same kinds of errors at the peaks as at the troughs? Did he or she, for example, make directional errors such as missing a turn or giving a false signal? What was the total/average number of such errors? It seems that these games never end. This is the second time we have wandered down dimly lit definitional corridors! Again precedence comes to the rescue.

Let us take the issues in turn: 1) There is no general answer to the question of over how many years to calculate the average. It is usually a function of data availability and the purpose at hand;[4] averages are indeed taken, mostly unweighted means, occasionally medians, of the deviations of predictions from actuals. As well, a simple unweighted average of squared errors, the "mean square error," is regularly reported.[5] 2) Measures of the variation in the errors are reported, usually the range and the standard deviation. This is done both directly, and indirectly, the latter through decomposing statistically the mean square error into its "bias" (i.e. the difference between the average prediction and the average actual), "variance" (the difference of the standard deviations of the predictions from the actuals' standard deviation), and "residual" components.[6] 3) The signs of the errors are collected and also used to report on bias.' Directional errors are particularly important, and, wherever possible, they are analysed separately.[7] 4) Finally other measures not alluded to above are also used. The correlation of forecasts with actuals is also a favourite; regressions of predictions on actuals another possible approach. Where various forecasts are available for the same horizon, quarterly forecasts being an example, the manner in which errors vary with changes in the forecast horizon, or as the forecaster gets closer to a given future point, is interesting (i.e. is he or she astigmatic or myopic?). Where components of an aggregate such as GNP and its expenditure sector components are available, which ones have the larger error is also of interest.

"Relative" Measures

Each of these particular approaches to absolute accuracy analysis has its place and its particular associated problems. Consider the unweighted, unsquared, mean error measure. What are we to make of the fact that it was, for example, −2.1 per cent for the Toronto Dominion Bank's predictions of the change in nominal GNP over the period 1956–69? The answer is: very little by itself except possibly that the sign was negative, indicating an underestimation on average of general economic growth. Without some relative sense such as the size of the actual change itself on average, or whether the error was significantly different statistically from zero, or how others did, we know little.

For this reason one usually proceeds quite directly to relative measures, the most immediate of which involves testing the various absolute measures such as the mean error, its variance, the number of over-versus underestimates, the correlation coefficient, and the slope and intercept coefficients for their statistical significance. On the surface these may not appear to be relative measures, but they clearly are, primarily because they require a choice of "significance level." In statistical theory this significance level is generally chosen as a function of the cost (probability) of making a wrong inference, a directly relative consideration here. Changing the specified significance level will change the definition of accuracy.[8] This, therefore, makes one's conclusions on the absolute accuracy measures directly relative to the cost of making a wrong inference about whether the average forecast error is significant. Again, precedence adopts the usual 5 per cent significance specification. But, as suggested, the choice in each case must be made by the assessor as a function of his or her direct cost of error. Being wrong one time in twenty may be too often, or not often enough, as the case may be.[9]

If significance testing is the most immediate sense of "relativeness," the most human is surely "How well did that other bunch do?" This gives rise quite naturally to inter-forecaster comparisons, usually involving the testing of the significance of the differences in the various absolute measures obtained for each.[10] Of these, the most frequent involves the comparison of mean errors. Again one has to be careful statistically not only because of the significance level choice, or the small sample problems, but also because there may well be correlation between the two sets of errors. Forecasters talk to each other all the time. As a consequence, how can one know if their forecasts are really independent of one another, or what the exact amount of overlap is, something that the statistical test requires?[11] One cannot. If one is careful, the correlation is estimated and the test statistic adjusted accordingly. Usually, of course, no such thing is done. One just goes ahead and tests!

An alternative approach is to compare the absolute error measures of a given forecaster or group of forecasters against those associated with an alternative method. Customarily this involves using simple, relatively costless alternatives such as those naive time series models discussed earlier. The reference to larceny should now be recalled. Various relative measures are possible. The one most frequently cited is the relative mean square error (RMSE), which compares the mean square error of the forecaster's predictions against those from the extrapolative method. One hopes that the RMSE will have a value of less than one. Another approach sometimes seen (Mincer 1969) involves regressing the forecaster's predictions on the actuals and the extrapolative predictions to discover whether the forecaster's method included at least the information available from simple extrapolative predictions.[12]

Most of these approaches to relativeness are straightforward. But they are also approximations to the correct measure of relativeness, which is what the inaccuracy brings forth, i.e. the error relative to the cost or loss from making it.[13] There are two important ways in which the accuracy of these aggregate economic forecasts leads to such costs/losses, independent, of course, of the individual economic agent's direct concerns. The first involves lost social welfare from formulating government policy on wrong information, the second lost profits, or often losses per se, to the firm using these inaccurate forecasts to make production, pricing, or other strategic plans.

Economists, and other social scientists, have had a great deal of difficulty modelling the concept of social welfare. Particularly unclear is exactly what the concept includes, especially in economics. Attempts have been made to develop social welfare functions that include such variables as GNP and unemployment.[14] There are a number of problems with this approach. Perhaps the most important involves determining the weighting scheme associated with these individual arguments. If one is to enact policies that maximize social welfare, a total measure of social welfare is needed. To arrive at that figure one must aggregate up over the individual arguments in the function. But how? For some, employment is more important than growth; for others the reverse is true; for still others prices are most important. And do preferences not change over time? The problem rapidly becomes unmanageable.

But were one able somehow to achieve agreement on such a weighting scheme, it would be relatively easy to estimate the lost social welfare from inaccurate forecasts. What social welfare would have been with perfectly accurate forecasts could be estimated from statistical models and compared to what it has been, given inaccurate forecasts. The difference, while still only an approximation to the true costs (because, for example, of self-alteration or "outside" random events), would be a much more appropriate measure of the inaccuracy of the forecasts than the mean or mean square error. However, for the reasons stated, it will likely always remain an un-attainable theoretical ideal.

However, it is posssible to estimate the true accuracy of these aggregate economic forecasts as seen from the vantage point of the firm, at least to the extent that one is willing to accept profits as the only element in the firm's welfare function. Insofar as this latter assumption holds, and there is general agreement among economists and others that it does, and to the extent that profits can be well measured, then so too can the costs of inaccuracy.

To demonstrate how this might be done, consider a company that is a monopolist in its major product market.[15] Assume that the quan-tity demanded is a function of price (p) and income (Y) (with error), that the production decision is made before the quantity demanded is observed, and that price adjusts to clear the market without the existence of inventories, back-ordering, or the like.

Suppose, as in Figure 1, that demand is forecast as D (Y^*). This implies that q^*_{y*} is the optimal quantity to produce. However, actual demand is $D(Y_A, e)$, resulting in profit $ABEF$. If income had been forecast perfectly, demand would have been predicted as $D(Y^* = Y_A)$, and q^* $(Y^* = Y_A)$ would have been the optimal quantity to pro-duce. Actual demand of $D(Y_A, e)$ would, therefore, have implied profit $ACDG$. The difference in profits that would have resulted from ac-curate forecasts of income, that is, $ACDG - ABEF$, is then a measure of the gross cost of aggregate forecast errors.[16]

Certainly the expectations of a given firm usually include several major inputs besides that firm's own aggregate economic forecast. These might include forecasts for the industry by trade associations and for the particular firms in question and/or the industry by se-curity analysts. Ideally, one would want to consider all these factors explicitly in developing any theory and obtaining estimates of the influence of inaccurate aggregate forecasts on the firm's actions. To the outside researcher some of these inputs are often unobservable or unavailable. As a result, while acknowledging that more generality would be desirable, one usually has to estimate the effects of inac-curate aggregate forecasts on an individual firm within a more lim-ited framework. Several such estimates, using somewhat different approaches, are given below.

These are then some of the possible senses one might give to the notion of the accuracy of these aggregate economic forecasts. That there are so many senses may be confusing. The reader may be heard to exclaim: "He or she damn well knows what inaccuracy means, and no amount of academic hair-splitting is going to change

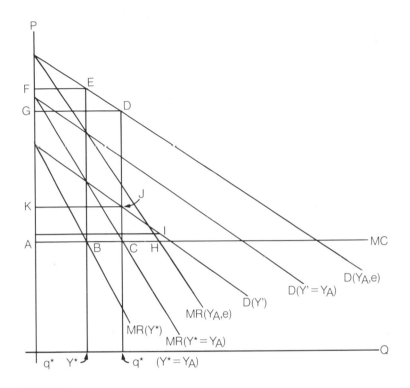

FIGURE 1

that." If so, chances are good that one of the measures described
here will come close to that idea of inaccuracy. The rest of us would
probably feel safer entertaining a broad range of measures, perhaps
seeing the actual results before making a choice. Let us, therefore,
consider those results, for the moment restricting ourselves to the
Canadian experience. I will report on larger, international comparisons in the next chapter.

THE CANADIAN RECORD

Introduction

The actual investigation of the accuracy of predictions of major
aggregate economic variables in the post-war period dates probably
from the early work of Theil (1955) and the (US) National Bureau
of Economic Research (1955). Hundreds of studies have appeared,
among the most important of which are Zarnowitz (1967), Nelson

(1972), McNees (1974), and, if I may say so, my own (Daub 1973; 1981), which is the principal work to date on Canadian forecasts.[17]

Much of this work is relatively recent. The explanation is quite simple. As we have seen, aggregate economic forecasting is essentially a post–Second World War phenomenon. Moreover, until quite recently, and principally for data-related reasons, most such forecasts were made only on an annual basis. Thus if one had been interested in evaluating the accuracy of those forecasts, and wanted to delay at least a few years to permit a reasonable estimate of the "typical" error, it would have been necessary to wait until at least 1955 to start the work, perhaps even 1965. This would have been true not only for short-term forecasts, i.e. those that predict, for example, real GNP or prices next year, but even more so for longer-term forecasts, such as investment in five years, or energy consumption in ten, where one would have undoubtedly had to wait even longer.

As a consequence, much of the work is recent, and based on a relatively few data points, at least as far as statistical ideals are concerned.[18] That does not mean, however, that there has been an absence of effort to evaluate accuracy, whether in Canada or abroad. I will look at the strictly Canadian results reported in some of this work, leaving international comparison to the next chapters. Let us begin by looking at some of my results, reported in Daub (1981) and updated where needed.

GNP and Its Expenditure Sector Components

By including the early 1980s, we have a record of over a quarter-century of Canadian short-term aggregate economic forecasts of gross national product (GNP) and its expenditure sector components, which one can use to assess accuracy. As noted, there are far fewer forecasts available from earlier in this period than later. And naturally one cannot look at all of them. But a representative sample will do.[19] Keeping in mind what was said above about accuracy measures, you will see that Table 6 summarizes the more important statistics for an evaluation of the absolute accuracy of one-year-ahead predictions made by Canadian forecasters of annual Canadian GNP, perhaps the key economic variable.

As indicated, over the period 1956–84 these forecasters made mean (mean absolute) errors of − 1.1 per cent (2.1 per cent) in their predictions of the annual percentage change in current-dollar GNP.[20] This mean absolute error was 21.0 per cent of the average actual increase of 10.0 per cent over this same period.

A breakdown by decades is interesting. It indicates, for example,

TABLE 6
Summary Statistics for an Evaluation of the Accuracy of Annual GNP Forecasts in Canada 1956–84[a] (in current dollars)

	Actuals (A): mean percentage change in GNP[b]	Mean error in percentage change predictions	Mean absolute error in percentage change prediction[c]
1956–69	7.9% ($\sigma_A = 2.82$)	−1.9%	2.5%* ($\sigma_{PE} = 0.47$)
1970–9	12.5% ($\sigma_A = 2.54$)	−1.2%	1.9%* ($\sigma_{PE} = 1.54$)
1980–4	9.2% ($\sigma_A = 2.45$)	0.5%	1.7%* ($\sigma_{PE} = 2.21$)
1956–84	10.0% ($\sigma_A = 3.37$)	−1.1%	2.1%* ($\sigma_{PE} = 2.46$)

	1956–69	1970–9	1980–4	1956–84
Type of errors in percentage change predictions				
Underestimated increases (u)	68 (82%)	61 (74%)	21 (52%)	150 (73%)
Overestimated increases (o)	15 (18%)	20 (24%)	18 (45%)	53 (26%)
Directional errors	0	0	0	0
Perfect forecasts	—	1 (1%)	1 (2%)	2 (1%)
Decomposition of the mean square error of the predictions[d]				
Mean square error	8.82	6.48	5.20	7.25
Mean "bias" coefficient	0.43	0.22	0.05	0.16
Mean "variance" coefficient	0.17	0.01	0.17	0.01
Mean "covariance" coefficient	0.40	0.77	0.63	0.83

Regression and test statistics

1956–69	1970–9	1980–4	1956–84
$A_2 = 2.46 + 0.91P + u$	$A_2 = 5.92 + 0.58P + u$	$A_2 = 2.24 + .72P + u$	$A_2 = 3.28 + 0.76P + u$
$R = 0.37$	$R = 0.28$	$R = 2.20$	$R = 0.52$
$t(\beta = 1) = -1.50$	$t(\beta = 1) = -4.04*$	$t(\beta = 1) = -1.21$	$t(\beta = 1) = -4.63*$

[a] All statistics are weighted for the duration of the reporting period of the set. In the period 1956–69 there were 8 sets and a total of 83 observations, in 1970–9 there were 10 sets and 82 ($n_{70-9} = 82$) observations, and in 1980–4 there were 8 sets and 40 ($n_{80-1} = 40$) observations. Thus overall $n_{56-84} = 205$ observations.
[b] First estimates of the actuals as given in the March or April issues of the *Canadian Statistical Review* are used here.
[c] An asterisk indicates significance from zero at the 0.05 level.
[d] The mean square error is defined as $E(P - A)^2$. The "bias," "variance," and "covariance" components are then, according to the well-known decomposition, $([P - A]^2/E[P - A]^2)$ $([\sigma_2 - \sigma_A]^2/E[P - A]^2)$, and $(2[1 - \rho_{AP}]\sigma_P\sigma_A/E[(P - A]^2)$ respectively (where P and A are predictions and actuals, P, A, $\sigma_P\sigma_A$ population means and standard deviations, ρ_{AP} the population coefficient).

that during 1970–9, Canadian forecasters made mean (mean absolute) errors of − 1.2 per cent (1.9 per cent), the mean absolute error being 15.2 per cent of the mean actual change of 12.5 per cent. When compared to the mean (mean absolute) errors of − 1.9 per cent (2.5 per cent) made during 1956–69, the latter mean absolute error being 31.6 per cent of the relevant mean actual change (7.9 per cent), it suggests that average prediction errors were in fact lower during the period 1970–9 than in 1956–69.[21] Another somewhat surprising result is that while, as one expects, the average actual increase in GNP during 1970–9 was higher (12.5 per cent v. 7.9 per cent), the variance was in fact smaller! Perhaps the one thing that is consistent with prior expectations was that the standard deviation of the absolute errors was higher during 1970–9 (1.54 v. 0.47), despite the fact that the average error was lower.

Data for the first half of the 1980s indicate that the mean error (0.5 percent) has changed somewhat, both in size and sign, from the 1970s. But the mean absolute error (1.7 per cent) is virtually unchanged, especially as a percentage of actual GNP in the period of (18.5 per cent actual GNP v. 15.2 per cent for the 1970s). This may be surprising to the reader, who will recall that the 1980s includes the second largest recession of the century after the Depression.

Several additional pieces of evidence on the size and kind of error are also reported in Table 6. These include a classification of the forecasts on the basis of whether they under- or over-estimate the actuals; a calculation of the mean square error and its "Theil" decomposition into bias, variance, and covariance; and finally the estimation of regression and test statistics.

A detailed examination of the results is left to the reader. Forecasters seem on average to underestimate the growth in current-dollar GNP. As mentioned above, conclusions like this must be qualified for a host of reasons relating to the validity of traditional statistical tests of significance in the presence of the high degree of serial and contemporaneous correlation that exists between forecast sets, to the unknown small-sample distributional characteristics of the inequality coefficients, and indeed to what the choice of a significance level implies about the very definition of accuracy itself. But the persistence of the tendency over time suggests that research to clear up these methodological problems, and to investigate, if the findings hold up, why forecasters show such a conservative bias, would be in order.

Until the mid-1970s few Canadian forecasters systematically recorded the decomposition of these nominal GNP predictions into real and price components. However, along with continued inflation, economic recession, and the growing importance of econometric modelling, there has developed a concern with these two measures and how accurately they are being anticipated.

As regards real GNP, Table 7 indicates that the mean forecasting error changed dramatically, from underestimation in the 1960s (-1.27 per cent) to a slight overestimation in the 1970s and 1980s. Further, comparing the size of the mean absolute error relative to the actuals, the changes in the sign profiles of the individual errors, the shift in the bias coefficients, and the regression results shows that real GNP was better forecast in the 1970s than either earlier or more recently. However, the tendency remains one of underestimating growth (-0.26 per cent) for the entire period 1957–84, and for the early 1980s, the severity of the recession.

However, underestimation of changes in the implicit price deflator (IPD) increased during the 1970s. Mean errors increased from 0.68 to 1.40, with the mean absolute errors increasing from 0.95 to 1.84. However, as a percentage of the actual change in the respective periods, the mean absolute error fell from 31.4 per cent in the 1960s to 22.2 per cent in the 1970s. There is little question that the main contributing factors to errors in predictions of changes in GNP changed from being real-related in the 1960s to price-related in the 1970s and early 1980s, and then back to real-related most recently. Mean errors in predicting real GNP were 64 per cent of errors in predicting nominal GNP in the 1960s (i.e. $-1.3/1.9$), whereas they acted in a small way to offset the large price-related errors during the 1970s. Over the entire period, mean errors in predicting nominal GNP were about 70 per cent price-related and 30 per cent real-related.[22]

Another piece of evidence concerns the correlation between errors made in forecasting the three variables. Further research indicates that nominal GNP errors were quite highly correlated with real GNP, and less so with price errors during 1957–69, whereas the reverse was true in the 1970s. The 1980s data are unclear. But over the entire period, nominal GNP errors were more highly correlated with price errors than with real GNP errors. In all the sub-periods errors in predictions of real GNP and prices were negatively correlated, suggesting that some 'offsetting' tendencies were at play, thereby benefiting forecasts of GNP in current dollars. As Zarnowitz (1979) has noted, "These observations ... are consistent with a view of the world in which nominal GNP changes are predicted directly and relatively well, but their division into real and price changes continues to pose great problems."[23]

TABLE 7
Summary Statistics for an Evaluation of the Accuracy of Annual Forecasts of Real GNP and the Implicit Price Deflator 1957–84[a]

	Real GNP				Implicit price deflator (IPD)			
	1957–69	1970–9	1980–4	1957–84	1957–69	1970–9	1980–4	1957–84
Actuals[b]	5.10%	4.16%	1.20%	3.62%	3.02%	8.26%	8.04%	6.59%
	(1.86)	(1.90)	(3.35)	(2.84)	(1.27)	(2.96)	(3.04)	(2.43)
Prediction errors								
Mean error	–1.27	0.10	0.31	–0.26	–0.68	–1.40	0.20	–0.72
Mean absolute error	1.67	1.03	1.81	1.41	0.95	1.84	1.01	1.32
	(1.05)	(0.74)	(2.51)	(1.89)	(0.66)	(2.23)	(1.16)	(1.93)
Type of error								
Underestimated increases	34 (78%)	29 (48%)	25 (62%)	88 (61%)	25 (80%)	45 (75%)	16 (40%)	96 (67%)
Overestimated increases	9 (20%)	30 (50%)	10 (25%)	49 (34%)	8 (18%)	12 (20%)	24 (60%)	44 (30%)
Directional errors	1 (2%)	–	4 (11%)	5 (3%)	–	–	–	–
Perfect forecasts	–	1 (2%)	1 (2%)	2 (1%)	1 (2%)	3 (5%)	–	4 (3%)
Decomposition of the MSE								
MSE	3.90	1.59	6.39	3.64	1.34	8.30	1.38	4.24
Bias coefficient	0.41	0.01	0.01	0.02	0.34	0.24	0.03	0.12
Variance	0.06	0.29	0.41	0.27	0.08	0.05	0.44	0.04
Covariance	0.53	0.70	0.58	0.72	0.58	0.71	0.50	0.86
Regression statistics $(A = \alpha + \beta P + u)$								
α	2.07	–0.78	–0.76	0.28	0.90	3.34	–2.49	1.04
β	0.79	1.18	1.31	1.16	0.90	0.72	1.28	0.95
$t(\beta = 1)$	0.19	1.32	1.34	1.85	0.64	2.01*	4.01*	1.02
r^2_{AP}	0.34	0.59	0.46	0.56	0.44	0.30	0.90	0.70

[a] All statistics are based on 44 observations, from 5 sets, for the period 1957–69, 60 observations, from 7 sets, during the period 1970–9, and 40 observations from 8 sets during 1980–4. There are thus 144 data points overall.
[b] First estimates of the actuals, to a base comparable to that which was forecast, have been used here. Figure in brackets is the standard deviation of the actuals.

Table 8 summarizes the result of the absolute accuracy analyses of forecasts of certain expenditure sector components of GNP. Four sets from 1958–69 and six from 1970–9 have been included.[24]

The mean absolute errors of total personal and government expenditures are smaller than those of the other components, particularly those that make up business gross fixed capital formation, all of which had mean absolute errors 1958–79 of 5–6 per cent. An examination of the record during 1970–9 as compared with that of the earlier period indicates that, like GNP forecasts, those of personal expenditures, new residential construction, new machinery and equipment, government expenditures, and exports all improved (with regards to mean errors – in absolute errors, export forecasts were worse), while those of new non-residential construction, net balance on current account, and imports worsened. Further, the average errors 1958–79 indicate that the long-standing belief in Canadian forecasting circles that exports are harder to predict than imports is justified by the record.

The mean errors are uniformly negative, with an average of over 60 per cent of all errors being underestimates. These results thus lend further credence to the earlier statement that any theory of expectations should be able to explain this tendency to underestimation, in this case in components as diverse as personal expenditures and new machinery and equipment. For components and/or periods in which there is more "uncertainty," as measured, for example, by greater variance, there will be less underestimation, relative to the size of the actual level. When forecasters are "well within themselves," as it were, they will almost certainly underestimate. Why?

Consider next the "relative" accuracy of these annual percentage change forecasts, comparing them to ex ante predictions generated from extrapolative models. Insofar as past data contain worthwhile information that can be obtained from relatively little cost, the forecaster ought to perform at least as well as forecasts that are mechanically generated.[25]

Table 9 indicates that GNP forecasts are superior to those generated from extrapolations. Over the period 1956–79 all ratios are less than one (further evidence from 1980–4 continues to support this conclusion as well). However, the forecasts provided only a small improvement in the mean square error over that of the best extrapolative alternative, which was obtained by using the "latest change" model.

This analysis implies that extrapolations are an alternative to the forecasts. Forecasters, in contrast, are likely to use extrapolations to develop predictions. Convention has thus identified two components

TABLE 8
Summary Measures of Errors in the Forecasts of Percentage Changes in Selected Components GNP 1958–79[a]

	Mean error	Mean absolute error (σ_{PE})	Type of error			
			Total number	Number of underestimates	Number of overestimates	Directional errors
Gross national product						
1958–69[b]	−2.0%	2.3% (1.45)	37	31 (83.8%)	6	—
1970–9[b,c]	−0.9	1.9 (1.44)	55	37 (67.3%)	17	—
1958–79[b,c]	−1.3	2.16 (1.44)	92	68 (73.9%)	23	—
Total personal expenditures						
1958–69[b,c]	−1.2	1.5 (.89)	37	30 (81.1%)	5	—
1970–9[b,c]	−0.7	1.3 (1.22)	46	27 (58.7%)	17	—
1958–79[b,c]	−0.9	1.4 (1.07)	83	57 (68.7%)	22	—
New residential construction						
1958–69[c,d]	−3.9	6.0 (4.26)	22	17 (77.3%)	4	—
1970–9	−3.3	5.5 (4.54)	52	31 (59.6%)	18	3
1958–79[c,d]	−3.5	5.6 (4.46)	74	48 (64.9%)	22	3
New non-residential construction						
1958–69[c,d]	−0.4	4.1 (3.79)	22	9 (40.9%)	9	2
1970–9	−2.8	6.8 (4.63)	31	17 (54.8%)	13	1
1958–79[c,d]	−1.8	5.7 (4.28)	53	26 (49.0%)	22	3
New machinery and equipment						
1958–69[c]	−4.4	6.1 (4.59)	22	14 (63.6%)	4	2

1970–9[c]	−2.1	5.0 (3.75)	31	15 (48.4%)	13	1
1958–79[c]	−3.0	5.4 (4.10)	53	29 (54.7%)	17	3
Total government expenditures						
1958–69[b]	−1.9	3.0 (2.12)	37	28 (75.7%)	9	—
1970–9[b,c]	−0.8	2.4 (1.79)	46	27 (58.7%)	17	—
1958–79[b]	−1.3	2.7 (1.94)	83	55 (66.3%)	26	—
Net balance on current account[e]						
1958–69[c,d]	−0.02	0.25 (0.22)	34	19 (55.9%)	5	7
1970–9	−0.07	0.77 (0.61)	55	19 (34.5%)	23	13
1958–79[c,d]	−0.05	0.57 (0.46)	89	38 (42.7%)	28	20
Exports						
1958–69[b]	−4.8	5.1 (3.57)	16	14 (87.5%)	2	—
1970–9[b]	−3.5	6.4 (4.70)	26	18 (69.2%)	8	—
1958–79[b]	−4.0	5.9 (4.27)	42	32 (76.2%)	10	—
Imports						
1958–69[b,c]	−3.1	4.2 (2.01)	16	11 (68.8%)	4	—
1970–9[b]	−4.2	5.6 (4.79)	25	21 (84.0%)	4	—
1958–79[b,c]	−3.8	5.0 (3.70)	41	32 (78.0%)	8	—

[a]During the period 1958–69 four sets were considered; six sets from 1970–9 were included. Not all sets forecast all components. The number of observations included for each component is as indicated.
[b]All actuals were increases.
[c]Includes perfect forecasts.
[d]Includes no change in the actuals.
[e]Absolute change in billions of dollars.

TABLE 9
Summary Statistics of a Comparison with Extrapolations 1956–79[a]

	Weighted mean of the ratio of mean square error of forecasts to extrapolations[c]								
	R1			R2			RBJ[e]		
Component[b]	1956 to 1969	1970 to 1979	1956[d] to 1979	1956 to 1969	1970 to 1979	1956[d] to 1979	1956 to 1963	1970 to 1979	1956[d] to 1979
Gross national product	0.11	0.03	0.07	0.30	0.60	0.75*	0.79	0.23	0.51
Total personal expenditures	0.06	0.02	0.04	1.36	0.80	1.05*	0.99	0.97	0.98
New residential construction	0.41	0.17	0.24	1.27	0.22	0.53*	0.69	0.41	0.49
New non-residential construction	0.29	0.30	0.29	0.40	0.59	0.66*	0.43	0.67	0.57
New machinery and equipment	0.34	0.16	0.23	0.75	0.56	0.63*	0.26	0.73	0.53
Total government expenditures	0.17	0.05	0.10	1.43	0.73	1.04	1.80	0.62	1.15*
Net balance on current account	0.49	1.15	0.90	0.45	0.79	0.66	0.71	1.15	0.98*
Exports	0.30	0.22	0.25	2.26	0.66	1.28*	1.27	0.68	0.90
Imports	0.21	0.25	0.23	1.12	0.52	0.75	0.86	0.80	0.82*

[a] For periods and sets included see Tables 6 and 8.
[b] All variables are measured in terms of percentage changes except net balance on current account, which is in absolute ($) change units.
[c] For an explanation of the extrapolative benchmark models used see note 25.
[d] The figures given for the period 1956–79 are a weighted average of the two sub-period results. An asterisk indicates that this is the best extrapolative model relative to the forecasts, for the given components.
[e] The Box-Jenkins models reported in Daub (1973) have been reidentified/estimated to include 1970–9. The models used here are as follows: gross national product: $\% \Delta \mathrm{GNP}_t = 6.82 + 0.62a_{t-1} + a_t$; total personal expenditures: $\% \Delta \mathrm{C}_t = 2.49 + 0.90\% \Delta C_{t-1} - 0.26\% \Delta C_{t-2} + a_t$; new residential construction: $\% \Delta \mathrm{NR}_t = 9.58 + a_t$; new non-residential construction: $\% \Delta \mathrm{NNR}_t = 10.26 + 0.71a_{t-1} + a_t$; new machinery and equipment: $\% \Delta \mathrm{NME}_t = 9.88 + 0.31a_{t-1} + a_t$; total government expenditures: $\% \Delta \mathrm{TGE}_t = 4.60 + 0.46\% \Delta \mathrm{TGE}_{t-1} + a_t$; net balance on current account: $\$ \Delta \mathrm{CA}_t - 0.04 + a_t$; exports: $\% \Delta \mathrm{X}_t = 7.88 + 0.24a_{t-1} + a_t$; and imports: $\% \Delta \mathrm{IM}_t = 7.63 + 0.38a_{t-1} + a_t$.

of predictions, "extrapolative" and "autonomous." One measure of the role of this latter factor in forecast preparation is given by the partial correlation coefficient of actuals (A) with predictions (P), controlling for an extrapolative contribution (E), i.e. $r^2_{AP.E}$. Also of interest is how efficiently the predictions used available extrapolative information ($r^2_{AE.P}$). To evaluate the actual importance of extrapolations in forecast preparation, r^2_{PE} was calculated.

Further analysis indicates that predicted changes are better correlated (albeit less so in later periods than in earlier ones) with the actuals than were the extrapolated ones (i.e. $r^2_{AP} > r^2_{AE}$] and are thus to be preferred in this regard. Unlike the earlier period, when $r^2_{AP.E}$ was relatively larger, thereby indicating a substantial "autonomous" component, during later times it is very low. Since r^2_{PE} is low, most available extrapolative information appears to be included in the forecasts, although that actually used was about the same as the amount of autonomous information, inasmuch as r^2_{PE} was approximately equal to $r^2_{AP.E}$.

When compared to the best extrapolative alternatives, the forecasts of real GNP were relatively more accurate than those of price level. In neither case were the forecasts much of an improvement, however; their errors were only 30 per cent less than those that could have been obtained using the simple average historical change. In fact, someone who consistently used the latest change model to forecast price changes would have done almost as well over the years as the forecasters did. However, the correlation of actuals with the best extrapolative prediction for both variables is lower than that of the forecasts. This fact, plus the small improvement in the mean square error, is probably sufficient to exonerate the forecasts.

With respect to component forecasts, over the entire period 1958–79 the forecasters were at least as good as, or better, than the best extrapolations in all cases but total government expenditures and exports. Predictions of total personal and government expenditures, while superior on the absolute accuracy basis, continued to be worse relative to extrapolations than for the rest of the components, a finding that suggests that forecasts of personal expenditures in particular, a large component of GNP, would have been improved by greater consideration of extrapolative information.

Except for total personal expenditures, predictions of changes in the components were more highly correlated with the actuals than were the extrapolations. Overall, the predictive efficiency due to the autonomous components ($r^2_{AP.E}$) was reasonably decent, with most available extrapolative information having been included, except total personal expenditures.

It is next of interest to consider "relativity" by comparing individual forecasters one against the other. This is not as easy as it might seem, since forecasts must be for the same variable, apply to the same period, and be issued at about the same time. Even then, as mentioned earlier, contemporaneous correlation, that is, "across forecasters' errors," causes problems with statistical inference.

Nevertheless the question of who forecasts "best" remains of interest. Because of the small sample sizes involved, the choice of the period over which to compare sets is critical. The addition of one year may change one's judgment entirely. For this reason, conclusions about the "value" of forecasts in general, or of one set in particular, based as they often are on one or two years' experience, are very suspect indeed. Better to consider the longest horizon possible, which here covers three sets of forecasts available for the period 1960–79.

An examination of the errors indicates that one set has lower mean and mean square errors than the other two and about the same mean absolute error. However, a test of the difference in the mean errors indicates that that set's was not significantly lower than the others'. Because the mean can conceal variation in the ranks over the years, the sets were also ranked on absolute errors in each year, and an analysis of variance (ANOVA) by ranks was done. The results suggest no significant difference in the sets. As well, individual tests were done by decades. In both the earlier, and later, periods there is no significant difference between sets.[26]

Against such a backdrop of no apparent difference in accuracy, one issue is relevant to the later periods. One of the sets of forecasts considered from this period was based almost entirely on an econometric model. Thus it is possible to compare the mean absolute (or mean square errors, which here generally give similar results) of this method with that of a basically judgmental one as well as with pure extrapolation, being all the while aware that the extent to which any given method is independent from another, i.e. is more or less judgmental or extrapolative, is a very murky subject. Given this warning, the best (in terms of lowest mean absolute error) judgmental forecast had a lower mean absolute error over a common period than did the econometric model forecasts for all three variables, i.e. real GNP, price level, and nominal GNP. However, when compared to the average judgmental forecast, there was no difference. Compared with the best extrapolative model, the best judgmental forecast had the lowest mean absolute error, the econometric model next lowest, and the purely extrapolative model the highest. Thus the model did at least as well as the average judgmental forecast, and better than pure extrapolation.

The same basic tests were used to investigate the forecasts of four sets that reported on a common collection of components, namely total personal and government expenditures, new residential construction, and the net balance on current account over a common period 1975–9. Once again an ANOVA by ranks, using absolute errors of the forecasts for each component, indicated that for no such component was the ranking of a given set of forecasts significantly lower than for the rest. However, an examination of the sum of the ranks and the mean square errors did indicate that the econometric model forecasts were superior to the best judgmental forecast in predicting total personal and government expenditures and worse than the best (or the average) judgmental forecasts of new residential construction and net trade balance.[27]

The same approach can be used to investigate whether errors were noticeably larger or smaller in different years. The relevant tests on the absolute errors of GNP forecasts suggest a significant difference in the errors made in different years. This result is invariant with respect to decade. Consequently, since 1960, some years have been significantly harder to forecast, others easier. The differences across the years seem more important than those between forecasters. That is, it would seem to matter less to the size of error to be expected whether one has the "best" forecaster than it does to the nature of the situation which all forecasters face at a particular moment.

Just which factors "determine" the nature of this situation continues to be unclear. Figure 2 indicates that the larger-error years were 1964–5, 1973–4, and 1982, the small-error ones 1967, 1978, 1980, and 1983. Movements in the percentage change of GNP would appear to provide some explanation, but the correlation coefficient between the percentage change in GNP and the mean absolute error is only 0.35. Nor do the first differences of the changes, that is, increases or decreases in the rate of growth, correlate well, either. In addition to the "conservative bias" noted above, this area as well needs examination.

The next sense of relative accuracy to be considered is the amount of error "relative to the cost of being wrong."[28] Using an approach much as outlined earlier in Figure 2, I estimated the costs of inaccurate aggregate economic forecasts to a major Canadian steel company during the 1960s (Daub 1974). Two different approaches yielded roughly the same results, namely that net income was $7.8 million lower on average (20.1 per cent of average net income during the period) with imperfect aggregate forecasts than it would have been with ones that contained no errors. That is, total revenue would have been $89.2 million higher on average (19.4 per cent of average total revenue) with perfect forecasts, total costs $81.4 million higher on average (due to an inappropriate choice, on average, of about 3.8 million man-hours per year – i.e. about 1,800 men – and roughly

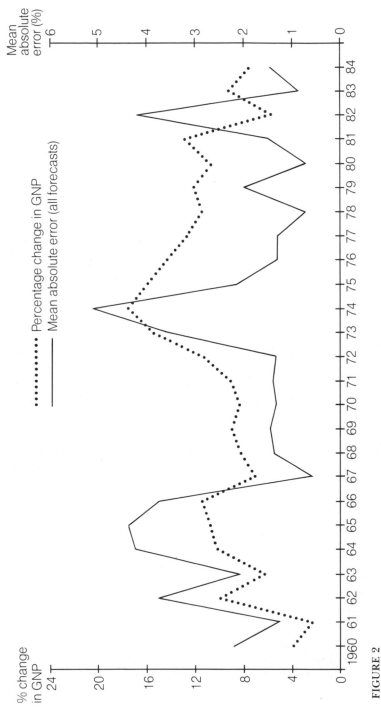

FIGURE 2
Percentage Change of the Mean Absolute Error in GNP Forecasts and Percentage Change in GNP 1960–84

$180 million in capital). Whether or not these figures are exactly correct, there being many problems with the estimation, they do indicate that the cumulative cost of aggregate forecasting error, not only to a company, but by extension to society as a whole, may well be quite large.

Some Additional Evidence

To conclude this section, I want to touch on three other studies that report on some of the approaches used by Canadian forecasters mentioned earlier and at the same time illustrate in greater detail certain aspects of accuracy evaluation noted above.

The first pertains to indicator analysis or, more generally, the turning point record. Several pieces of evidence can be brought to bear, in particular Daub and Savage (1973) and Daub and Sankaran (1984). In the former study we looked at the predictive power of nine leading indicators originally identified by Beckett. Using various criteria, such as average lead time and number of false or missed signals, we concluded, from a relatively limited examination, "that the usefulness of the leading indicators as tools for forecasting the Canadian business cycle is suspect."[29]

The latter study took up the question, in a slightly different fashion, with respect to the latest deep downturn, and subsequent turnaround, during the early 1980s. Here we chose a group of 16 forecasters who made at least four forecasts of changes in 1982 and 1983 real GNP before the end of the year that they were trying to forecast. Moreover, they had to have reported these forecasts to the public, in particular to have been summarized in the Conference Board's *Canadian Business Review*. Finally, we defined a turning point error as predicting growth [+] when there turned out to be decline [−], and decline when there turned out to be growth. The procedure used was a quarter-by-quarter tracking of the sign of the predictions from the first appearance of 1982 forecasts up to the end of 1984. In this way, it was possible to identify exactly when opinion as to the peak and trough developed. Table 10 shows their record in relation to the database available at the time of their forecast.

It can be seen that to the end of 1981:3 none of the 16 had made negative growth forecasts for 1982. The available information on actuals at that time shows that in the first two quarters of 1981 there had been positive economic growth, which, though slower than 1980:4, was better than the negative growth of the first two quarters of 1980. But by 1 January 1982, i.e. before that year began, and with only the additional information that 1981:3 had had negative growth, 7

TABLE 10
Timing of Real GNP Forecasts for 1982 (and Available Information Base)[a]

Forecast before	Information base: actuals	Frequency			Group point forecast		
		Negative growth	Zero growth	Positive growth	Average	Median	Range
Oct. 1/81	1981: 1 and 2	0/16	1/16	15/16	2.61	2.7	0.0 to 3.3
Jan. 1/82	1981: 1–3	5/16	2/16	9/16	0.0	0.0	−1.6 to 1.8
Apr. 1/82	All of 1981	8/16	1/16	7/16	−6.5	−1.0	−1.6 to 1.8
July 1/82	1982: 1	16/16	0/16	0/16	−2.91	−2.8	−4.0 to 1.8
Oct. 1/82	1982: 1 and 2	16/16	0/16	0/16	−3.95	−4.5	−5.2 to −3.3
Average of all five forecasts					−1.25	−1.5	−3.5 to 0.38

[a]For an explanation of the data used see the text.

of the 16 revised their forecast for 1982 to no positive growth, and 5 of them actually switched to negative growth. As well, the group average point forecast had also been revised from + 2.6 per cent to no growth. By April 1982, with the additional information that the last two quarters of 1981 had had negative growth, but with only incomplete indications that this might have extended to 1982:1, the group was now predicting negative growth for 1982. And by the end of the second quarter of 1982, all 16 were predicting negative growth, correctly identifying the turning point at the peak. Further, once a forecaster swung negative, he or she remained negative for the year. Finally, although not shown in Table 10, all forecasters correctly predicted the trough turning point for 1983 from their earliest forecast for that year (July 1982), and they stayed that way.

Several conclusions can be drawn from this exercise. If "more than one year ahead is far enough ahead to be judged ahead," then 5 of the 16 predicted the peak and all predicted the trough. If one is prepared to ease up slightly on the horizon over which the forecaster is expected to "forecast," the peak record improves considerably. Alternatively, cynics might suggest that forecasters were forecasting the actuals. Such a conclusion does not, however, explain the perfect trough turning point record. Nor does it meet the claim to the contrary that forecasters were simply making efficient use of the latest information. Others might perhaps suggest that first-quarter forecasts for a given year that are right on sign, and remain consistently so, are good enough.

In the final analysis, there is no way to judge except perhaps to consider what or who might have done better. Certainly no back-of-the-envelope extrapolation would have come close. Latest available estimates of the actuals for 1975–81 were 1.2 per cent, 5.5, 2.1, 3.6, 2.8, 0.5, and 3.1, per cent respectively. To have forecast ahead of time 1982's − 4.5 per cent or 1983's 3.5 per cent from any simple naive model would have taken some doing. Nor is there any previous Canadian evidence of a reduction in real GNP with which to compare. The 1954 period comes very near to being acceptable. Unfortunately, the available forecasts for the period do not support a similar analysis.

And so one is forced to the conclusion that the turning point evidence is somewhat contradictory. It is likely to remain so for a while, because GNP turning points don't come along every day! Alternatively, the evidence cited here was admittedly based on some rather simple analysis, and so a full-blown study of the evidence to date would be worthwhile. It might very well change the conclusions drawn here.

TABLE 11

Accuracy of Predictions of Percentage Changes in the Average Total Capital Investment of All Businesses by Forecast Span 1970–9

Absolute accuracy measures

All business	No. of obsns	Mean error[a]	Error sign u	o	Mean square error	Decomposition Bias	Var.	Cov.	Regression $P = \alpha + \beta_{A+e}$ $\hat{\alpha}$	$\hat{\beta}$
Span (in years)										
1	10	9.9 (9.9)*	0	10	165.2	0.59	0.02	0.39	13.55	0.62
2	9	0.25 (16.7)	6	3	378.0	0	0.10	0.82	23.12	0.05
3	8	4.8 (19.4)*	5	3	520.2	0.04	0.24	0.72	16.29	0.39
4	7	−20.6* (28.0)*	6	1	1134.6	0.37	0.04	0.59	53.07	−0.75
5	6	−37.5* (38.3)*	5	1	2229.4	0.60	0.40	0.00	−311.01	5.14

[a]Figure in brackets is the mean absolute error. Asterisk indicates that the mean (mean absolute) error is significantly different from 0 at the 0.05 level.

The second study I want to note concerns the accuracy of the investment intentions survey referred to in various places above (e.g. chapters 2 and 3). Table 11 presents some evidence on the predictions by all the firms in the sample of changes in their capital investment over various spans during the period 1970–6.[30] The mean error of the short-term, one-year-ahead annual predictions was 2.5 per cent. The actual change during these years relating to this horizon was 16.2 per cent suggesting that the average one-year-ahead annual prediction error was 15.7 per cent of the actual change. Longer term, i.e. over a five-year horizon, the mean error was 66.7 per cent versus an actual change of 58 per cent. That is, the predictions were 113 per cent wrong on average.

Perhaps as expected, the mean absolute and mean square errors were larger and increased regularly with the span. Rather more interestingly, the forecasts swung from overestimation in the short term to underestimation long term. This result is generally supported by the signs of the mean errors, the pattern of under- and overestimates, the change in the decomposition coefficients from variance to bias, and the regression results. Bearing in mind the statistical limitations associated with the conclusion that such a result is "significant," the evidence suggests that the forecasts became not only more inaccurate with span but also more biased towards underestimation. It is difficult to tell whether this says something about the organizational function of short-term investment predictions, about the way the question about intentions is framed ("Do you have *firm* plans today for the next N years?"), or simply about human nature i.e. more optimistic about finishing projects next year than is justified; more pessimistic about the future than is actually warranted).

A breakdown by industrial sector of some of the summary statistics reported in Table 11 was also considered. As with the results overall, in each instance the industries overestimated investment expenditures short term but changed to underestimation as the span lengthened. As well, the mean absolute (and mean square) errors increase regularly with the span, indicating worsening predictive accuracy with horizon. The fact that the results for total businesses are thus not due simply to one or two large sectors but are characteristic of all industries is also interesting. It suggests not only that future total forecasts should be viewed in this manner but also that there may be something peculiar about investment intentions in this regard. This is not to imply that there are no inter-industry differences in absolute accuracy, for clearly there are. The chemical industry, for example, is the worst over nearly all spans, whereas oil and gas companies seem to do rather well. However, without detailed investigation of the history of each industry during this period, there is nothing on the surface to suggest why one or the other ought to have been more or less accurate.

The same results hold for a breakdown of the sample by region. That is, mean absolute errors are seen to increase with the span, and there is a change in the nature of the errors from overestimation short term to underestimation long term. There are some regional differences. For example, Quebec does well in the short term, British Columbia better in the long term. But as with the individual industry results, the two general findings from the absolute accuracy analysis, namely decreasing accuracy over longer spans and a switch from overestimation short term to underestimation long term, would appear to be invariant with respect to region.

For all business taken together, average predictions of actual investment generally did better than extrapolative alternatives. However, the relative superiority of these predictions steadily deteriorated as the span lengthened. Beyond three years, extrapolative models did about as well, if not better. As with the discussions of the absolute accuracy of these forecasts, one must be careful about concluding that such differences are significant in a statistical sense. One simply cannot say. Rather they suggest that statements of investment intentions were better predictors of actual investment in the short run than the extrapolations, and worse in the long run.

The correlation analysis suggests that predicted changes were better correlated with the actual than the extrapolations. The results also indicate that some of the short-term efficiency of the forecasts is certainly due to information introduced by the forecasters and not found in the extrapolations, since $r^2_{AP.E}$ is positive. Some extrapolative information was used in the short-term forecasts, but the low value of r^2_{PE} indicates that it may well have come from other sources than the models assumed here.

Further investigation indicates that the finding concerning relative accuracy based on the total results must be altered somewhat depending on the sector under consideration. For example, in the oil/gas pipeline and electric utilities industries, the forecasts were always superior to the extrapolations, whereas in the chemical and pulp/paper sectors they were almost always worse. One result that is, however, consistent is that extrapolations do better vis-à-vis the forecasts as the span lengthens in virtually all cases. These same conclusions can be drawn from a regional breakdown of the data. In the prairies, the forecasts were always better than the best extrapolative alternative, in the Atlantic provinces almost always worse. As well, the relative value of the extrapolations generally increased with the span.

These seem to be several main conclusions one can draw from an investigation of the accuracy of the Canadian investment intentions survey over this period. One question that does, however, arise is whether the companies are better or worse predictors of investment relative to other types of aggregate forecasters. It may be recalled that the collection of forecasters predicting one-year-ahead, annual changes in non-residential construction and plant and equipment expenditures during the 1960s cited earlier made mean errors of 15 per cent and 30 per cent of the actual change respectively, whereas here the comparable figure was 15.7 per cent. The results on the relative accuracy, at least over a one-year span, are also roughly consistent with the findings reported above. Relative mean square errors for non-residential construction from similar extrapolative alternatives were 0.29 and 0.40, whereas here they are 0.18 and 0.15 for the average prediction of total investment.

Since the time periods and the variables involved are different, these earlier results are not strictly comparable. However, they are indicative of the kinds of accuracy results obtained for predictions of "investment" over similar forecasting horizons. As such, they suggest that the accuracy of the short-term predictions from the Canadian investment survey is roughly equivalent to that obtained in other circumstances. And thus so long as the short-term relevance of the findings is stressed, one is probably entitled to conclude that the investment intentions survey is a useful forecasting tool.[31]

The third, and final, piece of evidence on the accuracy of Canadian aggregate economic forecasts concerns another set of longer-term predictions, in this instance of total energy requirements. Daub and Petersen (1981) looked, in a systematic way, at the accuracy of the first 10 years of the National Energy Board's long-range forecasts of supply and demand made in the late 1960s for the period to 1990.

Table 12 summarizes the more important statistics for an evaluation of the absolute accuracy performance of these long-term energy demands. As indicated, the forecasters made mean (mean absolute) errors of -147.5 trillion (10^{12}) BTUs (151.1tBTU) in their predictions of total energy demand over the 10-year period, -0.13 per cent (2.06 per cent) in their predictions of the percentage change in total requirements. These change errors were 5.8 per cent (52.40 per cent) of the actual average change (increase) in BTUs (which was 4.12 per cent).

It is interesting to compare these results with the accuracy record associated with short-term predictions of GNP made during part of the same period as reported above (i.e. 1960–9). In that instance, mean (mean absolute) level errors were 2.22 per cent (2.62 per cent) of mean GNP, mean (mean absolute) percentage change errors 25 per cent (31.25 per cent) of the actual average change in GNP. Considering the nature of the problems involved, the conclusion would seem to be that the long-term forecasts compare quite favourably with the short-term ones, at least in this one instance and on this one statistic.

Interpreting the usual evidence on under- and overestimation, inequality coefficients, and regression in a manner consistent with that used in the studies of short-term forecasting accuracy indicates that there is probably no consistent sizeable bias towards underestimation of changes. This is not to imply that the forecasts are 'absolutely accurate,' as the mean absolute error, for example, is very large. What is also clear is that the forecasts, predicting, as they were, relatively stable growth in total energy demand (3.6–4.3 per cent), completely failed to anticipate the actual variability in demand, a type of error not nearly so evident in the short-term studies cited above. But on average they were not consistently "biased" in any identifiable way.

TABLE 12
Summary Statistics for an Evaluation of the Absolute Accuracy of Forecasts of Long-Term Energy Requirements in Canada 1967–76

Variable	Actuals[a] Mean Level (trillion BTU)	Actuals[a] Mean % change	Prediction errors Levels (TBTU) Mean error[b]	Levels (TBTU) Mean absolute error	Relative changes (%) Mean error	Relative changes (%) Mean absolute error	Type of error[c] U	O	D	Mean square error	Decomposition of mean square error Bias	Variance	Covariance	Regression statistics ($P_t = \alpha + \beta A_t + e_t$) $\hat{\alpha}$	$\hat{\beta}$	$t(\beta = 1)$[d]	R^2
By energy source																	
Petroleum	2648.0	3.29	−171.8 (79.62)	171.8	+0.18 (2.84)	2.21	6	3	1	7.22	0.005	0.972	0.023	87.09	−24.12	(−1.74)	0.28
Natural gas	985.0	7.83	−125.0 (63.78)	125.0	−0.67 (7.00)	5.50	7	1	2	44.00	0.010	0.774	0.216	17.04	−1.28	(−0.73)	0.02
Coal	241.1	−3.50	152.9 (29.38)	152.9	1.51 (9.14)	6.94	0	7	3	76.52	0.030	0.928	0.042	21.78	12.74	(2.06)*	0.42
Electricity	695.1	6.08	−16.8 (19.9)	21.0	0.18 (3.11)	1.84	8	1	1	8.63	0.004	0.944	0.052	37.80	−5.07	(−0.44)	0.02
Others	51.3	4.70	12.9 (13.03)	14.1	−6.91 (14.14)	11.08	2	3	4	225.57	0.212	0.741	0.043	−16.44	−9.52	(−1.86)*	0.29
By energy use																	
Res/comm.	1776.2	3.73	−157.0 (87.91)	157.0	−0.76 (5.30)	4.27	8	–	2	25.58	0.022	0.926	0.052	32.32	−9.59	(−2.12)*	0.34
Industrial	1521.9	4.09	70.7 (65.83)	75.5	0.55 (4.65)	2.66	7	2	1	19.55	0.015	0.883	0.102	21.15	−3.67	(−0.79)	0.05
Transport	1322.4	4.83	−61.2 (36.67)	61.2	−0.33 (2.23)	1.64	5	5	–	4.53	0.025	0.836	0.139	5.33	−0.11	(−0.18)	0.00
Total	4620.5	4.12	−147.5	151.1	−0.13	2.06	7	2	1	7.81	0.002	0.931	0.067	33.35	−7.34	(−2.25)*	0.36

[a] It is assumed that all actuals are measured without error. Percentage change (A % Δ[t]) is measured by (A[t − 1] − A[t])/A(t − 1).

[b] Figure in brackets is the standard deviation of the mean error. Mean error (Ē) is $\frac{1}{10}\sum_{t=1}^{10}(P[t] - A[t])$ for levels, $\frac{1}{10}\sum_{t=1}^{10}(P\% \, \Delta[t] - A\% \, \Delta[t])$ for relative changes.

[c] U = underestimate, O = overestimate, D = directional error. Where the figures do not sum to ten, it can be inferred that there were perfect forecasts.

[d] Asterisk indicates significance at the 0.05 level

When the absolute accuracy of the forecasts classified by source or use is examined, some interesting results emerge. As regards energy source, petroleum, by far the largest component, and particularly electricity seem to have been reasonably well forecast. The results are in many ways like those for the total energy forecasts, to wit, unbiased on average but with a poor prediction of the variability of the series in question. However, demands for natural gas and particularly coal and other sources were much more poorly forecast. As regards energy use by the three sectors, each of which accounts for about a third of total energy requirements, the poorest record by a considerable amount was recorded in predicting residential and commercial usage. The forecasts were biased, made some directional errors, and poorly anticipated the variability in the actuals. Alternatively, transportation usage was particularly well forecast.[32]

How does the accuracy of the forecasters vary over differing prediction spans? As regards total demand, the actual error made over the span in question is highly variable. However, the mean absolute error, perhaps a better measure of absolute accuracy over the entire span in question, is invariant with respect to span. This is contrary to earlier findings on the investment forecasts, where the size of the absolute error steadily increased with the span for all forecasters. The reason is rather straightforward. Most of the variables comprising total demand in fact generally behaved as one might have expected from the earlier study, that is, mean absolute errors increasing with span. However, the petroleum account was such a large part of the total that its contrary behaviour, a steadily decreasing mean absolute error out to five years and then a slight increase, was sufficient to offset the impact of the other variables. There is some increase in the errors with span but by no means as much as might have been expected a priori.

Relative accuracy measures were also considered. They indicated that the forecasts of both total demand and components were relatively more accurate than either extrapolative model considered. Since the forecasts themselves were for a relatively constant percentage change, an increase of 3.9 per cent, it can perhaps be said that the forecaster's extrapolations were better than the naive ones. Predicted changes were better correlated with the actuals than were the extrapolated ones, although the significance of the difference is difficult to establish. Neither correlation is particularly high.

This relative accuracy analysis is, however, very rigorous, if not outright unfair, for it allows the extrapolative model future information, namely the actuals, that the forecasters could not have had. A more appropriate basis for assessing relative accuracy in multi-

horizon circumstances such as these would be to choose simple extrapolative models that the forecasters might have chosen and project them out "unchanged" into the future, covering the same horizon
over which the forecasters are being judged. Relative accuracy could
then be measured not only over the total span but also over various
sub-spans as well. Two such extrapolative alternatives were constructed.

In general, with the important exception of petroleum (where the
forecasts were clearly better), most of the relative mean square errors
for the full 10-year period are close to one, indicating that, at least
on the basis of RMSEs, there is little to choose between the forecasts
and the extrapolative predictions. Here the RMSEs are much higher
than in the earlier case. This suggests the rather interesting idea that
the extrapolative models that had the benefit of more actual information were worse forecasting tools than those that had less! This
curiosity aside, the major implication of the results is that over the
entire span one could have done about as well as the forecasters did
by using simple extrapolations of the data available at the time.

To summarize, research into the accuracy of short-term economic
forecasts is relatively commonplace. However, little has been published on the accuracy of long-term forecasts, primarily because of
the dual problems of a certain "quantitative imprecision" on the part
of forecasters and a lack of record-keeping. Neither of these limitations applied with the long-term energy forecasts considered here.
A very precise prediction of each of a rich assortment of variables
was made and kept. As well, the actuals were all a matter of public
record. Because of this, it was possible to consider the accuracy of
such long-term forecasts. Besides providing a comparison with the
evaluations of short-term forecasts, thereby yielding information on
the influence that long spans have on forecasting accuracy, such a
study also serves as a guide to what might reasonably be expected
in similar longer-term forecasting circumstances in the future.

Further, because the methods used here are similar to those used
in the evaluation of the accuracy of annual short-term aggregate
economic predictions, the general conclusion that the accuracy of
these longer-term forecasts is not all that different is a bit surprising
and certainly interesting. It may well suggest that even in the case
of the more distant future, the degree of uncertainty and the inability
of the economy both to forsee and adjust to it are less than popularly
feared. Over the longer run, there may well be fundamental processes that determine economic activity. It may also be that economic
agents are sufficiently aware of these, and their slowly changing
character, to predict their future values as successfully as those of
potentially more volatile events closer at hand.[33]

SUMMARY AND CONCLUSIONS

I began this chapter by arguing that there were several reasons why one might be interested in the accuracy of economic forecasts. Not the least of these was a desire to understand the seeming contradiction between public complaints about accuracy and the evident prosperity of forecasting firms! Whatever the motives, as we moved to consider the entire subject area, it was clear that there were many conceptual barriers in need of surmounting. The first, and likely most important, involved the prediction dilemma posed by the possibility of self-altering predictions. While theoretically always a problem, it was explained away here by arguing that no forecaster, not even, indeed least of all, the government, enjoys sufficient prestige or power to be able to move people enough for the results to be reflected in the large aggregates we are talking about here, at least in any noticeably important way.

Many of the other difficulties that we noted, such as those relating to what the term "accuracy" could possibly mean and how exactly to measure it, were dealt with by relating to conventions that have grown up around the relatively young literature on accuracy assessment. This led us to talk of absolute and relative accuracy. Various measures were considered within each of these categories, their rationale was given, and possible problems with them were highlighted. By the time we had finished, it was evident that accuracy was a many-splendoured thing about which it was wise to take much care.

To illustrate some of these issues with hard data, some indication was given of the accuracy of several kinds of Canadian aggregate economic forecasts. Most attention was given to the relatively short-term annual forecasts of GNP and its expenditure sector components. Two longer-term forecasts were also considered, namely those from the investment intentions survey and from the National Energy Board's 1960 predictions of future energy demand in Canada.

Many detailed conclusions about the accuracy of these Canadian aggregate economic forecasts were drawn in connection with each of these reviews. There is little point in repeating all of them here. Several, however, stand out in my mind.

First, there appears to be no difference over the years among forecasters. This is important, for it suggests that the market in forecasting technology is more or less efficient. It also means that a "buy and hold" strategy with respect to purchasing forecasts is likely to be the best. Any preference for a particular forecaster should be based on things like price, service, or some other competitive variable.

Second, forecasters *underestimate* actuals. Certainly this tendency seems to be a function of the basic volatility of the actuals. But there has been no clear reason yet suggested why this should be so, and in particular why in the largest aggregate of them all, GNP, there is always this underestimation bias present.

Third, everyone seems to make the same kind of errors at the same time. This is really a corollary of the first two points, but it relates particularly to three observations: There are periods such as the 1960s when real factors are most important, and hence errors in predicting real factors are higher, and periods such as inflations when price is most important, in which case errors in forecasting prices are higher. There are large-error, and small-error, years, which coincide for almost all forecasters; why this is so is unclear at present.[34] And some components are harder for everyone to forecast than others, e.g. investment or exports as opposed to consumption. Again it is not necessarily obvious why errors should be relatively higher for some phenomena than for others. Volatility is no explanation at all.

Fourth, accuracy seems to vary with the span of the forecast but not in any clear way. Errors in the investment survey forecasts grew as the span lengthened, but they plateaued in the energy forecasts. Perhaps there is some point in the future beyond which everything is equally dim. From this evidence, three to five years looks like that point.

There is, evidently, one sense of the relative that we have not yet considered. And it may alter these perceptions of the accuracy of Canadian aggregate economic forecasts. That is, of course, the record of forecasters in other countries. So, in order to avoid being excessively parochial, and to provide as well some additional perspective on the results presented here, let us turn next to some international evidence.

CHAPTER EIGHT

International Comparisons

" ... in a world where all's unsure."

While this is a book principally about Canadian aggregate economic forecasting, Canadians are not alone in this game. The practice is world-wide. In some places such as the United States it is even proportionally much larger than it is in Canada. In others it is less consequential than one might expect. In some it is a free-market activity; in others it is dominated by one actor, usually the government. For our purposes here, it is of little interest to consider the forecasting activities of the centrally planned Eastern Bloc countries. That is not to say that the topic is not potentially interesting.[1] Rather, for various reasons, having principally to do with data definition and availability, one is best to restrict the discussion to the Western, capitalist economies. Economic forecasting, expectations-formation, and accuracy evaluation are very different things in the Eastern Bloc from what they are here in the West!

It is important, therefore, to have some understanding not only of the industry internationally but also of its forecasting record relative to our own. The first part of the task is straightforwardly descriptive; the second is more difficult, for two reasons.

The first relates to some of the same methodological questions as were raised when doing "within-country" comparisons of different forecasters but is exacerbated in international comparisons. Similar concepts may be measured, and thus forecast, differently; the same variables may not be forecast in all countries; forecasts may be made at different times in the year; prediction data may not be available for common periods from every country; more forecast sets may be available from some countries than from others; in some cases they will come only from private sources, in others only public, and in still others from some combination of the two. In addition, the implications of inaccuracy may vary between countries and over time.

Finally, the basic nature of the economies may well be different, some, for example, being more resource-based than others.

The second reason is that these economies are highly interdependent. Forecasting error in one country may well get transmitted abroad via trade and financial mechanisms, making it difficult to sort out whose error is whose. This problem also has its domestic counterpart, where it is caused by the close relations of forecasters leading to a high degree of correlation in these errors and concomitant difficulty in sorting out independent influence.

As we shall se below, these difficulties have been dealt with in various ways, ranging from simply ignoring them to trying to match country data sets as carefully as possible, or attempting to identify international error transmission. These efforts can never be anything more than partially satisfactory. But it is not necessary to throw in the towel, for some reasonably firm conclusions can be drawn. Before doing so, however, I want to describe briefly the industry internationally.[2]

INTERNATIONAL AGGREGATE ECONOMIC FORECASTING

There is little doubt that, as in many other economic institutions, in aggregate economic forecasting the dominant force in the world is the United States. Any number of pieces of evidence could be cited to support this claim. One will do. The publication *Economic Forecasts* reports monthly on economic forecasts made around the world for various different countries. Forecasts from 38 American sources are included, as opposed to 14 from the United Kingdom, 9 from Japan, 8 from France, 6 from Canada, and 5 each from Australia and West Germany. No doubt there are other sources in each country that might also have been cited. We know that for certain in the Canadian case. But the sheer weight of the American presence in the industry world-wide simply cannot be questioned.

There are many reasons for this dominance, which a full-blown international treatment of the subject, to my knowledge not yet attempted, would no doubt draw out. A highly individualistic, capitalist economy, with reasonably strict anti-trust laws, requires a lot of the "invisible-hand aid" of the kind that I have argued above (chapter 3) forecasts provide. Other factors motivating demand and supply also contribute: a well-educated managerial class, an abundant supply of economists (the main component of the industry's labour input) and computing technology, an increasingly litigious society, and the need to co-ordinate large, multinational corporate enterprises.

Because no study of the American forecasting industry similar to that of chapters 5 and 6 on the Canadian is available, one is forced to proceed on more or less ad hoc basis, using mostly personal knowledge and indirect evidence. Such an approach in fact indicates that the industry is rather similar in its structure to Canada's: there are several major actors and a collection of other institutions that play important supporting roles.

The former would certainly include Data Resources (DRI), originally founded by Eckstein of Harvard and having its head offices in the Boston area; and Wharton Consulting and Economic Information Services (WEFA-CEIS), the recently formed company which merged Wharton Econometric Forecasting Associations (an idea of Klein and Adams and located in Philadelphia) and Chase Econometrics (originally formed by Evans and until recently located in New York). Both DRI and WEFA-CEIS are now owned by larger corporate entities: a publishing house and a Swiss corporation respectively. But they continue to retain separate identities. An equivalent to the Conference Board also exists in the United States but enjoys nothing like the important forecasting role it has in Canada.

The group of majors would also include several actors that are also found in Canada but are less active in Canada than in the United States. For example, the Council of Economic Advisors is an important forecasting agent in the United States, perhaps more so than the Economic Council in Canada. The Bureau of Economic Analysis of the US Department of Commerce is certainly more important, because of its econometric model and its indicators work, than any published government-based forecasts in Canada.

Intimately linked with these majors are a host of institutions, including universities (e.g. Michigan); banks, trust and insurance companies (e.g. Harris Trust, various Federal Reserve banks, Prudential Insurance); publications (e.g. *Fortune* magazine); and a mixture of large corporations (e.g. IBM and General Electric), all of which regularly make aggregate economic forecasts. Some forecasts are available directly to the public; almost all are available indirectly, through at least three of the better-known sources of forecaster surveys, to say nothing of several lesser-known and/or private compendia. The first of these surveys is conducted by Livingston, a columnist for the *Philadelphia Inquirer*. Livingston has reported semi-annually (but most importantly in a late December issue each year) on some 40 to 60 forecasters for over 30 years now. His has been the database used in recent times for a considerable amount of empirical research in economics on expectation-formation. The second is the joint quarterly survey of between 40 and 80 forecasters by the American Statistical Association (ASA) and the National Bureau of Economic Research, published each quarter in the ASA's *AMSTAT News*. The third is the Blue Chip service, a private report available on subscription. To this one can add as well the more recent *Economic Forecasts* survey mentioned earlier, and one done by the Conference Board, which is similar to that reported in Canada by the same organization.

As indicated, very little is known in detail about the industry, in particular its conduct and performance. We can suppose that the nature of demand and supply will be pretty much as for the Canadian industry, with the important exception of the influence that technological developments abroad might have on the business. As we have seen, and with certain exceptions such as Canadian data handling contributions, most of the flow has been the other way: the American forecasting industry has been the major source of most technological developments. We can further suppose that such factors as the public good character of forecasts act to influence behaviour, and hence performance, in some of the ways they do in Canada. However, because of a very different regulatory and legal climate, the industry must behave differently in other respects.

As a consequence, and because of the absence of a thorough institutional-type study of the American industry, it is difficult to know much about the important characteristics with certainty. The little evidence that is available is largely anecdotal. The reader will recall evidence cited above (chapter 6) in connection, for example, with profitability. It was ambiguous and in any case is not acceptable as a basis for comparison. I would hasten to add that one is talking not about accuracy assessment alone, or even most importantly. Many major studies on this issue are available for the United States and will be examined in some detail below. Rather I am referring to the behaviour of the industry itself. The lack of such a study is unfortunate; US firms are the major players in the "free world's" forecasting market, and it is important that US motives and actions be well understood. Perhaps a study will be forthcoming.

Elsewhere in the world the situation is quite different. Consider, as an example, the United Kingdom, France, West Germany, and Japan. For the most part, and certainly until the last five years (in some instances even down to the present), almost all of the aggregate economic forecasting done in many of these countries was directly tied to "the accepted government forecast." Very little, and certainly no directly commercially available, "independent" forecasting was done. This was absolutely true for Japan and France, somewhat less so for the United Kingdom, and still less for West Germany, even though the indirect influence of the government there, through the "economic institutes," was always present. In Japan MITI played an all-important role; in France it was the Ministère des finances;[3] in Britain, the Treasury, with some independent contributions from the National Institute and several of the newspapers, such as the *Times* and the *Telegraph*.

As implied, this characterization of other forecasting "industries/ markets" (the words are obviously somewhat inappropriate to a government-monopoly situation) has begun to change in recent times. Other forecasts of the Japanese economy are becoming available, principally from securities and investment firms and the larger banks. This is only natural as the Japanese begin to open their market to foreign investment and to invest extensively themselves outside Japan. The French now have various different near-academic institutes as well as certain banks, all of which make relatively independent forecasts. This increased variety of forecasts in France is due in part to the death of central planning, in part to growing liberalization in economic matters. In the United Kingdom, several added sources have come to play important roles, especially because of "Thatcherism." The latter brought with it a distrust of all things Keynesian. Not the least suspect were the people at the Treasury, especially the forecasters. Forecasters at the London Business School were drawn into the arena, as were certain other non-traditional sources. At present there is thus considerable variety available where it wasn't before.

This same pattern of rather dramatic change can be seen elsewhere in the world as well. One now routinely can expect forecasts, from several different sources, of countries as diverse as Israel and Chile, Ireland and Australia.[4] The situation mirrors what has happened in Canada, albeit with some delay, and is due to many of the same forces – oil shocks, computer revolutions, and so on.[5] However, because of important advances in communications technology, a growing interdependence of financial markets has developed. Because money is now being committed world-wide, there is a need to know much more about prospects in diverse parts of the world. As well, trade has become much more important to many nations than it has been in the past. Part of trade policy planning inevitably requires forecasting. For these and other reasons, aggregate economic forecasting has grown throughout the world. There are simply many more forecasters at work in their respective countries now than ever before.

Mention need also be made of attempts to forecast the world economy as one large economic unit, i.e. to tie together the various economies and/or economic forecasts in a systematic way. Without question the major work in this regard has been carried out by Klein and others through their PROJECT LINK work. Ongoing since the 1960s, PROJECT LINK is, as the name implies, an effort to build a world-wide econometric model by knitting together various national models.[6] Extensive discussion of this work is not critical to our intentions here. Suffice to say, it has not been an unqualified success. As one can imagine, the problems that need to be overcome are horrendous. The effort is to be applauded simply because it is being made. Much remains to be done.

Also worthy of note is the work of the Organization for Economic Co-operation and Development (OECD) in Paris.[7] Because of its mandate, the OECD has the longest-running collection of in-house forecasts of the largest numbers of countries available anywhere in the world, dating from 1966. The organization argues that it has tried to ensure internal consistency when aggregating up these national forecasts to arrive at a prediction for the OECD "economy" as a whole. We will look at these forecasts, particularly at their accuracy, in some detail in a moment.

In summary, then, while there is considerable aggregate economic forecasting activity internationally, there seems to be a relative absence of recent institutional information on its exact nature. One is, however, able to piece together a general understanding from other sources. What such an attempt shows is that while there has been dramatic growth elsewhere in the world in very recent times, forecasters in the United States continue to dominate the industry, not only in the absolute and relative number of forecasts they make but also in terms of the issues, methodological or otherwise, of concern to the industry at any particular time. In these respects Canada is no different from the other countries I have mentioned. Indeed, after the United States, it may well be among the most active aggregate economic forecasting markets in the world.

COMPARISONS OF ACCURACY

Canada and the United States

Fortunately, the relative absence of recent institutional detail on the industry does not carry over to an absence of information about the accuracy of forecasts made in these various countries. Quite the contrary, for there is an embarrassment of riches from which to choose. It seems that people are always more interested in the accuracy of their forecasts than in how they happen to have been made! As a consequence, it is possible to gain some understanding about how well the Canadian industry has done relative to international standards.

Because of the pre-eminence of the US industry, it is natural to begin with a comparison of the Canadian and US records. There are other reasons why this is a good choice. It is a country that "matches" Canada well, at least with respect to forecasting communities. Many Canadian economic institutions have been strongly influenced by US experience. Not the least of these is the system of national accounting and, by implication, the variables that require forecasting. Because of this close similarity between methods for defining, measuring, and reporting aggregate economic data, some of the fundamental difficulties of comparative study can be overcome more easily than might otherwise be the case. Also, in both countries there is a sizeable private forecasting community, with records of forecasts, which, while never lengthy enough, do nonetheless refer to similar periods.

It is possible, with careful selection, to make almost the same comparisons as were made earlier in connection with Canadian forecasters themselves. If one further restricts the comparison to a common period, one major aggregate variable, such as seasonally adjusted nominal GNP, and only private forecasters, one can be fairly certain that any statements on relative accuracy are on safer technical grounds, at least in some "minimum required" sense. The major limitation of such a research strategy derives from the fact that the economies of the United States and Canada are quite different, both in size and nature. This raises questions as to whether any meaningful conclusions can be drawn from such a comparison. However, the two countries generally exist in the same economic environment, and such a comparison give some perspective to the performances of both American and Canadian forecasters. Also, differences in the two economies are controlled for when relative accuracy comparisons are made, that is, when the accuracy of the forecasts relative to that of extrapolative predictions is compared across the two countries. Clearly the approach is something of a compromise. However, it seems the only way to draw partially legitimate inferences about the relative accuracy of Canadian aggregate forecasts from inter-country comparisons without a lengthy series of methodological asides.

The evidence to be considered comes from patching together the results of three studies, namely Daub (1973a), Zarnowitz (1979), and Daub (1981). Doing so results in the following general observations:

1. During the 1960s, using a carefully chosen equivalent number

of "identical" forecasters, the general conclusion from my comparison of the absolute accuracy of American and Canadian predictions of percentage changes in nominal GNP and its expenditure sector components was that the former were more accurate (Daub 1974). The mean errors were fewer; the number of underestimates was smaller; the size of "correctable" errors was smaller; and the regression and test statistics were more favourable. However, when one considered relative accuracy, perhaps the more meaningful comparison in the case of the two economies, the American predictions seemed only about as accurate, perhaps even less so: the relative mean square errors associated with the "best" available extrapolative model were larger. Less autonomous input and information available from extrapolations appeared to have been included by American forecasts, although the extent to which extrapolations were actually used differed little between the two countries, neither of whose forecasts appeared to have contained much extrapolation.

2. Using Zarnowitz (1979) and Daub (1981), both of which updated respective earlier studies (i.e. Zarnowitz 1967; Daub 1973a), it is possible to compare evidence for the 1970s and over the longer run. The evidence comes from data which, if not exactly overlapping – United States 1953–76, Canada 1957–79 – are nevertheless nearly so, as is the actual number of years considered.

3. Zarnowitz (1979, 7) reports that the US record improved considerably during the late 1960s and the 1970s, "a turbulent period presumed to have been particularly difficult to forecast." This result is identical to the one reported in chapter 7 for Canadian forecasters.

4. The evidence over the longer run indicates that US forecasters (as represented by Zarnowitz's own selected group of private forecasts, ones directly comparable to the Canadian sample used in chapter 7) made mean (mean absolute) errors of −0.7 per cent (1.2 per cent) as compared to Canadian errors of −1.6 per cent (2.2 per cent) over the periods in question (roughly 1953–79). While absolutely smaller, when compared to the size of the actual change in the respective economies over time, *these mean absolute errors are virtually identical, i.e. 19 per cent v. 21 per cent respectively*. More elaborate relative accuracy analysis confirms this result.

5. Further comparisons of the results of accuracy analyses on the predictions of real GNP and the price deflator for common periods for which data are available give similar results.

6. The evidence indicates that the kinds of errors made in forecasting GNP, particularly underestimation of change, are common to both countries. Zarnowitz (1979) notes that turning point (directional) errors, while relatively few, are on average much larger than other errors, principally because of peak errors, the forecasting record

at the trough being good. They thus have an important effect on the overall accuracy of real GNP forecasts in the United States. Several of these conclusions, such as a better record at the trough than at the peaks, also hold for Canada, although the value of indicators as a forecasting tool may not apply as strongly in the Canadian case, at least on the basis of the early evidence presented above.[8]

These results are at once both satisfying and interesting. They mean that we do as well as others, a finding that is always satisfying. There is nothing either extraordinarily difficult about the Canadian economy or bad about our forecasting technology, at least relatively speaking, that requires attention. That they are interesting stems from the fact that as one widens the sample, there continues to be no difference in the accuracy of aggregate economic forecasters over time, regardless of where they might be.[9]

Before commenting on this finding directly, I will note several US accuracy evaluation studies that bear on it. Ahlers and Lakonishok (1983) did a systematic study of the accuracy of the Livingston collection of forecasts over the period 1947–78. Using a large number of variables, they confirm earlier findings that forecasting performance has improved through time, that there is a tendency to underestimate, and that the ability to predict different economic series varies substantially. Where they do differ from other findings is in their conclusion that forecasts do not outperform simple extrapolative alternatives, a result perhaps due to the rather different extrapolative alternatives they tested. This latter observation is important, for it serves to stress once again how important it is to match data and method when making these judgments.[10]

Several other US studies have in their own way underlined this finding of no difference. Armstrong (1978) surveyed the published empirical studies comparing the accuracy of econometric and time series methods. He concluded that econometric forecasts are not significantly better than time series ones.[11] Others such as Makridakis (1983) have shown that simple time series models will often do as well as more complicated ones; it depends very much on the variable. One could cite Nelson (1972), McNees and Reis (1983), and others as well. All the US studies contribute to the conclusion that there really is no difference between forecasters in accuracy over time, regardless of which methods are used or which economy they are forecasting.[12]

The Broader Picture

To test this conclusion directly I looked at a broader international sample of forecasters from four different countries, tried to be as technically careful as possible, and applied a series of fairly exhaustive tests to see if in fact there were any differences (Daub 1975; 1977). The results confirm that the errors, when taken relative to the size of the actual change or of the error made by extrapolative alternatives, were not significantly different in any of the cases considered. That is, the degree of accuracy achieved during the period in question, the 1960s, was invariant with respect to country.

Such a result is perhaps not as surprising as it might seem at first. Most of the major industrialized economies possess well-funded, responsible forecasting communities. Given the sizeable exchange of information and techniques through the literature, by personnel exchanges, and during conferences, it is not unrealistic to expect that methods of measurement, data collection, and development of predictions will show a strong degree of similarity. The logical extension of this reasoning would surely be that the degree of accuracy achieved should be about the same, on average, over a given period of time. That is, if the market in this know-how is at all efficient, the degree of accuracy that forecasters achieve should be about the same, on average, over a given period.

This argument can be carried even a step further. As has been well documented in the literature on financial markets, an efficient market hypothesis such as this may also suggest entertaining the theory that a random pattern exists in the errors over time, much in the way that an efficient stock market leads to the random nature of prices there. There are a number of ways to search for randomness in data. The methods most commonly used in economics and finance research involve runs testing and serial correlation analysis. As a result, I adopted them to examine whether the errors made by the forecasters in different countries were random over time. First-order serial correlation coefficients and a runs test were calculated for each forecast set individually, and for all sets taken together, using various relative accuracy measures.

The general conclusion would again seem clear. Neither the size of the first-order serial coefficients nor the number of runs, individually or aggregated, leads to the conclusion of non-randomness. This suggests that the forecasters did about as well as could have been expected in the circumstances. That is, ex post facto it may be possible to identify, for example, that the raw errors for some components contained a bias towards underestimation or that a given extrapolative model might have forecast "better." However, these are characteristics general to all forecasters, precisely because of shared technology. Hence, when one controls for them, the resulting errors are not only similar but also random. And thus, if we assume a free flow of information on techniques and the like, any forecaster will not only do about as well as any other over a specified period in forecasting given circumstances, but he or she will do about as well as available information permits.

Evidence for other countries, over varying periods – e.g. Bouysset (1974) for France, Ridker (1963) for Norway, Sims (1969) for Holland, Smyth (1966) for Australia, and Theil (1955) for a host of countries – could be introduced to expand the international comparison. In the absence of systematic reporting here of the record, the reader must take it on faith that, while the hypotheses are generally not directly examined, the evidence from this other research on accuracy generally supports the conclusions of no difference in accuracy and randomness in the errors.

One study involving the international aspects of forecasting errors, that by Llewelyn and others (1985) at the OECD, does, however, warrant closer examination, not only because of its large, multinational nature but also because it sought to look at the extent to which forecasting error originating in one country is "transmitted" via trade and financial channels to others. It therefore sheds light on the mechanisms underlying the assumption of efficient market in methods argued above.

It is useful to cite some of Llewelyn and his colleagues' basic accuracy-assessment statistics.[13] For the OECD as a whole, the mean absolute error over the period (17 years, 1966–82) was 1.0 per cent (about 30 per cent of the actual) in forecasting real GNP growth over the period, about 1.2 per cent in predicting the GNP deflator; slight underestimation was present; and the forecasts outperformed extrapolative alternatives. As well, the overall distribution of errors in single-country forecasts is approximately normal. Further, where both are available, there is no marked difference between the OECD forecasts and those of national forecasters. Finally, some years were clearly harder to forecast than others. All of this is quite similar to what we have seen earlier in Canada, although price forecasting errors elsewhere have not tended to offset real forecasting errors to the same degree.

The question of why some years were harder to forecast was examined by considering two sources of errors: those that originated within a country ("original sin"!) and those transmitted from outside (acquired sin). The researchers argued, quite ingeniously, as follows:[14]

If, in any given year, the forces acting on the OECD economy were broadly neutral, and if each single-country forecast were made essentially in isolation, with little contact between and discussion among those making forecasts for other countries, it might be expected that some country forecasters would over-predict domestic developments, while others would under-predict. Likewise, some would over-predict, or make too strong an assumption about, developments in the rest of the world, while others would do the reverse. Hence in a broadly normal year without significant discussion among forecasters it might be that:

i) the balance between the number of positive forecasting errors and the number of negative forecasting errors would be fairly close to zero; and

ii) the various single-country errors would approximately cancel one another, so that a forecast for the total OECD, made up from component country forecasts, would turn out to be relatively close to the actual outcome.

However, in addition to the years when the balance between positive and negative country errors is likely to be fairly close to zero – which could well represent the majority – there are also likely to be, from time to time, certain special, atypical years for which the single-country errors are rather far from randomly distributed. This could arise in any one of a variety of ways. It could be that the entire OECD economy is affected by an external shock. If the shock is unexpected, or the likely effects are fairly generally misunderstood, the result is likely to be a significant forecasting error, for the OECD area as a whole and thereby for most countries individually. Or, running the other way, it may be that something rather general happens and is misforecast *within* the OECD area, leading to errors for most countries individually and thereby for the OECD area as a whole.

Such considerations raise a presumption that, in at least many of the years when the balance between positive and negative forecasting errors across countries is markedly different from zero, that is to say when a significant majority of single-country forecasters either over-predict or under-predict likely developments in their countries, the forecasting error for the OECD economy as a whole is also likely to be relatively large.

They found that in many of the years from 1966 to 1982, errors for some countries were largely offset by errors in the opposite direction for others, suggesting that the main source of errors in forecasting originated within individual countries. This directly supports the conclusion drawn earlier from some of my work. However, in several of the years, a majority of the individual country forecasts made errors in the same direction, sometimes all overestimating, others all underestimating change. Careful study of these years indicated that they followed a large shock to the OECD economy as a whole, whether from within, because of important changes in policy, principally in the United States, or without, especially following the first oil shock. The effects of these shocks are poorly understood by all forecasters, not only for domestic reasons but more importantly

for "international" reasons. It would seem that the effects on economic activity abroad and hence, through feedback on one's own
economy, are particularly unclear. As a consequence, this increase
in uncertainty of all forecasters is "fed around" the larger world
economy via trade and financial channels and makes for larger errors
both overall and for each individual country's forecasters.[15]

This is an important result for Canadian forecasters, for it suggests
at least one explanation for those high-error years that we observed
earlier in Figure 3, especially the two most recent ones of 1974–5
and 1982. In these years immediately following a major shock to the
larger world economy (as represented by a change of at least 1 per
cent in the rate of change in the OECD real GNP), and particularly if
it involves parts of the trading or financial exchange channels that
are not well understood (because, for example, the problem of OPEC
had never arisen before), there will be larger forecasting errors
everywhere, including Canada. As a result, "it may well be appropriate in such circumstances to warn policy makers to place relatively
greater weight on the actuals as they come in through the year, and
relatively less weight on the forecasts, than would be appropriate in
normal years."[16]

Long-Term Forecasts

Finally a brief comment on the record elsewhere with respect to
longer-term forecasting. Just as was the case for Canada, the nature
of the evidence elsewhere is also extremely weak. This is not to say
that one is unaware of the accuracy of long-term predictions elsewhere. There is no end to the amount of "anecdotal" reference to
the inaccuracy, in the sense of "famous gaffes," of specific long-term
predictions whenever they have been made. One of my favourites
is the following summary of the report of a committee organized in
1486 at the command of the King and Queen of Spain to study
Columbus' plan to sail west to find a shorter route to India.[17] It
reported in 1490 that such a voyage was impossible because: "(1) A
voyage to Asia would require three years. (2) The Western Ocean
is infinite and perhaps unnavigable. (3) If he reached the Antipodes
[the land on the other side of the globe from Europe], he could not
get back. (4) There are no Antipodes because the greater part of
the globe is covered with water, and because Saint Augustine says
so ... (5) Of the five zones, only three are habitable. (6) So many
centuries after the Creation it was unlikely that anyone could find
hitherto unknown lands of any value."

A rather careful reading of the literature on the accuracy of more modern long-term forecasts elsewhere in the world, especially the summaries of Armstrong (1978) and Ascher (1978), suggests the following: 1) The further out one goes, the less accurate one becomes; 2) One should forget about forecasting variability or cycles; the trend is the best that can be hoped for; 3) No single method or source will prove more accurate than any other; 4) Certain periods are more difficult to forecast than others.

"I foresee an upturn within the next six to eight million years."

Further, assumptions would seem to be the key. Any given method works out only the implications. In this regard there are many caveats one can cite, in particular from the behavioural literature on forecasting. One of the ones stressed earlier is that in long-term forecasting the solution all too often gets driven by a sense of plausibility which is period-specific and generally conservative. Clarke (1984), the famous science fiction writer, stresses the failure of nerve and of imagination that this implies. Whether it is a "refusal to face facts" (and if so, why?!) or a "refusal to permit the flights of fancy their full rein" is difficult to measure. No doubt both play a role.

But there is little if anything in this cursory glimpse at the broader lierature on longer-term forecasting that is different from what we concluded earlier with respect to Canadian forecasting over the same horizons. In that respect the result is very similar to the short-term accuracy comparisons. As we have come to understand, it is probably to be expected.

CONCLUSIONS

What we have seen then is that there is a large international community of aggregate economic forecasters. They work at forecasting their domestic economics, as well as those of their major trading partners, and in most circumstances that of the United States as well. In addition, certain international organizations, in particular the OECD, attempt a kind of summing up to larger economic aggregations.[18]

Without question the largest of these communities is found in the United States. A cursory examination suggests that it is similar in many respects to the Canadian industry considered earlier, except that it is both absolutely and relatively larger and provides technological leadership rather than following it, as does the Canadian.

Aggregate economic forecasting elsewhere in the world is relatively less important, although this is beginning to change, especially as planning in many countries becomes less important and domestic economics more liberal as a result. Indeed a forecasting "industry" is beginning to develop in certain of these countries as dynamically as it did in Canada, albeit much later.

It is natural to want to compare our forecasting record with that of these other communities. It is quite another thing to be able to do so in anything like the way one can when comparing records within Canada. Various problems were identified. They all relate to the basic inability to match economies and forecasters successfully. If one tries to be as careful and thorough as possible, and takes as broad a sample as possible, several general conclusions seem to emerge, the most important of which is surely that there is likely no difference over time in the accuracy achieved by any given forecaster in any given country. Perhaps the second is that everyone tends to make the same kinds of errors at the same time.

It was argued that this is not surprising. Not only is there an almost "efficient-like market" in forecasting technology. Also, economies are tied together by trade and financial institutions that transmit the expectations-related thinking contained in aggregate economic forecasts back and forth between these economics. Thus on balance aggregate economic forecasters do about as well as the method permits. In this respect the results show that they are improving with time and are generally surprised together by events no one anywhere could have foreseen. Turning points, especially downturns, are particularly bothersome in this respect.

The observation was ventured that this is satisfying because it means that Canadians do about as well as others, i.e. there is nothing either extraordinarily difficult to forecast about the Canadian economy or bad about our forecasting technology that would require attention. It is also humbling, for it means that there is much to do internationally if one is to better understand, and hence predict, the kinds of thing that cause these aggregate economic forecasts to go wrong. Evidence from the 1970s indicates that unanticipated events, such as the OPEC price shocks or changes in behaviour patterns such as those involving fertility and labour force participation rates for women, have to be dealt with better.[19] Certainly forecasters have improved with time both in the tools of the trade and in their professionalism. It is to be hoped that the trend will continue. It is also devoutly to be wished that any shocks or changes that do come our way and do get missed will not be so completely destructive as to take us all down with them! But that is another story altogether, is it not?

CHAPTER NINE

Policy Considerations

"I don't altogether believe in forecasts ... "

As we have moved along through this story about aggregate economic forecasting in Canada, we have found ourselves on several occasions face to face with what might be thought of as policy considerations. In some instances the issues were addressed, in others ignored. It is now time to consider them in a systematic way.

The term "policy considerations" has been left deliberately vague for a reason. It is intended to cover two rather broad, and quite different, interpretations. The first relates to the use of aggregate economic forecasting in policy formation; the second to public issues related to "controlling" the industry itself, that is, policy versus it.

In a sense the first interpretation, that of the role of forecasting in policy formation, has been examined already both directly in chapter 5 and indirectly in some of the comments on accuracy evaluation in chapter 7. But it is important to draw all of this together in one place. A discussion of the second consideration, control of the industry, has not been covered at all. Let us consider each in turn.

ROLE IN POLICY FORMULATION

One of the major reasons why it is necessary to examine the role of aggregate economic forecasting in policy formulation is that its importance to the policy process seems increasingly of late to be questioned, whether by editorialists, executives, or finance ministers. Gone are the not so distant times when forecasting was king, when one could assert with the confidence of Lasswell in his foreword to Ascher (1978) that "forecasting is a fundamental component of public and private policy-making."[1] One wonders why there is this scepticism, especially in the face of continuing demand for the industry's products.

It could be due to a number of things. In chapter 5 we noted that forecasting tended to enter into the policy process, be it public or private, in one of two ways (via the "black box" or in a carefully programatic way, usually tied directly to the budgeting cycle) and to fulfil several expressed needs in so doing. Perhaps forecasts have disappointed policy-makers in some way with respect to meeting these needs. Alternatively the real causes of dissatisfaction may lie elsewhere. That is, other factors that masquerade as concern over forecasts may be responsible for this opinion about forecasting.

These aggregate economic forecasts are said, by those people who demand them, to contribute to, and guide, policy-making in one of several ways. To review briefly, we know that besides being a natural "seeking after a bit of revealed truth about the future," forecasting is also used as an organizational tool. It might serve, for example, to help ensure that the organization is being consistent in its thinking about the future. As well, it may aid in "rallying the troops to greater efforts." Yet another of these "sociological' reasons, indeed one of the more important, is to demonstrate, if only implicitly, that "reasonable care" has been taken in the way taxpayers', shareholders', or donors' funds have been committed. Not nearly so often acknowledged is the fact that failure is made easier if it can be shared with, or transferred entirely to, the forecasting community.

A more subtle purpose for demanding these forecasts, that is perhaps more global in nature and can be viewed from either a sociological or an economic perspective, is helping economic agents to "herd together." They are the vehicles whereby we declare, and hear declared, our individual thoughts about the future. Through such an exchange we come to understand better and deal with our mutual future. Economists might put it that forecasts have an informational value that in a market economy aids the "invisible hand" in working out collectively acceptable solutions.

Forecasting is but one of a number of ways in which policy-makers might choose to deal "economically" with an uncertain future. There are others: lobbying, hedging, or the stocking of inventory. Hedging against future interest rate fluctuations is similar to spending money to forecast those rates. The cost of lobbying to "arrange" the future may be less in certain instances than paying to forecast the "unarranged" future.

Perhaps then, the scepticism is due to the inaccuracy of the revealed vision fo the future. But it cannot be so. We also know that the record reviewed in chapters 7 and 8 indicates that no one Canadian forecaster is better than another and that Canadian forecasters are no worse or better than those in other countries. Further, it shows that the average error in forecasting percentage changes in nominal GNP, perhaps the single most general economic variable one might choose, is not significantly different from zero over a relatively long run of years. Moreover, accuracy has generally improved over time. So, despite what policy-makers may believe about accuracy, it just isn't so. Why then does it seem to them that forecasts are more inaccurate and thus to be rejected?

I would argue that criticizing the accuracy of the forecasts is merely a convenient way of summarizing a general feeling of dissatisfaction, not only, or even principally, with these traditional forecasts but, more important, with other aspects of economic activity. For one thing, the relative prices of some of the substitutes for traditional aggregate economic forecasting have fallen. Futures markets in interest and currency rates, for example, have become highly effective alternatives to forecasting. As the cost of hedging falls, and understanding of its use grows, the demand for traditional interest and exchange rate forecasts will fall.

Further, many more aggregate forecasts are now available in the public domain, partly because of increased regulatory activity. Whereas in the past more of such forecasts were privately produced and guarded, today, because of the public good characteristics of forecasting information, many potential demanders prefer to "piggy back" on published forecasts rather than pay the direct cost of acquiring the information. While this could be seen as merely a shift in demand from internal to external sources, I would argue that there has been a reduction in the total amount of forecasting services demanded because of the presence of these informational external economies.

As well, policy-makers are more sophisticated about how forecasts can be used to organize, manipulate, and otherwise direct activity. This, as well as the abuses that sometimes accompany such activity, has also altered the demand for forecasts.[2] These changes in demand have little to do with supposed inaccuracy. Rather they are motivated principally by relative price changes and changes in "tastes" (primarily education). As with many other goods, such substitution is frequently accompanied by a sense of dissatisfaction with the abandoned good or service, however justified or unjustified.

Equally important, some of the other roles that forecasts play are being addressed perhaps in the form of a complaint over accuracy simply because the real reason cannot be voiced. I would argue, for example, that much of the complaining about forecasts really relates to the "risk spreading" or "risk assumption" role that forecasters bear for policy-makers. Much of the anxiety that policy-makers have felt in facing greatly increased economic uncertainty since 1970, and the many disputes they have had about how to deal with it, have surfaced in the form of a lashing out at forecasters for not providing better scouting! The messenger is being shot for the message. It must be so, because it is hard to see how Canadian forecasters could have done any better.

Perhaps, too, policy-makers expected too much from the new technologies of the late 1960s and early 1970s. We saw how quickly the industry evolved in this period. Many people were carried away with its potential, only to be disappointed later with the quality of its product. It is a pattern that has been repeated elsewhere on many occasions and probably explains some of the current scepticism about the role of traditional forecasting in the policy process.

No doubt the industry itself was partly to blame for this. It oversold the product. There are other ways, too, in which it might be thought to be at fault. The first relates to what may be termed a "mismatch" of supply to demand. Canadian forecasters are part of a larger, world-wide intellectual community. As such, they have been influenced by work elsewhere, particularly in the United States. This is to be expected. These influences have contributed to the development of a kind of prism through which the Canadian economy is viewed, one formed mostly by American ideas about what constitute the important issues, and how (and what) data are to be gathered on these issues, and how (and in what way) they are to be studied (modelled).

This statement is not intended as yet another thinly disguised plea for Canadian nationalism. Nor is it meant to belittle the unique contributions of Canadian scholars and statisticians, or to comment on the appropriateness of monetary and fiscal theory, econometric modelling, and like considerations over the last half-century. No doubt it benefits substantially from hindsight. Rather, I intend to suggest that Canadian efforts may have focused unduly on concerns that, while also appropriate, were relatively less so in Canada than elsewhere.

Consider, for example, the issue of disaggregation. Canada's economic structure is regionally and jurisdictionally disparate. Yet, given Ontario and Quebec's preponderant influence, any aggregate models of the Canadian economy will relate principally only to them. These will be of little use to the policy-maker in Alberta or British Columbia whose economies bear little resemblance to those of Ontario or Quebec, or to those in the federal government who may wish to tailor policies to specific regions. Inasmuch as they are important to Canada, one would have thought that much early effort would have gone into provincial (or regional) models and data. Only recently has work gone forward on developing such regional data and models.

The same might be said for industrial sector disaggregation. Certainly CANDIDE did have structural detail. But the relative absence of good energy models to predict the effects on the oil and gas industry of the oil shocks or proposed National Energy Programme (NEP) legislation is only one example of the lack of specific sectoral models. Again, work has gone forward recently. The absence at a crucial time of these regional and sectoral models is suggested by some policy-makers as one of the reasons why they have become disillusioned with aggregate economic forecasts.[3]

This is not the only supply-related reason for disillusionment. Another is the advent of a new era in which the emphasis in theory and policy has shifted from short-term intervention to longer-term structural considerations. There is a perception that monetary and fiscal fine-tuning is relatively less important than it once was. The models, which were particularly designed to address them, seem somehow passé or irrelevant to the discussions of the "Japanese challenge" or industrial policy.

Yet another reason is the uncertainty caused by much of the debate in the economics profession since the late 1960s as to the appropriate theoretical characterization of the economy. One might call this "paradigm uncertainty." Policy-makers have become increasingly aware of this uncertainty. They have also become increasingly technically sophisticated. They are thus more informed about the inherent limitations of the major methods used to make predictions, the difficulty of exogenous variable prediction, structural-shift tracking problems, data, estimation, and so on. None of this makes them feel terribly like relying on forecasters when addressing their own problems. But it does provide an extremely convenient whipping boy at a time when one is really needed![4]

The forecaster is not immune from all this turmoil. Unfortunately, predictions are required. One cannot gracefully withdraw until a later time when all problems will have been solved and/or the world is more stable. Those forecasters thus provide a focus for many of the concerns discussed here. Therefore, the attack on the "inaccuracy" of these forecasters is probably at heart a reflection of dissatisfaction with the supposed uncertainties and inadequacies of economics and statistics more generally.

This is not to apologize for forecasting. Rather it is to argue that for much of the 1970s and early 1980s many policy initiatives appeared tied in all their most important respects to forecasts. Whether such initiatives lived or died often depended on whether they possessed the appropriate "seal of good forecasting." There is now a real danger that policy-makers and those who judge them are erring in the opposite direction. They now may well consider a forecast of little use whatsoever. They appear to have swung from an almost "rational modellism" to an equally strong sense of "forecasting atheism."

What is needed is some appreciation of the middle ground. Sophistication and maturity on the part of the user and humility and integrity on the part of the supplier should probably be the order of the day. Both sides should recognize that aggregate forecasts are nothing more or less than one element in the policy-maker's tool kit. Despite present concerns, it is likely that they will continue to be a uniquely appropriate vehicle for satisfying many of the traditional needs that policy-makers have when developing and selling initiatives, i.e. to show evidence of having used reasonable care, to spread responsibility, to provide a tool for organizational motivation, and to act as a signal of one's intentions to the larger world. Further, carefully developed and appropriately documented, such forecasts will probably continue to represent the best and most internally consistent guess about the future one can expect given current knowledge. For all these reasons, aggregate economic forecasting still has much to offer the policy-maker.

Such a thinly disguised plea for reasonableness all around may appeal to the kindly old Canadian academic in us all. Policy-makers have tended to react in other, more direct ways. They have, for example, moved to increase the flexibility and adaptability of their organizations to changing circumstances. Indeed these concepts have become one of the more important battle cries of modern management theory. "Adaptability the key to survival" reads many a headline! The Japanese, it is argued, "run very tight ships and are very quick on their feet." Policy-makers have also begun to plan "strategically," that is, to try to predict all possible futures and develop organization "escape routes" for all such eventualities.[5] Some even have "fire drills" to assess readiness, although most such preparation is stylized by using role-playing exercises and other kinds of "war games" exactly analogous to military planning exercises.

It will not escape the careful reader that neither of these responses implies eliminating forecasting completely. Indeed the latter requires, if anything, more prediction rather than less. All organizations will have to take one route or another off into the future. This will be done not blindly but rather on the basis of a reasonable "best-guess" about future circumstances. Being flexible, and prepared for all eventualities, is always wise. In no way does it eliminate having to make a choice as to which "road to take in a yellow wood."

PUBLIC POLICY TO CONTROL
THE INDUSTRY

Introduction

Yet another way in which policy-makers might have reacted would have been to make overt the forecaster's "assumption of risk" by suing the forecaster! Alternatively other remedies such as regulation or public ownership might have been forthcoming. Strangely enough, there has been little in the way of such a direct response. One can only imagine what might have happened in other circumstances where purchasers of products or services subsequently found that the seller had gotten the facts wrong to the buyer's detriment! To be sure, as we shall see, suits have been brought in recent times, but mostly in certain areas of forecasting and never with respect to aggregate economic forecasting in Canada. One wonders why. And in so wondering one raises the question of how, if at all, this very important industry is controlled in the public interest, and whether it ought to be.

At first blush it would seem that the industry is wide open. There has been almost no direct public intervention in the industry in the classical ways. For example, no price or territorial conspiracy or predation actions have ever been started under anti-competition provisions; no clauses about truth-in-advertising, product quality, or other practices in that same or similar appropriate legislation have been invoked; no direct regulation of the industry, whether for foreign owernship, monopoly returns, or various other reasons, has ever been considered. Moreover, there appears to be no self-regulation: there is a complete absence of a national trade or professional association paralleling those in medicine (CMA), law (CBA), accountancy (CIA, RIA), pharmacy (CDA), or even real estate and travel consulting.

It was not always so. In ancient times "soothsayers" were often placed under the benevolent protection of the state. And those in the business did their best to ensure that access to the services was strictly controlled. It is not completely clear why there seems to be such a difference today. That the difference is more apparent than real comes to light when one reflects on the ways in which the industry is controlled in the public interest other than, of course, by the market itself. Two avenues in particular are important, namely the law and competition from publicly owned forecasters. Let us consider each in turn.

The Law and Economic Forecasting

One of the major areas in which the industry has directly experienced public control is in connection with both common and statute law. Before looking at concepts of liability and intellectual property as they apply in Canada, I want to comment briefly on common and statute law interpretations found in the United States and Britain, because they inform Canadian laws to such a large extent. There is an added incentive in the US case because of the large forecasting community and an actively litigious society.

The field of common law most directly of relevance is torts.[6] In tort law there has always been an important difference for liability purposes (i.e. for error) between a statement of opinion and one of fact. Opinions are expected to exaggerate somewhat the actual situation (for example, to a seller's advantage) and hence enjoy greater leeway for error in the interpretation of the courts than do statements of supposed fact. There is a wonderful doctrine here called "puffing," which is held a responsible thing to expect. In recent times leeway has been narrowed, principally by the interpretation that opinions imply a reasonable basis for holding them, something that the courts are willing to require, especially in cases where the only remedy sought is restitution, not extra damages for deceit.

Forecasts are clearly statements of opinion. Further, what is probably implied is that they are honest beliefs and based on reasonable facts, especially if they are sold. To meet these standards one would have to show that there had been a reasonable analysis of available data and that the forecast reasonably reflected the competence of those who were selling it. That is, they could not claim much more for it than they themselves, who prepared it, could hope to deliver. What forecasters don't presumably have to worry about, and hence aren't liable for, is that the future failed to turn out as they predicted. They never guaranteed that it would.[7] Thus, in summary, there must be good faith, proper purpose, an honest belief in the estimate, and reasonable care in preparation.

Reasonable care is the main fly in the ointment. That is, to what extent has the forecaster been negligent such that there is misrepresentation, not deliberately, but unintentionally? Negligent but unintended misrepresentation is one of the more difficult areas of tort law. Since so many people might conceivably be injured (imagine all those who might hear a given forecast!), any potential damages that might be assessed would be virtually unlimited, and all because the forecaster, for example, had failed to use reasonable care. As a result, courts were hesitant to find for negligence except in quite restricted ways. This approach has been somewhat broadened recently, but the law is still unclear how far. So the liability for negligent forecasting is in some question as part of the uncertainty about negligent misrepresentation generally.

Most of the suits in the United States involving "forecasters" have been lodged not under common law but rather under securities (statute) law, which regardless of jurisdiction always has as its basic thrust the requirement of accurate information so as to avoid fraud or deception. Often these forecasters have been nothing more than stock salesmen making over-optimistic predictions of prices or earnings. Many of the common law aspects outlined above have been carried over to interpreting this requirement for accurate information under securities legislation. Thus there must be honest belief: if one has no reasonable basis in fact for the opinions stated, one is guilty of knowing misrepresentation. In a whole collection of cases involving the brokerage business, this honest belief requirement has been violated, or else there has been flagrant factual misrepresentation. Only on occasion has the common law "puffing" defence held up.

But these cases do not relate directly to forecasting as such. There are several in the United States, however, that do, although even there the number is limited, principally because the forecasting industry is rather young and the courts require a very rigorous burden of proof for negligent preparation. Consider several such early, securities-related cases and a recent weather forecasting, tort law case.

In *Milburg* v. *Western Pacific Railroad* (51 FRD 280 [SDNY 1970]) a suit was brought over an inaccurate earnings forecast that allegedly caused a loss to the purchaser plaintiff. The court disallowed the action, since there was no proof of "deliberate or reckless mistaking of the facts." Further it said: "Estimates are nothing more than estimates and can't reasonably be expected to be infallible. There is no such thing as absolute liability for error in this regard."[8] In *Dolgow* v. *Anderson* (53 FRD 664 [EDNY 1971]), perhaps *the* major early case on forecasting, the suit alleged the publication of false and misleading forecasts of earnings by executives at Monsanto Chemical while at the same time internal information to the contrary was withheld, all to permit the executives to sell their stock holdings at higher prices. As with *Milburg*, there was some consideration initially about whether the situation warranted a class action suit.

Class action suits are peculiar to US securities law, at least with respect to forecasting. Generally speaking, suit by one individual stockholder is not worth the candle, of legal fees in particular. However, if the suit can be broadened to include others through class action designation, then the legal fees can be spread over a much larger award. If one adds to this the US practice of contingency legal fees, that is, taking a case where fees will be a percentage of the award, one can readily understand the attempt in each forecasting-related case to try first to establish class action standing before the courts. To date the courts have been extremely reluctant to grant such status. The court didn't in *Dolgow*.

Moreover it found no merits on the principles of the action either: "Information submitted to the court and available through extensive discovery indicates that those forecasts were sound when made and that the subsequent failure of earnings to meet predictions was due to market and other changes that a reasonable businessman would not have foreseen or would have discounted in making predictions." The court also noted with approval that the firm had a regular practice of releasing plenty of information, including forecasts, so that people could judge for themselves what was happening. As part of checking for negligence the court carefully examined internal budgeting and other procedures to discover not only how the forecasts had been used and who had prepared them, but whether the same ones had been used for internal purposes as were released publicly. It found a great number of experts involved and the same forecasts used in both instances, thereby establishing both lack of negligence and honest belief.

The court went further in speculating about the potentially disruptive character of such suits if too strict an interpretation of liability were adopted (i.e. if predictions didn't come true). Corporate executives would have to spend all their time defending against suits of this form. Also, it would encourage executives not to report predictions of any kind whenever possible, not an ideal situation in an age of open corporations and government. It would also be tactically unwise, for competition is a function of difference in expectations as much as anything else. Knowing what the opposition thinks, and vice versa, is roughly tantamount to a legally enforced cartel!

Two other early American cases of lesser importance, *Butler Aviation* v. *Comprehensive Designers* (425 F. 2d 842 [2d Cir. 1970]) and *Spraygen* v. *Livingston Oil* (295 F. Supp. 1376 [SDNY 1968]), also contributed several points of note, all of which underline some of the requirements mentioned above. From *Butler Aviation* comes the requirement that while forecasts are not a warranty of the future, they must bear a reasonable relationship to the state of mind of the forecaster (i.e., there must be honest belief), and from *Spraygen* the need to have a close relationship between the forecast and available data.

To summarize from this early US case law, it would seem that "in principle the forecaster would not be liable simply because the forecast didn't come out if he/she made it in good faith and for a proper purpose, if it represented his/her actual belief about future prospects, and was prepared with reasonable care and diligence."[9] However, there is some question about disclosure obligations. The balance of opinion seems to be that except when forecasts indicate significant variation from past performance, the risk of witholding them, say by management, is less than the risk of releasing them (which may result in suit by shareholders or others, who place undue reliance on them). What is more, the latter provides too tempting a target for any disgruntled person to pass up. In any case the law seems clear that if a company does publish forecasts on one occasion for a purpose, it will generally have a duty to keep doing so. Thus to start implies not only immediate, but subsequent, liability.

The one more recent case of interest in the United States with respect to forecasting (there are others in the spirit of *Milburg* or *Dolgow* that do not add materially to the law) is a weather forecasting case, *Brown et al* v. *Government of the United States* (1985). Here the court held that the National Ocean and Atmospheric Administration was liable for the deaths of three fishermen when its forecasts failed through negligence to predict a storm off the New England coast. The court emphasized that the decision rested on the notion of negligence, not the fact that the forecast was wrong, something for which the court held weather forecasters cannot be held liable in normal circumstances. A weather buoy that would have helped to produce an accurate forecast of the storm had been out of commission for over three months, and no attempts had been made to repair it.

This case represented the first time that the law in respect to forecasting has been broadened to non-securities, non-contract areas. The fact that one can be liable if a "buoy is out of action" is somewhat troubling. By analogy one might be held negligent if one's investment sector equations weren't working as they ought to have been and hence an aggregate economic forecast missed a turning point, to the purchaser's detriment. Such an example may seem far-fetched, but then so does the decision here in *Brown et al*, which is currently being appealed.

British practice concerning forecasting liability is controlled by many similar statutes, such as the Companies Act and the Prevention of Fraud (Investments) Act, as well as codes of behaviour, for example, the Take-over and Merger Code. The codes have serious practical, if not exactly legal, consequences such as delisting if violated. To cite but a few provisions relating to forecasts, in takeovers or mergers all forecasts must be released, all assumptions stated, some sensitivity analysis presented, calculations explained, and all this duly noted and attested to by accountants and financial advisers! The Companies Act requires the stock prospectus to contain forecasts. Also relevant is the Fraud Act, which says (section 13): "Any person who by any ... forecast which he knows to be misleading, false or deceptive, ... or by the reckless making [dishonestly or otherwise] of any ... forecast which is misleading, false or deceptive induces or attempts to induce another person to buy or sell securities shall be guilty of a crime."

One recent case, *Esso Petroleum Co. Ltd.* v. *Mardon* (2 ALL ER, 5, 1976), stands out. In it, Lord Denning decided on appeal that "it had been established successfully that where one party who has special knowledge and expertise, and makes a forecast based on it with the intention of inducing another to enter into a contract, and in reliance on it the other party does so, it is open to the courts to construe that the forecasts are not merely an expression of opinion but constitute a warranty that the forecast has been made with reasonable care and skill." Since the forecast in this case had in fact been negligent (neither party disputed this), Esso was liable for breach of warranty, in addition to negligence. One of the other judges (Shaw) concurred, adding: "It is often assumed that a statement of opinion cannot involve the statement of a fact. In a case where the facts are equally well known to both parties, what one says to the other is frequently nothing but an expression of opinion ... But if the facts are not equally known to both, then a statement of opinion by the one who knows the facts best involves very often a statement of a material fact, for he impliedly states that he knows facts which justify his opinion."

This ruling would appear to be very generous and make for a much expanded sense of liability on the part of forecasters. Careful reading, however, indicates that the court is requiring a duty of care on the part of the forecaster to ensure that the forecast is reasonably prepared, commensurate with the level of skill one might reasonably expect of him or her. This is a very different thing from warranting the future if one makes forecasts. As we shall see, when this case has been cited in recent Canadian cases, this much narrower interpretation has been given to *Denning et al's* ruling.

Outright fraud aside, and even given *Esso* v. *Mardon*, it is unlikely that people who act on the strength of forecasts "in the ordinary way" have as much remedy under British law, statute or otherwise, as they do in the United States. Liability for negligent error in a forecast has not been much litigated beyond *Esso* v. *Mardon* because contingency fees are avoided by British lawyers and an unsuccessful plaintiff may be required to pay defendant's legal expenses in addition to costs. Both severely restrict class action, fishing expedition suits! As a consequence, forecasting is able to proceed with a good deal less concern about liability than in the United States.

The same can be said about Canadian law relative to the United States. As with the United Kingdom, the sources of control over forecasting are laws and codes: the federal Corporation Act, the various securities and companies acts of the provinces, the codes of the accounting profession, particularly the Canadian Institute of Chartered Accountants (CICA), and, of course, common law relating to torts. Many of the requirements about disclosure of financial forecasts, or for comments by the accountant, under CICA rules or those of the Ontario Securities Act (by far the most important), are similar to Britain's.

Consider first the principle that forecasts are statements of opinions, not fact, and that tort law holds that those making them are not liable for any resulting errors. Several recent cases adopt exactly this reasoning. In the real estate case *Blanchette et al* v. *Shakatowski et al* (8 ACWS [2d], 203, 1981) forecasts of farm income made by a seller to a buyer were so held, and hence the seller was not liable because they failed to pan out. The same reasoning was used in the franchise case of *Pepsi-Cola Canada and Pizza Hut* v. P.M. *Foods* (61 AR 340, 1985). P.M. *Foods* (the franchisee) accused Pizza Hut of among other alleged offences, fraudulent misrepresentation and negligence in respect to its forecasts of the likely success of a chain of Pizza Hut outlets that P.M. Foods opened in Edmonton (they subsequently failed!). The court held that there was neither fraudulent nor negligent misrepresentation involved in the forecasts. The Alberta Court of Queen's Bench stated: "To succeed for deceit, ... a false statement must be made knowing it to be false, with the intent it be acted upon, which the party did, to his detriment ... Where the representor honestly believes the statement complained of is true, he cannot be liable for deceit even though he is ill-advised, stupid, credulous or even negligent." This is exactly analogous to the honest belief requirement discussed above with respect to *Dolgow*. The court held further that there was no negligent misrepresentation because the forecasts were just statements of opinions. They were not held out as existing fact. In any event the court found that P.M. Foods had completely ignored all the opinions and assistance offered by the franchiser so that it obviously had not relied on the forecasts! Hence there was no possible liability for negligence.[10]

Both of these cases indirectly involve representations on contract that involved forecasts as part of a larger picture. *Shields et al* v. *Broderick et al* (46 OR [2d], 19, 1984), another real estate case, involved forecasts directly. In it an agent was not held liable for oral reassurances about the ability of the buyer to resell quickly a house because "the signs that the boom market was losing momentum ... were not so clear and compelling that the agent ought to have known the market was going to decline as it did. The agent's assurances to the defendants were no more than the normal puffing to be expected from any salesperson." This case shows the principle of puffery applied directly to forecasts.

These three recent cases take a very narrow, torts-dominated view of forecasting liability, completely consistent with what might be expected from the British tradition. Somewhat broader interpretations, perhaps more in keeping with recent American decisions, can also be found. They relate to several aspects of proving liability in respect of negligent forecasting, particularly to the requirement for reasonable care in preparation. *Lister Ltd* v. *Dunlop Canada Ltd (25 OR, 2d, 155*, 1978)*, a franchising case, and *Hamather et al* v. *Gregory et al* (CCH, DRS, 1985, 90-830), an accounting case, both suggest that reasonable care in preparation is required. What constitutes "reasonable" can be inferred from the standards used. In *Hamther et al*, the accountants were liable for "failing to use that skill and diligence which a reasonably competent accountant would exercise"; in *Lister Ltd* "a franchiser owes ... a duty of care in respect of ... predicted future performance of the proposed franchise." Both echo *Esso* v. *Mardon* strongly in this respect.

Disclosure of forecasts, an important question in both US and British law, has also been litigated recently in Canada, again, as with these two countries, in respect of securities law, particularly in merger cases. In *Dunford and Elliot Ltd.* v. *Johnson and Firth Brown Ltd.* (CCH DRS, 1971, p.1-972, NWT 1977) it was strongly established that confidential forecasts cannot be used by some shareholders, but not others. Once they are out of the bag and used by one, they must be made available to all. *Ridgewood Resources Ltd.* v. *Hemset* (BACWS [2d], 204, 1981) establishes that if the same forecasting information is effectively available elsewhere, one cannot be held liable for failure to disclose similar information in another context. This would seem to suggest that aggregate economic forecasts used in circumstances such as a merger or takeover could never be litigated for non-disclosure.

While all of these cases are important, the most specific with respect to the issue of liability for inaccurate forecasts is *Mercury International Ltd. (Messier, Trustee)* v. *Canada, Government of* (CCH DRS, p3-006, FCC, 1984). Mercury operated currency exchange and travel insurance concessions at Mirabel airport under leases granted through public tender. It alleged that it had lost large amounts of money because passenger traffic forecasts supplied by the federal Department of Transport to all tenderers had been substantially in error. It claimed damages equal to what profits would have been if the forecasts had been realized. The action was dismissed, and lost again on appeal.

The courts decided, first, that because of the highly uncertain nature of the realization of the government's plans and their associated forecasts, ones that Mercury could not have reasonably relied on, the government did not intend to bind itself contractually to the tenderers on this basis. The department had, in fact, explicitly stated to all tenderers that it would not be responsible if the forecasts proved inaccurate, an important factor, in the opinion of the courts. Second, they concluded that there had been no negligence in preparation that was in any way actionable. No one else could reasonably have done any differently, or better in making those forecasts.

In conclusion, then, there is a new body of law in Canada in respect of forecasting. Together with British and American law it establishes some requirements of forecasters in the public interest. It is interesting to speculate what might happen if more cases do come to be litigated or a much broader interpretation of liability comes to be adopted. One possibility might be the development of malpractice insurance for forecasters. Alternatively, and especially if such insurance is not possible, one might expect to see gradual erosion of the market for this kind of forecasting. These are admittedly somewhat hypothetical, and futuristic, concerns, since to date no one has brought a case against, for example, one of the majors. In that sense the law represents a kind of last line of defence for the public interest vis-à-vis these aggregate economic forecasters.

Competition from Public-Sector Forecasters

If the common law is a reasonably decent "last line of defence" of the public interest versus forecasting, the more immediate form comes from direct government intervention in the market in the form of public ownership of, and support for, certain forecasting operations. Some forecasting product from, for example, the Bank of Canada, the Department of Finance, Statistics Canada, and the Economic Council reaches market and thus provides direct competition for privately produced forecasts.

Some argue that, as a consequence, government provides a check on the industry. Should forecasts from the private sector become wildly inaccurate, or exorbitantly expensive, public-sector forecasts are always there to "take up the slack" from, or "undercut," the private sector. Others, in the industry, regard it as "unfair competition," arguing that making public-sector-based forecasts available to the market is highly improper for governments in a non-centrally planned, private-enterprise system. For one thing, such forecasts are open to deliberate manipulation by the party in power. In some circumstances they may come to be viewed as a plan and not a forecast. When, in addition, different sources in the government issue different forecasts, as they often do, citizens are misled in the extreme. Still others argue that while it is acceptable for governments to issue forecasts, care should be taken to co-ordinate forecasting activities so that the government speaks with one voice. While no doubt an improvement, such a suggestion does not address the dirigiste criticism of the activity levelled by some in the industry.

There is some question in my mind whether the presence of these public-sector forecasts is a deliberate public policy instrument aimed at the industry at all or whether it is simply an incidental consequence of public policy in support of research into economic forecasting and information gathering. These latter two activities suffer in important ways from externalities. In the absence of public support, there would be an undersupply of both, much as there would be in health care, education, and defence.

While various options such as regulation, tax policy, or direct subsidy are always open to policy-makers wishing to control individual industries, in the forecasting area direct public ownership, especially in the research and development stages, seems to have been the norm. Whether for reasons of bureaucracy (i.e. once in place such programs are hard to eliminate), confidentiality (a certain need, for example, for secrecy in budget preparation), or the simple belief that it is more efficient to have such work in-house and at hand, these public-sector forecasting activities have remained in existence.

An added motive may be to act as an instrument for control of private-sector forecasting. But my guess is that this is a second-order intent, if intent it be at all. More likely, the actual release of public-sector forecasts is an incidental consequence of these internal activities, motivated more by a desire to demonstrate reasonable care in the carrying out of public policy, or a lack of favoritism (even imprudence) in relying on one private-sector forecast when so doing, than it is a means to control the private forecasting industry.

Regardless of which explanation is more important, there can be little question that public-sector forecasts provide some check on the activities of private-sector forecasting firms. Be it via price for services, the appropriateness of the technology employed, exogenous assumptions adopted, or ultimately accuracy claimed, public-sector forecasts can ensure certain behaviour on the part of the private sector.[11] As such, they can be said to exercise control of the Canadian aggregate economic forecasting industry in the public interest.

CONCLUSION

Two important interpretations of the link between aggregate economic forecasting in Canada and policy have been considered. The first involves its contribution to policy formation, the second controlling forecasting in the public interest.

With respect to the former, it was argued that there is nothing unique about forecasting's contribution to the formulation of policy that cannot be understood by considering the nature of the demand for these forecasts more generally. It aids policy formation because forecasts help to demonstrate reasonable care, spread risk, organize and rally complex organizations, and so on. Whether forecasting enters such policy formulation in some programatic way directly linked to budgeting, or via the "black box" that is the president's final policy decision-making procedure, depends on the individual organization.

There has been considerable scepticism of late about how much aid of this kind forecasts actually provide. Much of this is allegedly due to inaccuracy. The actual record, however, indicates that forecasts have been more accurate recently than in earlier times. It is likely, therefore, that these complaints reflect dissatisfaction over other things for which forecasting is the convenient whipping boy. Otherwise much of the dissatisfaction may simply be a much stronger manifestation than ever before of risk-spreading. These complaints may be a function of a host of possible factors, including a certain mismatching in the supply of certain kinds of forecasts to a very different policy demand need, theoretical and methodological uncertainty, early overselling of the potential of the new econometric methods, or others noted earlier. Risk-spreading via complaints about forecasting is almost certainly due to the perceived increase in the level of uncertainty generally with respect to business and the economy. Being aware of these considerations makes it less likely that policy-makers will reject forecasting completely, something that would be foolish to attempt and impossible to achieve. Recent suggestions of alternatives, which consist at heart of advocating flexibility and being prepared for any eventuality, are really sensible adjuncts to forecasting, not ways to eliminate the need to forecast.

Some of these concerns lead naturally to considerations of how forecasting is, or might be, controlled in the public interest. Other than the discipline in service to a certain sense of the public interest that markets themselves always supply, little control appears evident, either by self-regulation from within or by deliberate policy from without. Indeed the situation is made even worse by the fact that the basic nature of the product, especially relating to externalities, makes it almost impossible to internalize completely responsibility and benefit, in any meaningful way, via patenting, trademarking, or copyrighting.

Two basic safeguards exist, namely the law, in particular common and statute law, and public-sector forecasting competition. A review of the law relating to forecasting in Canada and the two jurisdictions most closely linked legally to it, the United States and the United Kingdom, indicates that the law can be an effective device for controlling excesses. It will not hold forecasters liable simply because their predictions do not in fact materialize, if they were made in good faith, for a proper purpose, used reasonable care and skill, and represent the forecaster's actual belief about the future. Violation of any of these rquirements may lead to liability for the consequences that flow from the erroneous forecasts.

Much of the legal protection is a posteriori. Public-sector forecasting is a more immediate instrument for control. Some, be they interventionists or free-marketers, see it as a deliberately chosen route to control the industry that is more or less acceptable depending on their ideological position. For others, myself included, it is an incidental consequence of other public policy measures, in particular those in support of research into economic forecasting and information gathering, that are necessary because of the externalities attached to these activities, among other reasons.

Whether or not these two approaches are all that is needed in the way of control is always open to debate. Other alternatives are, after all, available. They could include, for example, the use of provisions in the Competition Act. But to this reasonably detached observer (!) the present public policy stance with respect to the industry is about right. Because of the nature of the product, a large degree of self-regulation by the market can be expected. Everyone can make forecasts (or so they believe); no one takes any given forecast too literally; and so on. Moreover, the existence of public-sector forecasts provides an ongoing standard against which to check excessive claims by the industry. It also helps keep prices down. Finally, the common law, does, after all, provide the ultimate fallback if the industry were to get badly out of hand.

It is generally recognized that democratic societies are becoming increasingly litigious. It is reasonable, therefore, to expect that economic forecasters will also come under greater legal threat, much as their weather forecasting colleagues have begun to in recent times. It is not difficult to envisage the management of a corporation that is on the brink of bankruptcy off-loading formally some of the responsibility and cost for failure by bringing suit against the forecaster rather than simply informally laying some of the blame on him or her as at present. To the extent that such suits are successful, some equivalent to professional malpractice insurance for forecasters would have to be developed or the open market for aggregate economic forecasts of the kind considered here would quickly disappear.

CHAPTER TEN

Conclusions

" ... come to second thoughts on such."

THE HIGH POINTS

It is always good at the end of a trip to reflect systematically on its important events. It is one of the main reasons many people keep a travel diary. By so reflecting one brings the trip alive briefly once more and fixes its moment in the memory. We have had a trip of sorts here, and it is wise now to do likewise. The following points, 30 or so, are those that I would hope the reader will take with him or her.

1. "Foretelling/casting" is an important part of desires and efforts to control one's destiny in an uncertain future. Generally speaking, it is a rational response, done rationally. We happen to live in a period in human history when it is an important and socially well-organized activity. There have been ages when it was less so. Because the prediction of a nation's economic future is perhaps the most important manifestation of forecasting in our age, careful consideration of such aggregate economic forecasting should in principle help us to understand better the general role that forecasting plays in human affairs.

2. Before doing so with particular reference to the Canadian case, we discussed briefly how forecasts are made. Through time almost every conceivable method for making forecasts has been tried. Admitting that there are various ways of categorizing modern approaches, we classified them into three groups by method. The first was based on the concept that the appropriate way to forecast is to survey people about their present or intended actions. The other two, ultimately both causative in concept but separable on the basis of a different interpretation of the sense of "causativeness," were designated directly causative and time series analytic.

3. The first of these two contains methods that use causative "bridges"

to model behaviour and thus make predictions. These bridges can be small and simple in conception, or large and complicated. For several reasons, this class of methods today enjoys the most use in making aggregate economic forecasts in Canada. The second group involves a broader sense of causation. It supposes that a host of factors "causes" a given variable. The best representation we have of their net impact is contained in the values of the variables themselves over time. Thus the study of these values for regularities, and the projection of these patterns into the future, are legitimate ways to make forecasts.

4. We took some time to show that each of these classes of approaches, and all the different individual methods that go to make them up, have strengths and weaknesses, advantages and disadvantages. Each is more or less appropriate given the circumstances. The "circumstances" in question generally relate to the time horizon over which one is forecasting; the availability of data; the accuracy desired; the speed required; and the cost to be tolerated. Every one of these factors have to be weighed constantly, traded off both within and across techniques. Knowing which to use evolves with experience. This suggests that economic forecasting continues to be an art, despite attempts over the years to reduce it to a science.

5. The history of some of these attempts, indeed of aggregate economic forecasting in Canada more generally, is a rich one. Because of a decided absence of written material, the version given here was based on interviews with many of those who played a part in the events and activities discussed.

6. Aggregate economic forecasting in Canada as we know it is essentially a post – Second World War phenomenon. It grew out of work in the 1930s that was interrupted, but also aided, by activities during that war. The recognizable roots of econometric model forecasts, investment intentions surveying, flow of funds, and agricultural and labour market predicting can all be found in the immediate post-war period, that of indicator approaches in the early 1950s.

7. After a natural hiatus in the late 1950s and early 1960s during which these new methodological developments were gradually diffused throughout the economy, and during which time the survey of Canadian consumer attitudes and buying intentions was introduced, the industry embarked on a new round of technological innovation. Several reasons for this second leap forward were discussed. Increased regulatory and other governmental activity related to environmental and other concerns was cited with respect to demand, while increased computing power was particularly important with respect to supply.

8. This next cycle in the industry's history mirrored in important

ways the earlier one. Early on there was a burst of methodological work on several fronts, but principally with respect to econometric modelling. Teams of researchers in various institutions such as the Bank of Canada, the Economic Council, the University of Toronto, and the Department of Agriculture all built large-scale, multi-equation models, which came to be used for forecasting purposes. As in the earlier cycle, most of this work was done by public-sector organizations, principally because of the large externalities associated with basic research of this type.

9. An implementation phase followed. It was perhaps made more dynamic than it might otherwise have been by events such as the first oil shocks, dramatically higher inflation, and floating exchange rates, all of which contributed to a suddenly more uncertain world. Abundant evidence exists to indicate that the industry as we know it today took on its character during this period. Several private forecasting firms came into existence; organizations everywhere, but especially in the private sector, began crash programs to integrate the new method into their planning activities.

10. This activity lasted for about five years before an almost predictable hiatus again set in. It has continued down to the present, aided by a certain maturity about the uses and limitations of the newer methods, considerable disarray in economic theory about some of the important theory underlying the models, a shift in emphasis from short-term to longer-term considerations in the wake of inflation abetting and the success elsewhere, as in Japan, of industrial policies with a longer-term orientation, and finally the development of "substitutes" for some methods, in particular of futures markets in stocks and currencies, and of the personal computer with its spreadsheet programs.

11. Thus it can be seen that the industry has its cycles, much as other industries do. At present it consists of four major firms, the Conference Board and Informetrica in Ottawa and Data Resources and Wharton Economic Canada in Toronto. In addition, there is a group of institutions and individuals that exist on the periphery of the business, sometimes acting much as retailers of the majors' main products, sometimes as independent producers. Collectively they are of considerably less importance than are the majors.

12. Careful examination of the demand for the outputs of the industry, i.e. for aggregate economic forecasts of the Canadian economy, revealed that these forecasts are needed for other reasons besides the security or assistance that a possible glimpse of the future might supply. They are used to demonstrate reasonable care in the commitment of resources; to spread the risk of failure from man-

agement or administration to the forecaster; and to organize institutions around common assumptions or to motivate them. In the larger context, they also help to organize society at large by acting as devices through which we exchange signals about how we are thinking about the future, and by implication how we intend to act in moving into it.

13. Exactly how they are used varies from organization to organization but can be characterized as being either programatically directly linked to, for example, one's budgeting, or essentially without structure, something I refer to as the "black box" process. The latter was in reference to the knowledge one can never have about exactly what role any given input plays in a decision-maker's calculus when that person does not explain exactly how he or she goes about making decisions.

14. Based on these arguments, an attempt was made to examine statistically the nature of demand. Various measures such as the size of the forecasting error, the amount of government spending, and others were considered. Because the data are not extensive, results can only be suggestive. They indicate that demand is likely positively related to the level of overall business activity, particularly to government spending. Relative price, especially measured implicitly by the size of the forecasting error, is also important, as is the educational level of those who use the forecasts. Increased uncertainty, at least as represented by days lost to strikes, does not seem to be a factor.

15. In supplying these aggregate economic forecasts to the Canadian public, the firms rely on a sizeable amount of human capital, something typical of the business services sector of the economy of which it is a part. This human capital is generally both highly professional and highly mobile. The other major inputs are physical plant and, particularly, computing machinery. The "arrival" of both seems to be scale-related and tends to make not only for a discontinuous production function but also for an optimal size. This size can be seen to be bi-modal, firms being either quite small (less than 7 people) or rather large (more than 20); they are seldom of medium size. Entry can be expensive, principally because the entrant will need a model sufficiently large to convince the market of a certain quality of product. It is one of the factors contributing to the restricted number of majors.

16. Consistent with our earlier discussions about the methods used in forecasting, one finds various approaches being adopted, the most important of which is econometric modelling. The horizons over which forecasts stretch have changed from the older, one-year-ahead,

annual prediction, which was the standard in the past. Much greater emphasis is steadily being given to both shorter-term (e.g. the next two quarters) and medium-term (usually five-year-ahead) forecasts. Extremely long-horizon predictions have been important at times since the war. But at present there is less emphasis on this product.

17. Because of data problems similar to those encountered with demand, supply modelling of the preferred type, that is, involving estimates of production functions and cost curves, is not possible. However, summary data from several sources tend in a broad way to support these assertions about the nature of supply.

18. I argued that the industry that emerges from the interplay of these demand and supply characteristics can be thought of as an oligopoly of four firms which, if not exactly dominated by the US industry, does feel its strong indirect influence. It tends to be concentrated in central Canada for obvious reasons and has grown both by internal expansion due to diversification and by entry. There is a relatively limited domestic, and virtually no export, market for the industry's main products. The industry is also somewhat circumscribed by the availability of similar products from public-sector sources.

19. An investigation of conduct relating to pricing, promotion, product differentiation, and other behaviour revealed a rich array of strategic practices in many ways typical of rational competition in an oligopolistic setting. Price changes are, for example, infrequent and tentative; attempts at product differentiation supported by R&D are the norm.

20. Several pieces of evidence suggest that as a consequence of these structural arrangements and industrial behaviour, the industry makes higher profits than business in general but no more so than other business service groups such as advertising agencies or engineering consultants; and the industry is at least as efficient as similar business service industries, comparing favourably with other business as well.

21. Because of the evident prosperity of the aggregate economic forecasting industry in Canada, I indicated that complaints heard regularly about the accuracy of its forecasts, surely one of their more important aspects, were contradictory, to say the least. It is as though drug companies were seen to prosper while the consumers of their products regularly complained that they didn't work very well! As we have seen, there may be other reasons for wanting to consume forecasts, just as one can imagine there being other reasons for consuming drugs. Indeed, some of these "other" reasons, such as a need to spread the risk, may be common to the need for both fore-

casts and drugs. But regardless of motive, the accuracy of forecasts seems always to be at issue.

22. Accuracy is not an easy issue to consider. Conceptual problems abound. The first involves the prediction dilemma posed by the possibility of self-altering predictions. While in principle always a difficulty for which no really satisfactory answer can be given, it is generally ignored on the grounds that in practice no single forecaster has sufficient power or prestige to move people or their governments enough for the results to be reflected in the large economic aggregates being forecast. Many of the other difficulties centre on what the term "accuracy" could possibly mean, and how to measure it. These were dealt with by referring to the conventions that have developed in the literature on accuracy assessment. This led to talk about the absolute and relative aspects of accuracy, the identification of various measurs considered within each, and possible problems to be expected.

23. Some indication of the accuracy of several kinds of Canadian aggregate economic forecasts was considered, special emphasis being given to the annual forecasts of GNP and its expenditure sector components which, as we have already mentioned, have been the most commonly available forecasts through time. Many detailed conclusions were drawn, some perhaps more important than others. In this category would surely be the finding that there appears to be no difference over the years between forecasters. This suggests that the market in forecasting technology is more or less efficient. It also means that a "buy and hold" strategy with respect to purchasing forecasts is likely to be the best.

24. Another important finding is that forecasters underestimate actuals. There has been no clear reason yet suggested why this should be so, in particular why for the largest aggregate of them all, GNP measured at current market prices, there is always this bias present. A third discovery of interest is that everyone seems to make the same kind of errors at the same time. There are periods when real factors are most important (e.g. the 1960s) and where errors in predicting real factors are higher as compared to periods when price (i.e. inflation) is most important, in which case errors in forecasting prices are higher. Also large-error and small-error years coincide for almost all forecasters. As well, some components such as exports or investment are harder for everyone to forecast than others such as consumption. It is not obvious why these things happen. Volatility, for example, is no explanation at all.

25. An important, relative perspective on the accuracy of Canadian

forecasters is provided by considering the record of forecasters in other countries with similar economic systems. There is a large community of such individuals, the most important concentration of which is to be found in the United States. Comparisons are made difficult for many of the same reasons it is difficult to compare Canadian forecasters to one another. Being as careful as possible, I made several conclusions from such a comparison. First, there is likely no difference over time in the relative accuracy achieved by any given forecaster in any given country. Second, everyone tends to make the same errors at the same time.

26. I argued that these results are not surprising: there is an almost "efficient-like market" in forecasting technology; and economies are tied together by trade and financial institutions that transmit the expectations-related thinking contained in aggregate economic forecasts back and forth between these economies. Thus on balance aggregate economic forecasters do about as well as the method permits. Further, the results show also that they are improving with time and are generally surprised together by events that no one of them anywhere could have foreseen. Turning points, especially downturns, are particularly bothersome in this respect.

27. Perhaps because of these findings, the issue of the control of the Canadian aggregate economic forecasting industry in the public interest is not exactly one of the burning political issues of the day. This is not to suggest, however, that it is completely absent, or that some people are not concerned. Besides the control that all markets provide, two principal avenues for control are used, namely legal recourse and competition from public forecasting sources. A review of the case law both here in Canada, and in the United States and Great Britain, indicates a developing jurisprudence on the issue of liability related to forecasting. Fraudulent preparation and use are never tolerated.

28. The issue of negligent forecasting is, however, less certain. On balance, the judgments suggest that forecasters are not liable for erroneous forecasts that were prepared in good faith, with honest belief, and using reasonable care and skill in preparation. They will not, for example, be held liable in the sense that the forecast constitutes a warranty or guarantee that the future will turn out as they have predicted. Were anything approaching such an "absolute" standard to be adopted, the aggregate economic forecasting industry would disappear, at least in the absence of some notion of malpractice insurance. Some forecasters, especially in the United States, are worried that the increasingly litigious spirit of the times will eventually lead to this.

29. If civil suit is seen as the last line of defence of the public interest, competition from public forecasting sources is clearly the more immediate. There is much debate about the validity of such a practice, characterized by some of the more traditional ideological arguments over the role of the state in a modern capitalist society. In my opinion the balance of the two influences, public and private, is about right. Government will always have to preserve some independent "productive capacity" both to "verify" private-sector forecasts and for confidentiality reasons. Moreover, the "heavy hand" of government is not so oppressive as it might be, or indeed is elsewhere. In this respect, as in certain others I have noted, the industry is somehow typically Canadian!

SOME FINAL THOUGHTS

These then are the highlights of the journey. What of the overall verdict? Can one now, for example, "believe in forecasts, come to second thoughts on such," or not? Or is the conclusion as qualified as it was for Hardy, whose judgment, it will be recalled, was one of "not altogether" believing? If the story has gone at all as intended, the reader should be able to make some judgment in this regard.

As a result of thinking through some of this over the years, I have become convinced that in the absence of a completely integrative philosophy such as Zen Buddism, forecasting of one form or another is indispensable to life. Because of the age, or individual circumstances such as that overactive childhood of mine referred to in the preface, it is more or less a requirement. But there is also more to it than a simple requirement that is deliberately entered into for utilitarian purposes.

I would argue that forecasting is an integral part of our pysche, inextricably linked to our sense of "time." Just as there is some question about whether we structure time as past, present, and future because we find it somehow useful, i.e. something that each human in time comes to choose as a rational contribution to living, or whether it is somehow "innate" to us, a kind of subconscious archetype like the others we collectively possess, so too is there a question about the origins of forecasting itself. Regardless of which approach one favours (both obviously make a contribution to understanding), it is likely that forecasting is in some way a derivative issue to the larger one of time-sense, much as is the wholly different derivative issue of "keeping track of time," for example, by clocks. That is, the mind either contains, or consciously adopts, a sense of time out of which grows both the practice of measuring it and that of trying to leap ahead, anticipate, or see into it. By this reasoning, history would close the temporal circle, reporting as it does on time past.

If one adopts this approach, it likely also follows that the process of forecasting is far more important than any specific forecast. Further it would explain the varying, and extremely subtle, motives for forecasting that we discussed earlier. Sometimes we will need a vehicle for spreading the risk or blame to others, especially if personal or collective anxiety is too high. At other times we will need to organize for a common purpose; or show others that we are taking reasonable care; or point to what we're planning to do. Forecasting, whether collectively chosen or innately driven, is the vehicle that permits this. In this way it is enormously socially useful, much as is the structuring of time by the institution of "keeping track of it." Pushed even further, it is clearly socio-biologically useful so long as there remains an uncertain element to life.

There should be nothing surprising in this. Nor should it be surprising that forecasting tends to "adhere" to the more important concerns of an age. It must be drawn there because of the social role it fulfils. Because getting soaked to the skin has never been pleasant in any age, weather forecasting has always been one such important concern. As critical to us, indeed much more so today, is our ongoing economic well-being. As such, it is the principal focus of our personal and collective forecasting efforts.

Because of this, it is reasonable to expect that in our age someone, or a group of people, will come to address this need or concern of society by developing and distributing economic forecasting, just as in the past, and most certainly in the future, others did, and will do, likewise for travel, battles, or other major human activities of concern. Moreover, we can expect these "forecasters" on whom we rely to do on average about what they can to meet society's wishes, consistent with their own concerns. In that respect they will be no different from farmers or those who build clocks. Given this position, various explanations of the way the practice is carried out follow. Clearly it will reflect the capabilities, and the philosophy or beliefs, of an age. Since we are the distant product of the Renaissance and live in a "scientific" age, the practice of forecasting for us means "rational," "logical," "causative." And thus we require "rational expectations." Moreover we use large machines; make careful measurements; employ all the technology available to us. To our predecessors, who needed the same institution for many of the same reasons, but had very different philosophies and beliefs, and certainly a much different technological base, forecasting practice meant an important role for the gods, entrails, and the position of the stars.

We consider the evolution from "superstition" to "science" a good thing. But it really depends on one's perspective and profits much from hindsight, itself an interesting concept relative to our discussions here of foresight.

The impact of technological change is the most obvious way to illustrate this contention. Consider again clocks. Landes (1983), on whom I am evidently drawing here, reflects on the effect of several technological innovations in the art of timekeeping on our sense of time. Two in particular are of interest – greater precision in measuring divisions of time down to the fractions of seconds, and the ability to carry time-pieces with us rather than having to leave them in one place so they might continue to work. Both dramatically altered how we thought of time, its role, and its importance in our lives.

The same is true of forecasting. Today we expect forecasts of a whole collection of economic variables, down to the decimal point of precision. We expect those forecasts to be based on all the accumulated economic wisdom of the ages, and in recent times to be available virtually instantaneously from a device we can carry around with us! This has as dramatically altered how we think about the future as changes in clock-making have altered how we conceive of time.

This realization suggests that what we have found from examining the accuracy of Canadian, and other, aggregate economic forecasting is about what we should have expected. That is, it is unlikely that anyone anywhere in the world will excel at the activity with respect to all others for any length of time. Moreover, everyone will do about as well as is possible given the technological capabilities of the age. All will make about the same mistakes at about the same time. The situation is analogous to what happens elsewhere when information on the new finds its way to other parts of those world "corners." Certainly there may be temporary disequilibriums, a favourite phrase of economists, when, for example, the Chinese are able to make better clocks than the Swiss, and in turn the Swiss than the Americans, and after them the Japanese than anybody else ... Thus there will be a time when the United States can forecast better than the rest of the world, or when one approach is better than another. But this will not persist. Indeed in our time it will hardly persist at all, so quickly is technology dispersed.

In this sense then there is no Rosetta Stone to be captured by the intrepid "Raider of the Lost Forecasting Ark." Indeed it is foolish to expect to be handed the future in this way. One might even venture that that is childish somehow, which is what complaints at present about forecasting are if they are not simply so much spreading of blame, anxiety, and fear in the recently more uncertain times.

Nor would I personally wish to have the future handed to me in this way. It, and the imagination's approach to it, are a vital and important part of living. Institutionalizing that imaginative casting about with regard to the future, and talking over the respective visions so generated, are one way of organizing discussion of our individual, and collective, destiny. Further, they are ultimately an important shaper of that destiny. In that sense Bacon was right for exactly the wrong reasons, or at least for reasons that he did not fully appreciate, when he said: "I mean not to speak of divine prophecies; nor of heathen oracles; nor of natural predictions; but only of prophesies that have been of certain memory, and from hidden causes ... My judgement is, that they ought all to be despised; and ought to serve but for winter talk by the fireside ... Almost all of them, being infinite in number, have been impostures, and by idle and empty brains merely contrived and feigned after the event past" ("Of Prophecies," Essay xxxv, *The Essays of Francis Bacon,* 1675).

As Canadians we take part in, and contribute to, the winter fireside chatting about those visions. Again there is nothing surprising about this. A careful study of Canadian aggregate economic forecasting, that particular branch of "envisioning" most important to our age, time, and place, indicates that there is a rich history to the chatting about our northern visions. Its focus and concerns shift and alter with the decades in an almost ebb-and-flow-like way. With time it has become a socially very complex activity. Indeed that complexity is itself an important sign of the key role we give it. But the complexity should not hide from us its essential social purpose.

I am thus led by these considerations, and those presented in the chapters foregone, to "believe in forecasts come to second thoughts." But it is in a much broader sense than Hardy no doubt intended. I believe in it the way I believe in the concept of time. Indeed my belief in it is an outgrowth of my acceptance of the concept of time. Using whatever term suits, "envisioning," "forecasting," or "predicting" is a rich and important part of life. It puts an emotional edge on the present, makes for joy or for fear. Without it we would have no sense of "hope." "Hope," one of the three greatest of Christian virtues, would vanish into a kind of Orwellian emptiness of the spirit if perfect certainty were about.

This belief is not meant to suggest that we should not expect of ourselves and others the very best envisioning that our age permits. But paradoxical as it may seem, we should equally well be certain it never becomes a perfect thing. That day would be a very black one indeed for the species. This conclusion may not have been one that the reader might reasonably have expected from a journey through the land of Canadian aggregate economic forecasting. But then life has a way of surprising us somehow. Apparently, it has something to do with the fact that it is uncertain ...

Notes

1 That there are many more data absolutely available in the modern era to aid in this arranging of the future than was true for the ancients can hardly be questioned. And hence we are better off than they. However, we should not flatter ourselves too much. For certain classes of ancient society, the importance of the future and one's ability to "manage" it successfully enough made it a major element in everyday life, much as is the case today. Julius Caesar would not have gone to battle without examining his dreams and consulting his astrologer or augurs, just as no modern general would think of going to war without consulting projections from his game-theoretic, computer-based models. Dreams and oracles are not so distant conceptually from models. Besides, who among us has not sneaked a look at astrology charts, or flipped a coin, at one time or another? We cannot thus afford to be all that smug.

2 It should be clear from this that the terms "forecasting" and "prediction" can be used interchangeably, although it is equally clear, from the title of the book and this passage of text, where my preference lies. As will become clear, they are quite distinct from a term such as "extrapolate," which is given a more precise meaning later (in chapter 2).

3 For example, a statement, such as "the world is coming to an end" would not be considered a forecast under the definition being discussed here. Similarly there must be no ambiguity in the concept used. Such ambiguity was a favourite escape-hatch for oracles of old. We moderns require a more specific assumption of responsibility. For example, a prediction of the dollar amount of a firm's assets at a specific point in the future should identify whether or not the measuring stick was the lower of costs or market. If it does not, it is not, for the purposes one wishes to use the term here, a forecast.

4 It is for this additional reason that it is impossible to consider the statement "the world is coming to an end" a forecast. There is little hard
data on the period leading up to previous such occurrences to go on.

5 It should be noted at this point that nothing has been said here about
the specific nature of the forecast over and above the fact that it is a
statement about an unknown future. Thus it is possible to entertain the
idea that this statement may well come in many forms. For example,
one such traditional form is a simple "point" estimate of the unknown
future in the sense of the statement that "gross national product measured at market value will increase 8 per cent from the fourth quarter
of 1975 to the fourth quarter of 1976." This is as opposed to an alternative statement concerning the unknown future of the form: "I am 95
per cent sure that the increase in gross national product measured at
market value will be between 5 per cent and 10 per cent for the period
from the fourth quarter of 1975 to the fourth quarter of 1976." This
statement is often referred to as an "interval" forecast (with a probability
assessment attached). It should be clear that these are very different
statements about the nature of the unknown future.

6 Like other theoretical generalizations, this statement leaves as much
unanswered as it addresses. How, for example, are benefits measured
– in terms of more accurately knowing the future (an answer given in
chapters 7 and 8)? Perhaps, but then what is the appropriate measure
of that increased accuracy – social welfare, profits? The theoretical principle gives little guidance.

7 This simple example serves to point out the key role that "accuracy"
plays in much of the theory of forecasting. It is a question dealt with at
considerable length in chapters 7 and 8.

8 Following Daub and Mohr (1985), the argument is also advanced in
chapter 5 that forecasts act as a signalling device for economic agents,
helping them to co-ordinate economic activity, thereby aiding in the
work of the famous "invisible hand" of Adam Smith's.

9 There is also a recent literature in game theory that is instructive with
respect to expectations. But it has had little influence on theory more
generally, relative to this "rational expectations" revolution in
macroeconomics.

10 For a period in the late 1960s, when macroeconomics had finally begun
to model expectations in an explicit way, it took a highly, and a typically,
irrational approach to the subject. Consider this rather simplified example from MacMillan (1983, 256–64) which illustrates an "expecta-
tions-augmented Philips curve" analysis of wages, prices and
unemployment:

For purposes of our example, let us suppose that labour requires compensation this year for last year's inflation rate. If we like, we can think of it as compensation for *expected inflation* this year – *where for simplicity the inflation rate expected this year is assumed to be the actual inflation rate last year:*

... To start things off in as simple a manner as possible, let us suppose that the economy has been sitting at an 8 percent unemployment rate for some time, with a steady 3 percent rate of inflation. Consequently, expectations are geared up for a 3 percent rate of inflation and this amount of compensation has become built into wage gains each year.

... However, all is not well in this economy. There is considerable social unrest over the 8 percent rate of unemployment. In fact, a recent election has seen the opposition party elected on a platform to reduce unemployment to a more socially acceptable level of 6 percent.

... Government analysts clearly know that there would be a one-year tradeoff between inflation and unemployment and forecast that to move the economy (by expansionary monetary and fiscal policy) to 6 percent unemployment would cost the economy – in the same year – a 1 percent boost to the inflation rate (moving it from 3 percent to 4 percent). As a result, not feeling that this additional amount of inflation would be politically harmful, the government decided to make good on its election promise. The money supply was increased and taxes reduced by enough to stimulate aggregate demand and cause a reduction in the unemployment rate to 6 percent. As expected, the reduced unemployment caused pressure in the labour market, forcing up wage rates faster and producing a 4 percent rate of inflation.

... No one appeared too angry about the 4 percent inflation rate in year 1 and, in fact, there was considerably favourable publicity concerning the reduction in unemployment. The government, therefore, decided to follow whatever monetary and fiscal expansion would be necessary to maintain the level of unemployment at 6 percent for an indefinite period.

Unfortunately, labour realized they had negotiated for what they had thought would be a 3 percent increase in real wage rates, only to find out that they had received real increases of only 2 percent – as a result of the 4 percent inflation. (Remember, they obtained 6 percent nominal wage gains and expected a 3 percent inflation would erode this to a 3 percent gain in purchasing power terms.) Therefore, in year 2, they demanded a further 1 percent compensation for inflation in addition to their other wage demands. This demand for 4 percent inflationary compensation – combined with an unemployment rate remaining at 6 percent – led to wage rate increases in year 2 of 7 percent and unfortunately, therefore, an inflation rate in year 2 of 5 percent.

Labour is again frustrated. Again they thought they had negotiated 3 percent real wage rate increases in year 2. (They obtained 7 percent nominal wage gains and expected a 4 percent inflation would erode this to a 3 percent gain in purchasing power terms.) But again, inflation has held their real wage rate increases to only 2 percent. (Remember, that because of business pricing behaviour, labour is only ever going to get 2 percent annual increases in real wage rates – since in this example, 2 percent is the annual rate of productivity advance.)

At this point, labour having been fooled a second time concerning the expected inflation rate, is slightly more angry, and again (in year 3) adjusts its required compensation for inflation and wage demands upwards. Supposing this process continues for 8 years. By the end of year 8, there is considerable unrest in the economy. No one talks much about unemployment anymore, but inflation is on everyone's lips. The newspapers speak of the plight of those on fixed incomes and the value of money halving every seven years or so at the current inflation rate. Consequently, a new election is forced on the issue of inflation.

The point of this is simply to suggest that no "rational" worker would ever be fooled eight times in a row by such a "non-rational" price forecast, i.e. that $P_{t+1} = P_t$. He/She would quickly switch to a more rational forecast that incorporated his/her knowledge of the past errors. As well, the reader should ask, as economists soon did, why the government is the only one assumed to have knowledge of the exact price/employment tradeoff. If, on the contrary, and more realistically, everyone has about the same information on the economy, everyone will form about the same expectations of what money supply changes will mean. This led economists for a time in the 1970s to fear that they had reduced the government to fiscal and monetary policy impotence (see, for example, Maddock and Carter 1982) unless all such changes were "unanticipated." This closed a wonderfully tautological circle but gave no practical or theoretical guidance as to how the distinction between "anticipated" and "unanticipated" changes was to be made.

11 Hogarth (1980), 72.
12 Simon (1979a), for example, argues strongly for this sense of "bounded rationality." He says: "The capacity of the human mind for formulating and solving complex problems is very small compared with the size of the problems whose solution is required for objectively rational behaviour in the real world – or even for a reasonable approximation to such objective rationality."
13 See, for example, Capon et al. (1984) and Dymsza (1984) for examples for these strategic planning practices.
14 It goes without saying that this approach is much more consistent with the recent work in macroeconomics, the area where, as indicated earlier, much of the theoretical interest of the profession has been concentrated.

CHAPTER TWO

1 As we shall see below, there are two possible cases here. One is to survey intended actions, the other is to survey present actions and deduce or infer from them future actions. Both are done.
2 What we clearly are discussing here is univariate time series approaches. Below we shall see that modern multivariate stochastic approaches have muddied considerably this distinction between causative families. Indeed it is at the heart of the "causality debate" that has raged in econometrics since the 1970s. For the moment, however, we are dealing with simpler things.

3 Thus one would group all short-term-related, as distinct from longer-term-related, methods for discussion purposes.

4 We shall see below (chapter 6) that this belief about the greater inaccuracy of longer-term forecasts is not necessarily true. Indeed Samuelson (1976), among others, has argued that the opposite will be true in certain instances. However, for the time being, we will accept here the conventional view that the longer term is harder to forecast than the short term.

5 Prediction over such a longer-term horizon is thus sometimes referred to as "technological forecasting."

6 As mentioned, the statistical literature on regression is vast. The reader is referred to any number of fine textbooks on the subject available in econometrics or the other branches of applied statistics. One such book is Intriligator (1984).

7 These large models involving simultaneous equations systems are often called "econometric models" after that group of economists that concentrates on the theoretical and applied statistical aspects of the subject. Technically speaking all models they work on, even the simplest univariate regression model, are "econometric" models. But the term often takes on the former, restricted notion when used colloquially.

8 A further assumption is usually made in the multivariate case that these multiple influences are additive in their combined influence, rather than multiplicative (as will be the influences in, for example, the traditional time series decomposition method discussed below).

9 In the univariate case, if, as is customary, Y is the dependent variable (e.g. consumption) and X the independent variable (e.g. income), then the regression equation would generally be $Y = \alpha + \beta X + e$ where α measures the intercept and β the slope terms of the line, and e is considered to be some random influence affecting Y that is not captured by its relationship to X (it is assumed to be zero on average but in any given period can take on non-zero values) or by the intercept (which can be viewed as a summary of other regular influences on Y not "caused" by X). Thus a series of past observations on both X and Y (by convention at time t, $t + 1$, $t + 2$, etc) permits the estimation of $\hat{\alpha}$, $\hat{\beta}$, and $\hat{\sigma}_e^2$ (the variance of the errors) under the sum of the squared errors criterion discussed in the text proper (see also figure below). Often calculated as well is the amount of "variance" in the dependent variable that is "explained" by the variance in the independent variable. Called the "coefficient of determination," or R^2, this descriptive statistic is one of the most misused of all regression statistics (particularly by those who think that a higher R^2 means a better fit; it does not necessarily mean anything of the sort). The formulae for all these statistics are well known as are those for the multivariate case parameters (i.e. where $Y = \alpha + \beta_1 X_1$

$+\beta_2 X_2 + \dots + e_i$; $X_1, X_2, \dots$ being a series of "causative" forces acting on Y and $\alpha, \beta_1, \beta_2, \ldots, \sigma_e^2$, and R^2 the measures requiring estimation; the one additional statistic often calculated is the "coefficient of partial determination" which reports on the amount of variance in the dependent variable explained by a given independent variable, all other variances held constant).

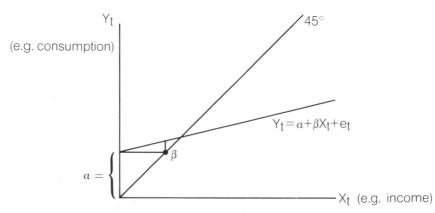

NOTE: t is defined as yearly. Thus if the data are taken from the years 1950–85, $t = 1950$, $t + 1 = 1951$, $\ldots$, $t + 35 = 1985$.

10 The word "linear" here is used to indicate the general character of such models. It should be noted, however, that such systems of equations can, and usually do, include important non-linearities and asymmetries where required.

11 Both variables in the first equation are said to be "endogenous" to the system because they are determined by the simultaneous solution of the two equations. The equation itself is referred to as "behavioural," as opposed to the second one, which is an "identity." The only other type of equation sometimes found in these systems is called "technical." It might, for example, be one relating output to labour and capital inputs, i.e. a production function.

12 Suppose the first equation is estimated as $C_i = 1.0 + 0.9Y_i$. Further, the government decides I_i will be equal to 5. Then the second equation becomes $C_i + 5 = Y_i$. Using public school algebra, solving two equations in two unknowns yields $C_i = 55$ and $Y_i = 60$ as equilibrium values.

13 There was considerable dispute in the econometrics profession for some time on this point, but most model builders and users now use the same estimation techniques discussed in connection with straightforward single equation estimation (usually referred to as OLS procedures, for ordinary least squares).

14 These second-order effects are sometimes further subdivided into strictly "indirect" effects, which would be the reduced (increased) purchases of the passenger transport (television) industries, and the "income-induced" effects, which would be triggered by the discharged (newly hired) workers.

15 For details on how this is done see Leontief (1966).

16 See, for example, Statistics Canada (1977).

17 One would need more than the I-O tables to pick up the "income-induced" effects distinguished in note 14. The "total requirements" table thus relates only to direct and indirect effects as defined in that note and the text proper.

18 The reader is referred to Pindyck and Rubenfeld (1981) for a more extensive discussion of what follows.

19 Mathematically, $P^*_{t+1} = P_t$, $P^*_{t+1} = P_t + (P_t - P_{t-1})$, $P^*_{t+1} = \frac{1}{2} (P_t + P_{t-1})$, $P^*_{t+1} = P_{t-1}$, etc.

20 Thus, $P^*_{t+1} = \alpha P_t + \alpha(1 - \alpha) P_{t-1} + \alpha(1 - \alpha)^2 P_{t-2} + \dots$ or after transformation $P^*_{t+1} = \alpha P_t + \alpha(1 - \alpha) \bar{P}_{t-1}$, where $\bar{P}_{t-1} = (P_t + \alpha(1 - \alpha)P_{t-1} + \alpha(1 - \alpha)^2 P_{t-2} + \dots)/(1 + (1 - \alpha) + \alpha(1 - \alpha)^2 + \dots)$.

21 These may be represented mathematically as $P_t = \alpha + \beta t$ (a simple linear function, in time), $P_t = \alpha + \beta_1 t + \beta_2 t^2 + \beta_3 t^3$ (a more complicated polynominal), $P_t = Ae^{rt}$ (an exponential function), and $P_t = 1/(K + ab^t)$ (a logistic curve).

22 This statement is perhaps too strong. Early researchers in the field were heavily criticized for doing "measurement without theory." This opinion was later somewhat muted by the recognition that there was, after all, a certain theory that led one to expect, for example, a housing start series to precede a GNP series, since the latter measures activity "further down the economic stream." But indicator analysis was not based on anything like the theoretical richness of econometric modelling and as such always suffered for it in terms of professional acceptance. Certainly in the community at large, it enjoyed much greater success, being considerably easier to understand.

23 Thus $P_t = P_{t-1} + e_t$ where $E(e_t = 0)$ and $E(e_t, e_{t-i} = 0)$ for all $i = 0$. This model is obviously related to the naive model discussed above with the noted exception of the stochastic error term.

24 Further reflection will suggest that this distinction is just conceptual: an autoregression model can be rewritten by successive substitution as one in terms of past errors. However, certain series are better conceived of one way, others the other, and still others as some combination of both.

25 Thus, $P_t = \alpha + \beta_1 P_{t-1} + \beta_2 P_{t-2} + \dots + \beta_p P_{t-p} + e_t$ is an AR model of order (length) p, $P_t = \alpha' + \beta_1' e_{t-1} + \beta_2' e_{t-2} + \dots + \beta_q' e_{t-q} + e_t$ is an MA model of order q, and $P_t = \alpha + \beta_1 P_{t-1} + \dots + \beta_p P_{t-p} + \beta_1' e_{t-1} + \dots \beta_q' e_{t-q} + e_t$ an ARMA model of order p, q.

26 This analysis could be expanded to include, for example, seasonal processes that may be at work either by themselves or in conjunction with
the original process. The seasonal processes can, as one might guess, be
autoregressive, moving average, or some combination. Thus in its most
general form one might have a SARIMA model of order (p, d, q, P, D, Q),.
As I said, it is all very complicated in conception but generally quite
straightforward in practice!

27 Clearly correlation does not imply causation. It might simply be better
to call X an "indicator" of Y. The direct relationship to the earlier indicator work is obvious. The old indicator series has thus been re-ex-
amined using these new methods. With respect to the correlation-causation
issue, careful reflection led to various criteria being specified, by different authors, whereby "causality" could be deemed to exist. Thus one
can speak, for example, of "Granger causality" – see, for example, Sims
(1977).

28 See, for example, Leamer (1983).

29 At least 100 observations are considered a minimum for the univariate
case, while 200 are preferred for dependable results. The multivariate
case positively devours data.

30 The survey is useful not only in directly confirming, modifying, or rejecting forecasts made by other methods but also as a guide to the
appropriate modelling choice within these approaches. Thus, for example, surveys can be used as an aid in determining which regression
specification is most appropriate.

31 If, of course, the population is small and/or the cost of error in predicting
high, a census of the population may be both possible and practical.
However, this will not generally be the case.

32 It is important to keep in mind that a vast literature on the subject of
surveys is being summarized. The purpose is to identify the general
issues in surveying so that the reader has a rough grasp of what is
involved. References such as Stephan and McCarthy (1958) can be used
to direct any further interest.

33 In certain areas of marketing research such as those touching on advertising, direct observation of respondents by such psychometric techniques as eye cameras and the like is possible. But surveys with respect
to aggregate economic activity almost inevitably use direct questioning.

34 The entire problem area ("pit" is the operative word!) that is questionnaire design is not considered either. Whether to use open- or closed-
ended questions, how many to use, and in what order are all important
to the success of surveys. It is an area, if ever there was one, for professional help. I would suggest only one rule: field test the questionnaire
extensively before using it. It will always be true for at least one question

that what is perfectly clear to the writer is completely garbled to the interviewee. It is good to know this ahead of time.

35 This is really statistical estimation, the third one being hypothesis testing. Both are given slightly different interpretations here.

36 This may be true for many of the reasons discussed earlier, i.e. respondents don't form predictions about home heating oil, or they change their minds before actually buying, and so on.

37 There are others, in particular the purchasing agents' and labour force surveys. However, they are much smaller, more recent, or less reliable. Hence they are not considered here. Nor for that matter is that investment survey of Statistics Canada, which is more recent and for a much shorter horizon (one year ahead only).

38 Such an approach also helps to average out the effect of "individual bias, ignorance, and idiosyncratic hobby horses."

39 One is talking here of "serious" approaches to the making of forecasts. There is a whole class of instruments that economic agents might use from time to time which, while "serious" to them, do not strike the rest of us that way! Such approaches as astrology, Tarot cards, palmistry, dream interpretation, and even coin tossing come to mind. This is perhaps cruel and unusual punishment, for who is to assert that one day they will not say the same thing about regression analysis? Some even do today! One is likely, therefore, better advised to fall back on the absence of general usage as the main reason for a less than equal treatment of these methods vis-à-vis those discussed above.

CHAPTER THREE

1 Some of what follows in this and the succeeding chapter is taken from my paper "A History of Canadian Aggregate Forecasting," *Journal of Business Administration* 15, no. 1/2 (Fall 1985): 139–58.

2 As an example of one such definition, consider an "industry" as "any grouping of firms which operate *similar processes* and could produce *technically identical products* within a given planning horizon" (Nightingale 1978, 35).

3 Such a designation depends critically on the sense of "similar" and "technically identical" and, more generally, of course, on the length of the planning horizon. Thus one might argue that all modellers operate "similar processes," all non-modellers "dissimilar processes." Thus the former are one "industry," the latter another, as would be steel versus wood truss manufacturers (Nightingale 1978). But one person's non-model is another's model. For example, is DRI's model a sufficiently "similar process" to Informetrica's? Probably, but then surely so is the

Bank of Canada's, the Economic Council's, Statistic Canada's, and others'. Moreover, which of the two conditions of the definition predominates, i.e. "similar process" or "technically identical products"? If the latter, one is inclined to a much broader sense of "industry" than the former, in that a forecast of real GNP is an arguably "technically identical product" to forecast of real GNP, regardless of its methodological basis, be it derived from an econometric model, indicators, or surveys. As noted above, taken to its extreme, one would swallow up definitionally all sense of "industry." The important point is that no one has a sense that this is true empirically. Rather, again as noted, there is a definite belief that there is something called a forecasting "industry" the history of which can sensibly be told.

4 A list of the more important contributors to this history is available on request to anyone wishing to pursue the subject further.

5 Some might argue that it is even younger than is suggested here, dating principally from the late 1960s. This view is not adopted here for reasons that the history itself makes clear.

6 For an excellent book on the subject see Clarke (1984).

7 Crawford (1955), 36.

8 Blankenship, Chakrapani, and Poole (1985). It was joined during this period by Canadian Facts and Elliot Research, among others, both of which continue in existence today.

9 "Before the war there were some data particularly on firms and some industries but there was no real way that we had at the time of tying the thing together" (personal interview, 1983).

10 Maintained by several different government departments at various times, this survey of investment intentions has been continued to the present (see chapter 2). Other investment-related surveys of, for example, inventory anticipations appeared briefly somewhat later in this period but died out rather quickly because of problems with data timeliness and imprecision.

11 Such a survey of labour force intentions has continued to exist, again in various forms and places (e.g. plant gate v. worker, Department of Labour v. Employment and Immigration) to the present. But because labour markets are so difficult to forecast, regardless of the method used, these surveys have never enjoyed the same respect as other intentions surveys. It is the surveying of labour force intentions, not the use of surveys to report actual labour force behaviour, that is poor. The quality of the latter is quite good. For an excellent early article on the subject see Hartle (1958).

12 When this department was disbanded after the war, the Economic Analysis group that was working on the models was transferred to the Department of Trade and Commerce, where it was joined most notably

by May in 1949. It continued work in this department to 1964 (Brown leaving in 1959), when the model group was again moved, this time to Finance, where the last two versions of this family of models were built.

13 Bodkin, Klein, and Marwah (1985), 7.

14 May in particular talks of the constant need through this period to keep reprogramming and redesigning as machine capabilities changed. It was interesting to hear talk of estimating equations with calculators and adding machines. The inversion of even simple matrices must have been a finger-flattening exercise of excruciating boredom. Along with May, Leduc in particular made important contributions to the computing side of the work in its embryonic phases, albeit later during the 1960s.

15 See Beckett (1961).

16 The *OECD* (1965) report "Techniques of Economic Forecasting" gives a detailed description in the chapter on Canada of the governmental consultation and co-ordination process that had developed during the latter part of this period and that was to carry over well into the 1960s.

17 The surveying of consumer attitudes and intentions, along the line of work of Katona and Mueller and Michigan's Survey Research Center begun in the early 1950s, was actively under consideration by a Canadian advertising agency in the 1955/56 but in fact did not arrive on the scene until 1960, principally because of a lack of interest in the product (see below).

18 A Toronto-based group, ECONTRO, organized by Rogers and Patterson, developed somewhat later in the 1950s. Both organizations have been preserved to the present, again in various forms. The Canadian Association of Business Economists, a loose federation of regional associations, plays a similar role, although membership does include some public-sector people.

19 The Beckett organization was to undergo several transformations. In 1974–5, when Beckett left, the firm became known as Singer and Associates. It has recently amalgamated with the management consulting firm of Currie, Coopers, and Lybrand, where some of the original group remains. There is further discussion in chapter 4 of some of the factors underlying these changes.

20 Bodkin, Klein, and Marwah (1985), 16.

CHAPTER FOUR

1 It is seldom certain throughout this history whether technology drives demand in the fashion of Say's Law or whether demand factors are more important. The text mentions both but tends to pay more attention to supply. The nature of the demand for forecasts is not discussed

explicity. Briefly stated, besides the obvious desire to obtain a more accurate idea of what is likely to happen in the future, sometimes known as the "revealed truth" motive, forecasts are used to help rally organizations to a common good, to aid in consistent thinking at budget time, to share blame, and to demonstrate that reasonable care has been used. An extensive discussion of these factors and their effect on the changing nature of the demand for forecasts appears below, in chapter 5.

2 A comprehensive chronology of these efforts would require more space than is available. What is possible is a brief listing of the more important work and a discussion in some detail of selected parts of it. With respect to some of the econometric modelling work, the reader is once again referred to Bodkin, Klein, and Marwah (1985), from which some of what follows is taken.

3 For this, one needs the public good argument advanced in the text. Beckett and Associates, the major private forecasting organization, might well have been at the forefront of this work. It was not. It is interesting to speculate on why this was the case. This is done below in some detail. While not conclusive, this consideration of Beckett and Associates tends to confirm the public good recapture hypothesis adopted here.

4 Bodkin, Klein, and Marwah (1985), 14.

5 Grady reports (personal correspondence, 1985) that during this hiatus the department experimented with using several existing models for policy analysis – first QFM (see below in the text for a discussion of this University of Toronto product), then RDX2/Red (modified somewhat by Finance itself). But in the late 1970s dissatisfaction with all models led to development of Finance's own model, QFS, which was first used to produce the official government forecast in the fall of 1982.

6 Officer published another model in this period (see Officer 1968) from his doctoral work at Harvard. "Primarily of interest for historical reasons, it was a useful training ground for one of the principal authors of RDX1 and RDX2 i.e., Officer" (Bodkin, Klein, and Marwah 1985, 22). Shapiro and Steward (the latter another author of RDX) had also each previously constructed, estimated, and simulated complete models of Canada as part of their graduate work at Princeton and Cornell respectively.

7 See, for example, Helliwell et al (1971a and b).

8 In addition to Helliwell et al (1971a and b) and Bodkin, Klein, and Marwah (1985), see also de Bever and Maxwell (1979) and O'Reilly (1985).

9 A note of the "might-have-been" variety is of interest here. Officer, Wilson, Sparks, and Dobell, all important contributors to work in this period, were intending to go to McGill as a group from their respective us schools in 1967. Arrangements fell through at the last moment. Wil-

son then went to the University of Toronto, the others elsewhere. Had McGill delivered, it and Montreal, with its computing capacity, would have been the unquestioned centre of much of what happened in this entire area over the next 10–15 years.

10 See, for example, Carr, Jump, and Sawyer (1976).

11 See, for example, Bodkin, Klein, and Marwah (1985).

12 This is certainly true of the more sociologically based work of this period, perhaps less so of the systems work of, for example, Meadows. But even with respect to the latter, the econometric work was much more complex.

13 There is little doubt that the first oil crisis in the 1970s was itself directly responsible for a second development/implementation rush on all fronts into energy modelling. Some work on energy modelling had been carried out by people at the National Energy Board throughout the 1967–73 period. A long-term energy demand forecast was made publicly available in 1967–8. However, there is no question that the first oil shock gave energy modelling and forecasting an important boost.

14 Chase Econometrics also entered the market briefly in this period. As noted below, it abandoned the effort only to reappear again in 1980.

15 Of note as well as a reflection of the times was the fact that the leading financial newspapers, in particular the *Financial Post*, began in 1974–5 to publish regularly a summary of economic forecasts because "we sensed a desire to know about these forecasts."

16 There are many other issues relating to industrial organization besides product differentiation. They include entry strategies, pricing, profitability, and eventual industry structural characteristics. They are discussed in chapter 6.

17 One important activity affecting all work in this period was the need to re-estimate models with the appearance of Statistics Canada's new 1971 base data in 1977–8. This work involved a substantial capital investment and in itself helps explain the calm that prevailed early in this period. The same effect occurred after the 1980s revisions.

18 See, for example, Nelles (1983).

CHAPTER FIVE

1 While its modelling-based forecasting activities date from about the same point as the rest, i.e. the mid-1970s there is an earlier, somewhat irregular, consensual-based history dating back to the 1960s that can be used to justify this claim. It is independent of the us organization of the same name.

2 As chapters 3 and 4 indicated, many of these organizations and individuals have a long tradition of aggregate economic forecasting stretching back to the early 1950s. Indeed they constituted the industry in its

early days. Naturally the relative importance of organizations and individuals changes with time, but there is a stability in many of the operations that requires that they be included as part of the industry.

3 Departments with major sectoral responsibilities, and thus fairly substantial forecasting departments, such as Transport, Agriculture, and Employment, are possible candidates, but I do not consider them members of the industry in the same way as say Finance or the Bank of Canada.

4 That is, my criticism of this work is identical to that made of indicator approaches by traditional economics, i.e. there is a statistical explanation but no economic one.

5 To this can be added the great bulk of the Austrian and German historical school traditions in economics, which argue, quite independent of justification given here in the text proper, that institutional studies, if not exactly the sine qua non of economics, are nonetheless extremely important to any attempt to understand economic behaviour.

6 Because of the way in which the industry has been defined, the concepts of demand and supply are somewhat more difficult to separate here than in other cases. That is, those in the loose group of non-majors may buy from the majors, incorporate their own work, and then "resell," even to the point of publication, and in competition with the majors. Thus it is less clear what is demand, what supply. This is conceptually similar to the case of a retailer who buys from a basic producer, puts his brand on the product, and resells it in competition with the basic producer's branded product (e.g. Sears and tires). In this instance, tradition in industry studies treats the retailer as part of supply. This is done here as well so that, for example, expenditures on forecasting personnel by the Royal Bank are considered part of supply.

However, total expenditures on forecasting by the same bank can also be seen as part of ultimate demand insofar as that organization's management requires forecasts from several sources, including its own in-house suppliers. Thus, whether these expenditures are related to total sales, a traditional type of demand hypothesis in industry studies, is of legitimate concern here.

Accordingly, in the discussion to follow, demand is taken to refer generally to ultimate demand; all else is supply. However, the data from the loose group of non-majors will be considered as part of both demand and supply.

7 This discovery was a decided discomfort to one schooled in "rational" decision-making, scientific methods, ex post analyses, and other evidently tangential paradigms! However, it is perhaps to be expected, for it is the executive's function to conduct the affairs of the organization, in particular (with discretion) to explain or not explain exactly how the

forecasts determined his/her actions. It is the forecaster's job merely to supply one of the services necessary to do so.

8 It has been suggested that a demand-inspired boom for aggregate economic forecasts would occur if Canadian competition policy were more strongly enforced. Because of stricter anti-trust laws, competitors in the United States talk with one another at their peril. Hence each needs "outside," predictive information about the collective sense of the economy, the industry, and the competition. In Canada so much mutual discussion goes on that this need for forecasting is considerably diminished. The organization does not, therefore, have to provide it (or have it provided). One *knows* what his/her competitors and others think. It is another most interesting consequence of the sorry state of Canadian competition policy.

9 "If the forecasters are saying circumstances will improve, and we act in accordance with this opinion and they fail to do so, the forecasters are to blame as much as ourselves (if not completely to blame in most cases ...)." Some suppliers of forecasts directly acknowledge their responsibilities in this regard, suggesting that one benefit they contribute is precisely that of "hand-holding" (as executives presumably grope through the "cold, uncertain dawn").

10 As we shall see below in chapter 9, the small amount of case law that has developed on liability in forecasting supports such an argument as a valid extension of the "reasonable person/reasonable care" obligations of common law more generally.

11 Since all such evidence is ultimately in the public domain, it probably also suggests why regulated companies have a much more structured system for incorporating aggregate economic forecasts into their decision-making than do most other organizations.

12 A more subtle theoretical extension of this point would be to argue that forecasts fulfil a "signalling" function in the economy as a whole. They are the vehicles by which we declare, and hear declared, competing opinions about the future. In a market economy under uncertainty, they are thus a major element in the invisible hand's working out of collectively acceptable solutions (Daub and Mohr 1985).

13 There are other factors at work. For example, subscription fees (price) are annual in nature. It is therefore inappropriate to think of using quarterly data. Because of the youth of the industry, annual data are available for only 11 years, not nearly enough to warrant estimating the model that is suggested in note 14, or any simpler one either, even if cross-sectional data had been available for pooling, which they weren't, for the reasons given in the text.

14 What that model might have been can be at least indicated. Summarized in equation form with indicated proxy measures for individual variables:

$$q_{F,t} = \beta_o + \beta_1 P_{F,t} + \beta_2 P_{b,t} + \beta_3 P_{c,t} + \beta_4 S_t + \beta_5 PG_t + \beta_6 O_t + e_t,$$

where: $q_{F,t}$ = total number of clients of forecaster F during period t (output proxy),

$P_{F,t}$ = real subscription fee, or the size of error in forecasting nominal GNP, of forecaster F (price proxy),

$P_{b,t}$ = standard real futures market brokerage charges (substitute price proxy),

$P_{c,t}$ = index of real computer costs (complement proxy),

S_t = average size of clients' real assets or sales (wealth/income proxy),

PG_t = number of forecasters listed in the *Financial Post*'s annual competition (public good proxy), and

O_t = growth in real GNP, or days lost to strikes, or number of MBA's graduated, or real growth in government spending ("other" factors).

15 This practice is well established in both the forecast accuracy assessment and industry study literatures; see, for example, Zarnowitz (1967; 1984a) and Daub (1981) as well as discussions below in chapters 7 and 8.

16 The Conference Board annual reports yield considerably less precise data. For example, the number of clients ("associates") is given infrequently and only approximately. As well, total revenue comes from other sources besides forecasting, such as conferences. Moreover, membership fee revenue, which is broken out of total revenue, itself covers other services besides forecasting. Finally, as noted, there are only five data points available.

17 This figure was derived in three different ways, too lengthy to detail here, which gave approximately the same results. The sample departments accounted for an estimated $9 million, 70 per cent of the estimated total spent on forecasting.

18 Implicit price indices are available for this category (STATSCAN 61–213). They were divided by the implicit GNP price deflator to obtain a generalized relative price variable.

19 The SIC category "services to business management" (861–9) includes lawyers, architects, accountants, advertising agencies, and engineering/scientific and computing services, in addition to "other business services, n.e.s." (861, 866, 869 – which includes the forecasters).

20 Since a firm helps to develop the human capital involved (whether by formal or informal training), it is thus a loss when professionals depart. Quite obviously, there is conversely a substantial premium captured by the ex-employee when he/she moves elsewhere.

21 As an example, the arrival of personal computers with their spreadsheet programs has altered not only the demand for forecasts but also their

supply. Suppliers are now finding it economic to write forecasting and communication software in order to allow individual buyers to access the firm's data banks and larger models, as well as to do simulations. In addition, of course, the substantial reduction in cost due to the increased capacity of mainframes has directly reduced supplier computing costs. So both aspects of computing technological change have had an effect on supply.

22 Supply-related changes are a factor here as well: greater machine and communication capacity has allowed better reporting and more analytical capability, thus enhancing quarterly estimation and prediction.

CHAPTER SIX

1 Green (1980), 15.

2 It is also my belief that the majors account for about 80 per cent of Canada's basic aggregate economic forecasting. This estimate is based on the relatively narrow client base served by similar concentrations of forecasting human capital outside the four (e.g. Finance, the Bank, the Policy Institute, the Economic Council, the Royal Bank), interview findings on "net" forecasting done in addition to considering the majors' forecasts, and similar considerations.

3 One piece of evidence is a simple head count of the number of forecasters cited, or who could be cited, in international compendia of forecasts such as *Economic Forecasts* (North Holland, monthly).

4 Some of the product line of DRI, Wharton Canada, and the Conference Board is imported from the United States and sold directly in Canada as part of the Canadian firms' offerings. To that extent there is some import competition. But it is not of the classic type.

5 WEFA-CEIS (Wharton Consulting) entered the Canadian market directly only very recently, although, as noted in chapter 4, the University of Toronto's TRACE model was part of Klein's "PROJECT LINK" from the earliest times. Of course, to the extent that they are really the old Chase Econometrics operation, they have actually been in Canada since 1980.

6 Generalizations about the actual price elasticity are therefore difficult. The sketchy evidence from chapter 5 indicates the sign at least is as expected. If the data from the confidential firm are typical, and they are analysed in the traditional way (which is suspect because of the small number of data points), then the price elasticity of demand as measured by number of clients and annual relative real subscription fees is -0.22 in the region of the means. A piece of anecdotal evidence suggests that at least one supplier believes that the price elasticities on the simulation and data access parts of the business are quite high, principally because

the most sophisticated buyers are to be found there. If true, it would tend to negate somewhat the tie-in argument made in the text. I am less inclined to this view than I am to the more generally accepted one.

7 Another interviewee observed that the situation was indeed like cars. "You need a new product every so often, or people get bored." An attempt to compile some rudimentary statistics on the number of product innovations was unsuccessful. However, anecdote after anecdote from the major suppliers confirms that they are acutely aware of what the others are offering and continually at work to find new ways of changing the product, viewed in its broadest sense, to keep up with, or to differentiate themselves more firmly from, the competition.

8 These calculations are approximations at best. For example, there is some question about how for tax purposes to depreciate a large-scale econometric model or one's data bases. There are similar accounting/ tax definition problems with arriving at a comparable average *equity* figure. A careful attempt has also been made to ensure that all such calculations are compatible with the STATSCAN figures cited later in the text proper. But they are estimates only.

9 The figure thus likely overstates the return on investment ROI: the same profits would be considerably diluted if retained earnings remained the same but shareholders' equity were present.

10 "A Squabble Stalls the Wharton Deal," *Business Week,* 28 February 1983, 49.

11 "Chase Reveals Sale Discussed," *Globe and Mail,* 28 December 1984, 84. As noted earlier, Chase in the United States was subsequently sold in 1987 to WEF Assoc. AG, a Swiss company.

12 Green (1980), 131.

13 As noted earlier in the chapter, there is some controversy over whether the industry has been quick enough to introduce recent technological advances forthcoming from the latest econometric research. There was, for example, some discussion of this point at the First Canadian Econometric Study Group conference at Queen's University in October 1984. Some academics would argue that it has not, some industry representatives that they are doing the best they possibly can.

14 The implication is thus that while it is correct to speak of forecasts as being rational if they fulfil accuracy requirements or can be demonstrated to be consistent with mathematical specifications that use available information in appropriate ways (see, for example, Caskey [1985]), it is incomplete, misleading, and inconsistent with traditional economic theory to view expectations formation in only these essentially "statistical" ways. A more correct approach, in my view, is to conceive of it as yet another product or service with demand and supply characteristics that rationally explain its economic character.

CHAPTER SEVEN

1 Henschel (1978), 100. The reader is referred to this paper for an excellent treatment of the problem, which might be called the "circularity" or "verification" difficulty in another context. It is known also as the Epimenides paradox, after the Cretan prophet and philosopher whose example was: "All Cretans are liars." There is also an Arab epigram: "He who foretells the future lies even if he tells the truth." This prediction dilemma lay at the heart of the "impotency" deduction made from the rational expectations assumption in macroeconomics discussed in chapter 1.

2 Nagel (1961), 468.

3 However, if the completely revised figure is regarded as the "true" realization to be forecast, it is important to comment on the differences in the accuracy assessment introduced by using different estimates of the actuals. This is also a problem in statistical reporting more generally, where one always hopes to have more accurate data earlier. Several studies e.g. Cole 1969 indicate that better provisional estimates would generally decrease forecasting error, sometimes noticeably.

4 Thus an academic researcher interested in basic research might use all the data possibly available after months of searching, whereas the policy analyst for a large bank, perhaps more interested in the recent record, might use only five years.

5 Averages are unweighted because the various users of the assessment results may have varying ideas about which years deserve more weight. The most conservative and general scheme is thus to weight each error equally.

6 Mathematically,

$$\frac{1}{n} \sum_{i=1}^{n} (P_i - \bar{A}_i)^2 = (\bar{P} - \bar{A})^2 + (\sigma_P - \sigma_A)^2 + 2(1 - R_{AP})\sigma_P\sigma_A,$$

where P_i and A_i are predictions and actuals; $\bar{A}$, $\bar{P}$, σ_P and σ_A population means and standard deviations; and R_{AP} the population correlation coefficient. This approach was first suggested by Theil (1958). Dividing through each side by the left-hand variable yielded the fraction of the mean square error due to bias (the "bias inequality coefficient"), variance, and residual factors, respectively.

7 Cycles in general economic activity, as measured, for example, by real GNP, have been relatively absent from economic activity since the Second World War. However, individual aggregate variables, such as various aspects of investment activity, show much more volatility. Forecasts of

these variables are thus more amenable to turning point error analysis. This latter point applies most directly, of course, to indicator, or bivariate stochastic, time series methods, the major raison d'être of which is turning point signalling.

8 See Daub (1973), 95, where I showed (Note 13) the important difference that this made to some earlier judgments that Zarnowitz (1967) had made about US forecasts.

9 Other than this, there are few direct statistical problems, inasmuch as the tests are well known. The one important difficulty is the small size of the sample that one is forced to use when annual forecasts are the rule. Significance testing with 5 or 10 data points is a highly risky business. Even 25 points (e.g. annual real GNP predictions from 1960 to 1985) can be somewhat questionable. Assuming no highly dramatic changes in the structure of the economy, in 20 or 30 years we will be on firmer inferential grounds.

10 Quite obviously, one is not restricted to any particular group of "other forecasters." The usual distinction made is domestic versus foreign. We will follow it here, considering Canadian forecasters first by themselves, and then relative to those in other countries forecasting their particular economic aggregates (chapter 8).

11 If no adjustment is made for this, the inferences about differences between forecasters will be wrong. The same problem would develop if one were to test the significance of the average error of a group of forecasters over time against zero error (Daub 1973, 95). In this latter instance the extent of bias in the forecast would likely be overstated.

12 Correlation analysis will do the same thing, i.e. comparing r^2_{AP} to r^2_{AE} (where E represents the extrapolative predictions) or checking $r^2_{AP.E}$ and $r^2_{AE.P}$. Again there are small sample and statistical problems. But the approach can at least be entertained.

13 That they are approximations to the "true" measure of inaccuracy (the cost or loss flowing from the inaccurate forecast) should be clear. The mean forecasting error will equal this "true" measure only under some extremely restricted theoretical conditions (i.e. linear loss function).

14 The most recent attempt to do so can be found in the optimal control literature of the early 1980s.

15 What follows is taken from some of my earlier work (Daub 1974). The same applies to the empirical results cited below in the next subsection.

16 This explanation treats the case of a period in which Y^* underestimates Y_A and realized demand contains a positive random error. Various other possibilities could also have been considered. For example, relabelling $D(Y_A,e)$ as $D(Y^*)$ and $D(Y^*)$ as $D(Y_A,e)$ suggests a cost to inaccurate aggregate forecasts, in the case of an overestimation of actual income

(which contains a negative random component), of AHIL – ACJK. These are "gross" measures of the cost of inaccuracy, since they ignore the cost of increasing the accuracy of the forecasts.

17 Other studies on the accuracy of Canadian aggregate forecasts are available, the most important of which is that of Kenward and Jenkins (1977). However, their study related exclusively to econometric models, reported on only a very small number of ex post forecasting periods, and did not use as extensive a method for accuracy analysis as is used here. This is not meant as criticism of their work, for it was well done, especially in regard to controlling for common estimation techniques, where it went much further than what is done here. However, it was less extensive in other aspects. The surveys of forecasts and their accuracy made annually in recent years by the *Financial Times* and the Conference Board are also available. However, they present virtually no analysis of accuracy and no historical perspective. They are thus of limited aid.

18 The advent of quarterly forecasting has helped, but here the records of past forecasts are very sketchy. This matter of record-keeping has always been a severe constraint on accuracy research. Nothing is as stale as old forecasts, except old news; they are seldom, if ever, kept. Reaching back is thus difficult. As always, one does what one can.

19 As Table 6, note a, suggests, in regard to GNP, for example, in the period 1956–69 there were 8 forecaster/sets and 83 observations, in 1970–9 10 sets and 82 observations, and in 1980–4 8 sets and 40 observations. Some of the sets from the earlier period are continued throughout. Others, being discontinued, have been replaced with as nearly identical types of forecasters as possible, that is, near-government for government, business forecasting for business forecasting, and so on. Most of the unpublished forecasts were supplied only on the grounds of anonymity. I continue to honour this request for confidentiality, even though with time more and more forecasts of this type are being made public. Some forecasters still do, however, insist on anonymity. As well, to have violated promises of anonymity made to the original group well after the fact would be unconscionable . Thus no source is identified. The continued co-operation of all contributors is acknowledged with thanks.

20 All errors were calculated relative to preliminary actuals, a practice the defence for which is given in Daub (1973). Evidence on any influence that using the latest actual may have had indicates that measurement error continued to account for the same amount by which the "latest" prediction error differed from the one calculated using first estimates. The other prediction-related source of error lies in estimating the current position of the actual. Far fewer forecasters in recent times have specified the level of actual GNP from which they were predicting per-

centage changes. However, evidence from 1956–79 indicated a mean error of about −0.16 billion, which is not excessively large relative to GNP (approximately 0.2 per cent of average GNP) during that period.

21 A significance test of the difference indicates that the mean absolute errors in the two periods are significantly different at the 0.05 level. It will be recalled that this test has its problems in the present circumstances.

22 The numbers in Tables 6 and 7 do not exactly sum up (i.e. −0.26 + −0.72 does not equal −1.1) because somewhat different samples are involved.

23 Zarnowitz (1979), 16.

24 Data from the 1980s on current-dollar component forecasts were not as readily available as before. Because of inflationary concerns, forecasters began switching to constant-dollar predictions of components. This makes the two sets of data incomparable, since no individual component deflator forecasts accompanied the original sets. Updated component results are not, therefore, reported here.

25 Here the extrapolations used are the "no change" model (1), that the prediction for next year is this year's actual; the "same change" model (2), which predicts the "latest change"; and a class of models (BJ) based on Box-Jenkins techniques. The measure of comparison used here is a weighted average, overall sets, of the ratio of the mean square error of the judgmental predictions to those of the extrapolative predictions. Thus a ratio of less than one indicates that the forecasts are superior. These are presented as R_1, and R_2, and R_{BJ} respectively.

26 It would have been of interest to compare the four core firms. Because Chase is such a recent entrant to the industry, this was considered unwise, especially as a deep recession occurred almost immediately after that entrance. However, it will certainly be one piece of research worth doing in about five years' time, when sufficient data have accumulated.

27 After consideration of the accuracy of quarterly forecasts from four econometric models, over a very short period in the 1970s, Kenward and Jenkins (1977) reached much the same conclusions: "Not surprisingly, none of the models dominates all others ... [In addition] the economic models generally perform very well vis à vis the economically naive alternative used here, univariate B.J. models." Stokes (1982), in a study restricted to the Conference Board's models, also concludes "that the errors [made by QCF (the Board's forecast)] are certainly comparable to those made by other Canadian forecasters [i.e. as reported by Daub (1981)]." So there is some supporting evidence for the conclusions drawn here. It is admittedly rather thin.

28 The careful reader will remark that the story seems to be passing along without any mention being made of quarterly forecasts. Unfortunately, the data are much more limited than is the case with annual forecasts.

Nonetheless I made an attempt to consider the question in Daub (1973) but dropped it for Daub (1981) because, and rather surprisingly, availability of quarterly data has not increased much with time. Indeed, in very recent years, perhaps as a function of the sense of humility that has entered the business, interest in quarterly forecasts seems to have died down somewhat. As a consequence, here is yet another topic in need of further work. However, it is one best left until better data finally become available. All is not lost, though, at least on the methodological side: some of the issues associated with multi-horizon accuracy assessment are illustrated below in connection with the investment intentions, and long-term energy, forecast investigations.

29 Daub and Savage (1973), 82.

30 In order to assemble a reasonably consistent data base from the collection and publication confusion that has recently characterized the investment intentions survey, I decided to use a period in which the Department of Industry, Trade and Commerce did most of the surveying and analysing of the data, published its results, and over which horizons of more than one year were included, that is 1970–6.

31 Investment intentions are sometimes used as "inputs" to the model forecasts so that the two approaches are not necessarily as disjoint as the text implies.

32 Fluctuations in weather may cause short-term problems in residential and commercial energy forecasts, because forecasters commonly include such variables but use historical averages. This is not an important factor in the prediction of transportation demand.

33 Thus a view, often associated with Keynes, about the great difficulties intrinsic in long-term forecasting may not be as appropriate as a looser version of the rational expectations hypothesis advanced above; i.e. on average in the long run people have a decent idea of what is likely to happen. One additional piece of evidence supporting this contention relates to the Gordon Commission forecasts of real GNP made in 1955 for 1980. This forecast, appropriately adjusted for base shifts, was in error by 5.3 per cent of actual (i.e. it predicted that 1980 real GNP would be $124.8 billion, and it turned out to be $131.8 billion). Viewed in terms of a compound growth rate forecast, it predicted 4.5 per cent growth on average, and the actual was 4.8 per cent. This is not bad over 25 years!

34 One explanation, not advanced above but sometimes thought by the industry to be important, might be called the "herd instinct." While analytically difficult to consider, this hypothesis suggests that because forecasters must sell their forecasts, and clients may not want, for reasons noted above, a major deviation in view from other forecasts, the forecasters may find their extreme positions "talked back to the conventional

view," i.e. to the consensus of other forecasters. As indicated, it is impossible to test this explanation with the data at hand.

CHAPTER EIGHT

1 Information on the Russian, and other, plans is available as a matter of course. But these "forecasts" are not at all what we mean by the term. Evidence on the process and record of something approaching our idea of forecasts is, of course, buried deep in the early stages of these plans, and quite zealously guarded. From time to time anecdotal evidence surfaces to suggest that the Russians are no better at forecasting the course of our economies, or their own, than we are (Russian participant in panel discussion at the Third International Symposium on Forecasting, Philadelphia, 1983).

2 The emphasis here is on the word "briefly," for one could spend pages and pages on this and on citing accuracy records as well. The intent is only to give the barest outlines of what happens elsewhere.

3 The "plan," with its "dirigiste" character, may be thought to have played a large role in causing this centralization. It is my impression that the French always paid much more attention to the annual forecasts released by the finance ministry. Centralization of the forecasting function in the governments of these countries was a natural consequence of the need to rebuild completely economies following the disastrous Second World War. It has withered away in varying degrees as this process became completed.

4 Accompanying this explosion world-wide, indeed a very good indirect measure of developments, is the availability in the past several years of international compendia such as the aforementioned *Economic Forecasts*, which reports on 23 countries.

5 No doubt we were somewhat quicker off the mark because of our proximity to the United States, where much of the action happened in the early to mid-1970s.

6 Bodkin, Klein, and Marwah (1985) contain a chapter summarizing work over the years on PROJECT LINK.

7 Global forecasts, with substantial country detail, are now also being produced by the large American firms such as DRI and WEFA-CEIS. Some include also groups of countries (e.g. WEFA-CEIS's European Service).

8 The reader will recall Daub and Savage (1973). Zarnowitz's evidence is not exactly congruent with that of Daub and Sankaran (1984) presented earlier, because the two studies do not overlap in time period or method. However, if forecasts available late in the previous year are the ones that count for turning point analysis (and not ones early in the year to

be forecast – recall the earlier discussion), then the 1982–3 errors would have been considered turning point errors, would have been very large, and indeed would give results consistent with Zarnowitz's. They dominate the 1980s record cited in chapter 7 for this very reason. So Zarnowitz's point is well taken, namely that "there are indeed strong reasons for makers and users of economic forecasts to give a great deal of attention to turning-point errors" (Zarnowitz 1979, 12).

9   McNees and Ries (1983) establish this for the United States internally.

10 One study that has always been a model in this respect is Fair's (1979b) analysis of the predictive accuracy of four us macroeconomic models. His procedures have been duplicated in the various macro "horse races" done with Canadian models in recent times and mentioned in chapter 4.

11 Nelson (1972), perhaps the first study to show this, came as a bombshell to the economic community! Others since, such as Fildes (1985) and Makridakis (1986), continue to discover this.

12 Some of the us studies of accuracy (e.g. Brown and Maital 1981) were done in an attempt to document the existence of rational expectations. This was especially true in the early days of the hypothesis, when it was thought to require strictly unbiased forecasts. This approach to the subject has, however, died out recently.

13 Fourteen countries in all reporting over the years 1966–82 were included. Real GNP and the deflator were considered. Unfortunately, in a number of the countries the study was restricted to only the OECD's forecast. However, because of the large number of countries used, and the rather sophisticated approach taken, the study may be forgiven this lack of "depth" in places.

14 Llewelyn et al. (1985), 21.

15 The study thus found that in all but one of these single-country, large-error years, the error in forecasting the OECD as whole was also large by comparison with its average error (Llewelyn et al. 1985, 35).

16 Llewelyn et al. (1985), 38.

17 "Faulty Forecasting through History," *The Futurist*, October 1983, 1.

18 No mention has been made of the United Nations, the International Monetary Fund, or the World Bank, all of which do similar kinds of forecasting but are far less important on the forecasting "scene."

19 McCracken (1983).

CHAPTER NINE

1   Ascher (1978), 11. Segments of this section are taken from Daub (1984b), where the reader may find a more specifc discussion of the issue.

2   Wachs (1982) is an excellent discussion of some of the difficulties that plague relations between policy-makers and forecasters. The one that

almost always takes pride of place, and amply illustrates one of the sociological functions of forecasting, is the request to alter a forecast to conform better to the policy-makers' wishes/needs/plans. In such circumstances, should the forecaster give them what they want, or what he/she really thinks? This ethical dilemma is particularly acute where the continued prosperity of the forecasting firm depends on client satisfaction. But the situation is no different from that of an accounting firm on an audit, or a management consulting team giving advice to a client. It is a problem that plagues all professionals (lawyers, management consultants, and others) who rely on a client's continued patronage. But it is probably fair to say that there is a collective sense of integrity in the business as a whole, particularly with respect to each of the majors. None, more than any other, is felt to "pull its punches." Certainly every forecaster has his or her little story of a colleague's succumbing to pressure and his or her own heroic stand in the face of similar efforts to force a specific result. There are enough places in the entire forecasting exercise where such pressure can play on one's own legitimate doubts to the point that one gives way. But the honour of the industry, broadly viewed, is not generally questioned – its accuracy always, its integrity sometimes, but a good deal less.

3 Waslander (1982), 2–5, suggests that forecasters are not necessarily completely to blame. The structural detail, for example, has, after all, been maintained (the same cannot be said for regional data, which continue to be unconscionably weak). The models have, however, been used mostly for macroeconomic analysis and policy guides. Waslander cites several reasons for this relative inattention to available sectoral forecasts. These include the feeling that politics (e.g. lobbying for quotas) and macro policies are likely to be more important to the outcomes of sectors than forecastable sector-specific factors. If this is so, it certainly warrants attention to the prediction of macro variables. It also suggests that policy-makers ignore sectoral forecasts for other reasons.

4 Yet another supply-related change has been the increased speed that the market place now demands of forecasters. One of the reasons for this is the explosion in the number of MBAs, economists, and others, who are much more sophisticated in the use of analytical systems. Many are also familiar with modern computer technology. As well, they recognize that with modern integrated capital markets any chance for differential gain from information must materialize quickly or be lost. For all these reasons, they have come to think in terms of, to need, and to expect speed. However, the re-estimation of a large model system may be something rarely done that well, that quickly. To be sure, estimation times are dropping dramatically because of simplification of models, better on-line data access, and improved software. But no one ought to expect

miracles. Accuracy is still a sacrifice one needs to make to speed. If such speed is absolutely required, subsequent faults are as much due to the unrealistic expectations of the user as they are to the inadequacies of the forecaster.

5 See, for example, Rutenberg (1985) and Wack (1985).

6 Part of what follows is taken from Herwitz (1973).

7 This absence of a warranty with respect to the future is obvious. What is perhaps less obvious, but broadly related, is the absense of intellectual property law with respect to forecasts. This might seem strange to some, for the propriety of the service, and ultimately the forecast, would seem worth protecting through patents, trademarks, or copyrights. Apart from obvious copyright activity, this part of the law has had little impact, for reasons primarily related to the public good aspects of much of the data and econometric technology involved. My forecast of GNP could be exactly identical to yours, and you could not, in virtually any but the most obvious passing-off circumstances, prove that I had stolen your forecast. The same goes for the method, which is available to all through academic textbooks and journals. Thus, not only is the forecast producer deprived of protection in this respect, but so also is the consumer, who, in other circumstances, can use the existence of branded goods as an implicit measure of goodness and, hence, specific liability. Some of these issues are addressed in *International Forecasting Corp.* v. *Stoll et al* (8 ACWS [2d], 299, 1981), as is the difficulty of getting court-enforced personal services contracts (which the supplying of forecasts was held to be).

8 The reader will recall the distinction made earlier between absolute and relative accuracy.

9 Herwitz (1973), 247.

10 This case, *Pepsi and Pizza Hut* v. P.M. *Foods* (1985), contains an excellent citation list on the question of liability for inaccurate forecasting in Canada. In particular *Esso* v. *Mardon* was cited. The court held that it did not apply because there was equality of knowledge on both sides and opinion only was present, not fact; there had been no gross negligence in preparation; forecasts had been generously made available; and they had been totally ignored!

11 Exactly the reverse is also true. Which represents the greater damage needing control by the other is partly what the dispute referred to in the text proper is all about. A decision in this regard is ultimately as much ideologically inspired as it is a matter of fact, for the record shows that neither public nor private-sector forecasting organizations have been guilty of outrageous behaviour needing control.

References

Ackoff, R.L, 1981. *Creating the Corporate Future.* New York: John Wiley & Sons.

Ahlers, D., and J. Lakonishok, 1983. "A Study of Economists' Consensus Forecasts." *Management Science* 29, no. 10 (October): 1113–25.

Angevine, G., 1974. "Forecasting Consumption with a Canadian Consumer Sentiment Measure." *Canadian Journal of Economics* 7, no. 2 (May): 274–89.

Armstrong, J.S., 1978. *Long-Range Forecasting: From Crystal Ball to Computer.* New York: John Wiley & Sons.

– 1979. "Forecasting with Econometric Methods: Folklore versus Fact." *Journal of Business* S1: 549–600.

– 1980. "The Seer-Sucker Theory: The Value of Experts in Forecasting," *Technology Review* 83: 18–24.

– 1984. "Forecasting by Extrapolation: Conclusion from 25 Years of Research," *Interfaces* 14, no. 6 (November–December): 52–66.

– 1986. "Research on Forecasting: A Quarter-Century Review, 1960–1984," *Interfaces* 16, no. 1 (January–February): 89–109.

Arrow, K., 1978. "The Future and Present in Economic Life," *Economic Inquiry* (April): 157–69.

Ash, J.C.K. and D.J. Smyth, 1973. "Who Forecasts the British Economy Best? An Assessment of Half-Yearly Forecasts of Gross Domestic Product Published by the Treasury, NIESR, OECD, the Sunday Times and the Sunday Telegraph," University of Reading Discussion Papers in Economics, Series A, No. 52.

Ascher, W., 1978. *Forecasting: An Appraisal for Policy Makers and Planners.* Baltimore: Johns Hopkins University Press.

Ayres, R., 1969. *Technological Forecasting.* New York: McGraw Hill.

Baille, R., R. Lippens, and P. McMahon, 1983. "Testing Rational Expectations and Efficiency in the Foreign Exchange Market," *Econometrica* 51, no. 3 (May): 553–63.

Bails, D.G., and L.C. Pepper 1982. *Business Fluctuations: Forecasting Techniques and Applications.* Englewood Cliffs, NJ: Prentice-Hall.

Bain, J., 1959. *Industrial Organization.* New York: Wiley and Sons.

Bakony, L., 1959. "A Quarterly Econometric Model of the Canadian Economy," *Econometrica* 27 (April): 296–7.

Barker, K.M., 1983. "World Economy Forecast Post Mortems: 1978–82," *National Institute Economic Review,* May.

Beckett, A., 1961. "Canadian Indicators," in G. Moore, ed., *Business Cycle Indicators,* vol. 1.

Blackwell, D., and M.A. Girshick, 1979. *Theory of Games and Statistical Decision.* New York: Dover.

Blankenship, A., C. Chakrapani, and H. Poole, 1985. *A History of Marketing Research in Canada.* Toronto: Professional Marketing Research Society.

Blohm, H., and K. Steinbuch, 1973. *Technological Forecasting in Practice.* Lexington, Mass.: Lexington Books.

Bodkin, R., V. Cano-Lamy, E. Chow, J. Fortin, I. Gunaratne, J. Kuiper, and C. Serrurier, 1979. "Ex Ante Forecasting with Several Econometric Models of the Canadian Economy," *Journal of Post Keynesian Economics* 1 (Spring): 16–40.

Bodkin, R., L. Klein, and K. Marwah, 1985. "Canadian Macroeconometric Modelling, 1947–1979 and Beyond," Research Paper 8502, Department of Economics, University of Ottawa.

Bouysset, J., 1974. "La précision des prévisions; la budget," Ministère de finance, Gouvernment de France.

Box, G.E.P., and G.M. Jenkins, 1976. *Time Series Analysis: Forecasting and Control.* Revised Edition. San Francisco: Holden-Day.

Bright, J.R., and M.E.F. Schoeman, eds. 1973. *A Guide to Practical Technological Forecasting.* Englewood Cliffs, NJ: Prentice-Hall.

Brock, G., 1982. *The Telecommunications Industry.* Boston: Harvard University Press.

Brown, B., and S. Maital, 1981. "What Do Economists Know? An Empirical Study of Experts' Expectations," *Econometrica* 49, no. 2 (March): 491–504.

Brown, R., 1963. *Smoothing, Forecasting and Prediction.* Englewood Cliffs, NJ: Prentice-Hall.

Brown, T., 1964. "A Forecast Determination of National Product, Employment, and Price Level in Canada, from an Econometric Model," *Studies in Income and Wealth,* vol. 28. National Bureau of Economic Research: Princeton University Press, 59–96.

– 1970. *Specification and Uses of Econometric Models.* Toronto: Macmillan.

Butler, W., and R. Kavesh, 1966. *How Business Economists Forecast.* Englewood Cliffs, NJ: Prentice-Hall.

Canada, Bank of Canada and Department of Finance, 1981. "Seminar on Responses of Various Models to Selected Policy Shocks," Bank of Canada, Ottawa.

Canada, Department of Finance, 1979. "Papers Presented at Seminar on Policy Simulations Sponsored by the Fiscal Policy Division of the Department of Finance on April 6, 1979," Department of Finance, Ottawa.

Capon, N., C. Christodoulou, J. Farley, and J. Hurbert, 1984. "A Comparison of Corporate Planning Practice in American and Australian Manufacturing Companies," *Journal of International Business Studies* 15, no. 2 (Fall): 41–54.

Carlson, J., 1975. "Are Price Expectations Normally Distributed?" *Journal of the American Statistical Association* 70 (December): 749–54.

Carr, J.L., G.V. Jump, and J.A. Sawyer, 1976. "The Operation of the Canadian Economy under Fixed and Flexible Exchange Rates: Simulation Results from the TRACE model," *Canadian Journal of Economics* 9, no. 1 (February): 102–20.

Caskey, J., 1985. "Modeling the Formation of Price Expectations," *American Economic Review* 75, no. 4 (September): 758–76.

Caves, R., 1962. *Air Transport and Its Regulators.* Cambridge: Harvard University Press.

Caves, R., and R. Holton, 1959. *The Canadian Economy: Prospect and Retrospect.* Cambridge, Mass.: Harvard University Press.

Chambers, J.C., S.K. Mullick, and D.D. Smith, 1971. "How to Choose the Right Forecasting Technique," *Harvard Business Review* (July–August): 45–57.

– 1974. *An Executive's Guide to Forecasting.* New York: John Wiley & Sons.

Choudhry, N.K., Y. Kotowitz, J.A. Sawyer, and J.W.L. Winder, 1971. *The TRACE Econometric Model of the Canadian Economy.* Toronto and Buffalo: University of Toronto Press.

Churchill, G., 1983. *Marketing Research.* Third edition. New York: Dryden.

Cipolletta, I., and D. de Roo, 1981. "Erreurs et ajustments successifs dans les prévisions macroéconomiques en Europe," *Prevision et analyse économique* 2, no. 4 (November/December).

Clarke, A., 1984. *Profiles of the Future: An Inquiry into the Limits of the Possible.* Revised edition. New York: Holt, Rinehart and Winston.

Cleary, J.P., 1975. "A Comparison of the Forecasting Performance of Box-Jenkins Transfer Function Models," in *Proceedings of the American Statistical Association* (August): 291–4.

Coddington, A., 1982. "Deficient Foresight: A Troublesome Theme in Keynesian Economics," *American Economic Review* 72, no. 3 (June): 480–7.

Cohan, J., 1972. *Psychological Probability: Or the Art of Doubt.* London: George Allen & Unwin.

Cole, R., 1969. "Errors in Provisional Estimates of Gross National Product,"

Studies in the Business Cycle No. 21, National Bureau of Economic Research, New York.

Conference Board In Canada, 1976. *The* AERIC *Short-Term Quarterly Forecasting Model of the Canadian Economy.* Revised edition. Ottawa: The Conference Board in Canada.

– *Annual Report* 1981, 1982, 1983, 1984.

Conner, M., 1982. *The Tangled Wing: Biological Constraints on the Human Spirit.* New York: Basic Books.

Craig, J., and B. Malkiel, 1982. *Expectations and the Structure of Share Prices.* National Bureau of Economic Research Monograph, Chicago: University of Chicago Press.

Crawford, C., 1955. *Sales Forecasting Methods of Selected Firms.* Bureau of Economic and Business Research, Bloomington, Ill.: University of Illinois Press.

Cyert, R.M., and J.G. March, 1963. *A Behavioral Theory of the Firm,* Englewood Cliffs, NJ: Prentice-Hall.

Cyert, R.M., and M.H. Degroot, 1974. "Rational Expectations and Bayesian Analysis," *Journal of Political Economy* 82 (May–June): 521–36.

Daly, D., 1959. "Seasonal Variations and Business Expectations," *Journal of Business* 32, no. 2 (July): 258–70.

Daniels, L.M. (ed) 1980. "Business Forecasting for the 1980's – and Beyond," unpublished paper, Graduate School of Business Administration (Buher Library), Harvard University.

Daub, M., 1973. "On the Accuracy of Canadian Short-Term Economic Forecasts," *Canadian Journal of Economics* 6, no. 1 (February): 90–107.

– 1974. "On the Cost to the Firm of Aggregate Prediction Errors," *Journal of Business* 47, no. 1 (January): 11–22.

– 1975. "An International Comparison of the Accuracy of Canadian Short-term Predictions of Gross National Product," *Applied Economics* 7: 235–40.

– 1977. "An Examination of the Nature of Errors in Aggregate Economic Prediction," *Review of Economics and Statistics* 59, no. 2 (May): 230–3.

– 1980. "An Investigation of the Accuracy of Canada's Capital Investment Intentions Survey," Discussion Paper 385, Institute for Economic Research, Queen's University, May.

– 1980. "The Accuracy of Canadian Short-term Economic Forecasts Revisited," *Canadian Journal of Economics* 14, no. 3 (August): 499–507.

– 1984a. "Some Evidence on the Accuracy and Uses of Long-Term Projections," Working paper 84–3, School of Business, Queen's University.

– 1984b. "Some Reflections on the Importance of Forecasting to Policy Making," *Canadian Public Policy* 10, no. 4 (December): 377–83.

– 1985. "A History of the Canadian Aggregate Economic Forecasting Industry," *Journal of Business Administration* 15, no. 1/2 (Fall): 139–58.

Daub, M., and E. Petersen, 1981. "The Accuracy of a Long-Term Forecast: The Canadian Energy Forecast," *International Journal of Energy Research* 5, no. 2 (May): 141–54.

Daub, M., and G. Savage, 1973 "A Note on the Predictive Power of Selected Canadian Leading Indicators," *Journal of Business Administration* 5, no. 1: 79–83.

Daub, M., and L. Mohr, 1983. "Modelling the Signalling Functions of Forecasts," unpublished paper, School of Business, Queen's University.

Daub, M., and S. Sankaran, 1984. "The Recent Turning-Point Record of Canadian Aggregate Economic Forecasts," Working Paper 84–5, School of Business, Queen's University.

de Bever, L., U. Kohli, and T. Maxwell, 1979. "An Analysis of Some of the Dynamic Properties of RDX2," *Canadian Journal of Economics* 12, no. 2 (May): 162–70.

de Bever, L., D.K. Foot, J.F. Helliwell, G.V. Jump, T. Maxwell, J.A. Sawyer, and H.E.L. Waslander, "Dynamic Properties of Four Canadian Macro-economic Models: A Collaborative Research Project," *Canadian Journal of Economics* 12, no. 2 (May): 133–9.

de Bever, L., and T. Maxwell, 1978. "An Analysis of the Major Dynamic Properties of *RDX2*," Bank of Canada, Technical Report 13, June.

Denton, F., and J. Kuiper, 1965. "The Effect of Measurement Errors on Parameter Estimates and Forecasts: A Case Study on the Canadian Preliminary National Accounts," *Review of Economics and Statistics* 37 (May): 198–206.

Di Caprio, U., R. Genesio, S. Pozzi, and A. Vicino, 1983. "Short Term Load Forecasting in Electric Power Systems," *Journal of Forecasting* 2, no. 1 (January–March): 59–76.

Diamond, P., and M. Rothschild, 1978. *Uncertainty in Economics.* New York: Academic Press.

Doucet, J.C., 1984. "Current Developments in RDXF: The December 1983 Version," Bank of Canada Memorandum, July.

Dungan, P., and J. Head, 1982. "The Response of FOCUS to Various Monetary Policy, Fiscal Policy and Exchange Rate Shocks," Paper presented to a seminar at the Department of Finance (Canada), July.

Dymsza, W., 1984. "Global Strategic Planning," *Journal of International Business Studies* 15, no. 2 (Fall): 169–84.

Economic Council of Canada, 1972. *The Years to 1980.* Ninth Annual Review. Ottawa: Information Canada.

Edwards, W., 1968. "Conservatism in Human Information Processing," in B. Kleinmuntz, ed., *Formal Representation of Human Judgment.* New York: Wiley.

Ehrenberg, A., 1975. *Data Reduction: Analyzing and Interpreting Statistical Data.* New York: Wiley.

Einhorn, H.J., in press. "Learning from Experience and Suboptimal Rules in Decision Making," in T. Wallsten, ed., *Cognitive Process in Choice and Decision Behavior*. Hillsdale, NJ: Erlbaum.

Einhorn, H.J., and R.M. Hogarth, 1978. "Confidence in Judgment: Persistence of the Illusion of Validity," *Psychological Review* 85: 395–416.

Einhorn, H.J., and R. Hogarth, 1982. "Prediction, Diagnosis and Causal Thinking in Forecasting," *Journal of Forecasting* 1, no. 1 (June): 23–36.

Evans, M., 1969. *Macroeconomic Activity*. New York: Harper and Row.

Fair, R., 1979a. "An Analysis of a Macroeconomic Model with Rational Expectations in the Bond and Stock Markets," *American Economic Review* 69, no. 4 (September): 539–52.

– 1979b. "An Analysis of the Accuracy of Four Macroeconometric Models," *Journal of Political Economy* 87, no. 4 (August): 701–18.

Feige, E., and D. Pearce, 1976. "Economically Rational Price Expectations," *Journal of Political Economy* 84, no. 3: 499–522.

Ferber, R. (ed.), 1974. *Handbook of Marketing Research*. New York: McGraw-Hill.

Fildes, R., 1985. "Quantitative Forecasting – the State of the Art: Econometric Models," *Journal of the Operational Research Society* 36, no. 7: 549–80.

Fischhoff, B., 1975. "Hindsight = Foresight: The Effect of Qutcome Knowledge on Judgment under Uncertainty," *Journal of Experimental Psychology: Human Perception and Performance* 1, no. 2: 288–99.

Firestone, O., 1965. *Problems of Economic Growth*. Ottawa: University of Ottawa Press.

Fontenau, A., 1982. "La fiabilité des prévisions macroéconomiques à court terme: 12 ans d'expériences françaises (1970–1981)," *Observations et diagnostics economiques* 2 (October).

Foot, D.K., and J.A. Sawyer, 1979. "Some Dynamic Properties of the TRACE Model," *Canadian Journal of Economics* 12, no. 2 (May): 176–81.

Forrester, J.W., 1971. *World Dynamics*. New York: Wright-Allen.

Friedman, B., 1979. "Optimal Expectations and the Extreme Information Assumptions of 'Rational Expectations' Macromodels," *Journal of Monetary Economics* 5, no. 1 (January): 23–41.

Frydman, R., and E.S. Phelps, 1983. *Individual Forecasting and Aggregate Outcomes: "Rational Expectations" Examined*. New York: Cambridge University Press.

Gorbet, F., 1973. "Econometric Models: Some Comments on Their Use in Policy Analysis," *Bank of Canada Review* (October): 3–14.

Grady, P., 1985. "The State of the Art in Canadian Macroeconomic Modelling," Department of Finance (Canada), March.

Granger, C.W.J., 1980. *Forecasting in Business and Economics*. New York: Academic Press.

Granger, C.W.J., and P. Newbold, 1973. "Some Comments on the Evaluation of Economic Forecasts," *Applied Economics* 35–47.

– 1976. *Forecasting Economic Time Series.* New York: Academic Press.

Green, C., 1980. *Canadian Industrial Organization and Policy.* Toronto: McGraw Hill-Ryerson.

Grether, D.M., and C.R. Plott, 1979. "Economic Theory of Choice and the Preference Reversal Reversal Phenomenon," *American Economic Review* 69, no. 4 (December): 623–38.

Grossman, S., 1975. "Rational Expectations and Econometric Modelling of Markets Subject to Uncertainty: A Bayesian Approach," *Journal of Econometrics* 44 (August): 255–72.

Hafer, R.W., and S.E. Hein, 1985. "On the Accuracy of Time-Series, Interest Rate, and Survey Forecasts of Inflation," *Journal of Business* 58, no. 4 (October): 377–88.

Hartle, D., 1958. "Predictions Derived from the Employment Forecast Survey," *Canadian Journal of Economics and Political Studies* (August): 388–9.

Hatjoullis, G., and D. Wood, 1979. "Economic Forecasts – An Analysis of Performance," *Business Economist* 10, no. 2 (Spring): 1–4.

Heimer, R., 1983. "The Origin of Predictable Behavior," *American Economic Review* 73, no. 4 (December): 560–95.

Helliwell, J.F., 1983. "Recent Evidence from Macroeconomic Models of the Canadian Economy," in G. Mason, ed., *Macroeconomics: Theory, Policy and Evidence.* Winnipeg: Institute for Social and Economic Research.

Helliwell, J.F., F.W. Gorbet, G.R. Sparks, and I.A. Stewart, 1973. "Comprehensive Linkage of Large Models: Canada and the United States," in R.J. Ball, ed., *The International Linkage of National Economic Models.* Amsterdam and London/New York: North Holland/American Elsevier.

Helliwell, J.F., H.T. Shapiro, G.R. Sparks, I.A. Stewart, F.W. Gorbet, and D.R. Stephenson, 1971a. "The Structure of RDX2 Part 1," Bank of Canada, Staff Research Study No. 7, 1971.

– 1971b. "the Structure of RDX2 Part 2," Bank of Canada, Staff Research Study No. 7.

– 1969a. "The Dynamics of RDX1," Bank of Canada, Staff Research Study No. 5.

Helliwell, J.F., L.H. Officer, H.T. Shapiro, and I.A. Stewart, 1969b. "The Structure of RDX1," Bank of Canada, Staff Research Study No. 3.

Helliwell, J.F., T. Maxwell, and H.E.L. Waslander, 1979. "Comparing the Dynamics of Canadian Macro Models," *Canadian Journal of Economics* 12, no. 2 (May): 181–94.

Henschel, R., 1978. "Self-altering Predictions," in P. Fowles, ed., *Handbook of Futures Research.* Westport: Greenwood Press.

Herwitz, D., 1973. "The Risk of Liability for Forecasting," unpublished paper, (US) Securities and Exchange Commission.

Hogarth, R.M., 1975. "Cognitive Processes and the Assessment of Subjective Probability Distributions," *Journal of the American Statistical Association* 70: 271–89.

– 1980. *Judgement and Choice.* New York: Wiley and Sons.

Holloway, C.A., 1979. *Decision Making under Uncertainty.* Englewood Cliffs, NJ: Prentice-Hall.

Hyndman, R.M., 1977. *The Data Resources Model of the Canadian Economy.* Toronto: Data Resources of Canada, November.

Institute for Policy Analysis, 1977. FOCUS: *Quarterly Forecasting and User Simulation Model of the Canadian Economy.* Toronto: Institute for Policy Analysis.

Intriligator, M., 1984. *Econometric Models, Techniques and Applications.* Second edition. Englewood Cliffs, NJ: Prentice-Hall.

Jacobs, R., and R. Jones, 1980. "Price Expectations in the United States," *American Economic Review* 70, no. 3 (June): 269–76.

Jenkins, G.M., and D.G. Watts, 1968. *Spectral Analysis and its Applications.* San Francisco: Holden-Day.

– 1979. *Practical Experience with Modelling and Forecasting Time Series.* Jersey, Channel Islands: GJ&P (Overseas) Ltd.

Jorgenson, D., J. Hunter, and M.I. Nadiri, 1979. "The Predictive Performance of Econometric Models of Quarterly Investment Behaviour," *Econometrica* 38, no. 2 (March): 213–24.

Jump. G.V., 1979. "The Quarterly Forecasting Model," *Canadian Journal of Economics* 12, no. 2 (May): 150–61.

Kahneman, D., and A. Tversky, 1973. "On the Psychology of Prediction," *Psychological Review* 80, no. 4: 237–51.

Kennedy, M., 1969. "How Well Does the National Institute Forecast?," *National Institute Economic Review,* 55: 40–9.

Kenward, L., and G. Jenkins, 1977. "The Comparitive Ex-post Forecasting Properties of General Canadian Quarterly Economic Models," Technical Report No. 7, Bank of Canada.

Keynes, J.M., 1936. *The General Theory of Employment, Interest and Money.* New York: Harcourt, Brace and World.

Klein, L., 1974. "Five-year Experience of Linking National Econometric Models and of Forecasting International Trade," unpublished paper, University of Pennsylvania.

Klein, L., and R.M. Young, 1980, *An Introduction to Econometric Forecasting and Forecasting Models.* Lexington, Mass.: D.C. Heath.

Krasker, W., 1984. "Heterogeneous Expectation and Capital Intensity in an Overlapping Generations Model," *Journal of Macroeconomics* 10, no. 4 (Fall): 433–46.

Kudrle, R., 1975. *Agricultural Tractors: A World Industry Study.* Cambridge: Ballinger Press.

Kuiper, J., 1970. "Model XVI – An Econometric Model of the Canadian Economy," mimeographed, Department of Finance (Canada), February.

Landes R., 1983. *Revolution in Time: Clocks and Making of the Modern World.* Cambridge, Mass.: Harvard University Press.

Leamer, E., 1983. "Let's Take the Con out of Econometrics," *American Economic Review* 73, no. 1 (March): 31–43.

Leontief, W., 1966. *Input-Output Economics.* New York: Oxford University Press.

Linstone, H.A., and M. Turoff, 1975. *The Delphi Method: Techniques and Applications.* Reading, Mass.: Addison-Wesley.

Lipinski, A., and D. Loveridge, 1982. "Institute for the Future's Study of the UK, 1978–85," *Futures* (June): 205–40.

Llewellyn, J., et al, 1985 "International Aspects of Forecasting Error," unpublished paper, OECD, Paris.

Llewellyn, J., S. Potter, and L. Samuelson, 1985. *Economic Forecasting and Policy.* London: Routledge and Kegan Paul.

Loasby, B.J., 1976. *Choice, Complexity and Ignorance.* Cambridge: Cambridge University Press.

London, A., and E. Stokes, 1982. *The Medium Term Forecasting Model* (MTFM): *An Overview.* Ottawa: The Conference Board in Canada, June.

Lucas, R.E., Jr., 1981. *Studies in Business Cycle Theory.* Cambridge: MIT Press.

Lucas, R.E., Jr., and L.A. Rapping, 1969. "Price Expectations and the Phillips Curve," *American Economic Review* 59, no. 3 (June): 342–50.

Lynes, B., 1983. *Astroeconomics: The Union of Astrology and Economics.* Springfield, Mass.: Lymes.

MacFarlane, I.J., and J.R. Hawkins, 1983. "Economic Forecasts and Their Assessment," Reserve Bank of Australia Research Discussion Paper, August.

MacMillan, A., 1983. *Macroeconomics.* Second edition. Toronto: Prentice-Hall.

Maddock, R., and M. Carter, 1982. "A Child's Guide to Rational Expectations," *Journal of Economic Literature* 20: 39–51.

Makridakis, S., 1986. "The Art and Science of Forecasting: An Assessment and Future Directions," *International Journal of Forecasting* 2, no. 1: 15–40.

– 1983. *The Accuracy of Major Extrapolation (Time Series) Methods.* New York: John Wiley & Sons.,

March, J.G., 1978. "Bounded Rationality, Ambiguity, and the Engineering of Choice," *Bell Journal of Economics* 9, no. 2: 587–608.

Masson, P.R., D.E. Rose, and J.G. Selody, 1980. "Building a Small Macro-

Model for Simulation: Some Issues," Bank of Canada, Technical Report 22, November.

May, S., 1966. "Dynamic Multipliers and Their Use for Fiscal Decision-Making," *Conference on Stabilization Policies.* Ottawa: Economic Council of Canada, 155–87.

McCracken., M.C., 1973. "An Overview of CANDIDE Model 1.0," CANDIDE Project Paper No. 1. Ottawa: Informetrica Canada.

– 1983. "Economic Forecasting: Humbling Experiences of the 1970's," unpublished paper, Informetrica Ltd., Ottawa.

McCloskey, D., 1982. "The Rhetoric of Economics," *Journal of Economic Literature* 21, no. 2 (June): 481–517.

McNees, S., 1974. "How Accurate Are Economic Forecasts?" *New England Economic Review* (November/December): 2–19.

– 1979. "Lessons from the Track Record of Macroeconomic Forecasters in the 1970s," *Studies in the Management Sciences,* 12: 227–64.

McNees, S., and J. Ries, 1983. "The Track Record of Macroeconomic Forecasts," *New England Economic Review* (November/December): 2–11.

Meadows, D.H., 1971. *Limits of Growth.* London: Earth Island Ltd.

Mincer, J. (ed), 1969. *Economic Forecasts and Expectations.* New York: Columbia University Press.

Modigliani, F., and O.H. Sauerlender, 1955. "Economic Expectations and Plans of Firms in Relation to Short-Term Forecasting," in *Short-Term Economic Forecasting.* Vol. 17 of Studies in Income and Wealth. Princeton: Princeton University Press, 288–9.

Montgomery, D.C., and L.A. Johnson, 1976. *Forecasting and Time Series Analysis.* New York: McGraw-Hill.

Moore, G.M., 1977. "The President's Economic Report: A Forecasting Record," NBER *Reporter* (April): 4–12.

Morrison, G.W., and D.H. Pike, 1977. "Kalman Filtering Applied to Statistical Forecasting," *Management Science* 23, no. 7 (March): 768–74.

Muth, J., 1961. "Rational Expectations and the Theory of Price Movements," *Econometrica* 29 (July): 315–35.

Nagel, E., 1961. *The Structure of Science.* London: Routledge and Kegan Paul.

National Bureau of Economic Research, 1955. *Short-Term Economic Forecasting.* Vol. 17 of Studies in Income and Wealth. Princeton: Princeton University Press.

National Energy Board, 1969. "Energy Supply and Demand in Canada and Export Demand for Canadian Energy 1967 to 1990," Discussion Paper NE23–669, Ottawa.

Nelles, V., 1983. "The Numbers Game," *Saturday Night* (July): 28–37.

Nelson, C., 1972. "The Prediction Performance of the FRB-MIT-PENN Model of the u.s. Economy," *American Economic Review* 62, no. 5 (December): 902–17.

Nelson, R., and S. Winter, 1982. *An Evolutionary Theory of Economic Capabilities and Behavior.* Cambridge: Harvard University Press.

Nightingale, J., 1978. "On the Definition of 'Industry' and 'Market,'" *Journal of Industrial Economics* 27, no. (September): 31–40.

Nisbett, R.E., and L.D. Ross, 1980. *Human Inference: Strategies and Short-comings of Social Judgement.* Englewood Cliffs, NJ: Prentice-Hall.

O'Carroll, F.M., 1977. "Subjective Probabilities and Short-Term Economic Forecasts: An Empirical Investigation," *Applied Statistics* 26, no. 3: 269–78.

Officer, L.H., 1968. *An Econometric Model of Canada under the Fluctuating Exchange Rate.* Cambridge, Mass.: Harvard University Press.

Okun, A., 1962. "The Predictive Value of Surveys of Business Intentions," *American Economic Review [Papers and Proceedings]* 52, no.: 33–69.

O'Reilly, B., 1985. "A Review of Models Developed within the Bank of Canada ... ," Research Department Paper RM–85–024, Bank of Canada.

Organization for Economic Co-operation and Development (OECD), 1965. *Technologies of Economic Forecasting.* Paris: OECD.

Pindyck, R., 1982. "Adjustment Costs, Uncertainty and the Behaviour of the Firm," *American Economic Review* 72, no. 2 (June): 415–26.

Pindyck, R., and D. Rubinfeld, 1981. *Econometric Models and Economic Forecasts.* Second edition. New York: McGraw-Hill.

Rathmell, J., 1974. *Marketing in the Service Sector.* Cambridge, Mass.: Winthrop.

Rege, U., W.J. Brennan, and W.H. Siwester, 1981. "A Case for the Disclosure of Corporate Financial Forecasts under Take-over Bid Situations," unpublished paper, School of Business, University of Saskatchewan.

Rhomberg, R., 1964. "A Model of the Canadian Economy under Fixed and Fluctuating Exchange Rates," *Journal of Political Economy* 72: 1–31.

Ridker, R., 1963. "An Evaluation of the Forecasting Ability of the Norwegian National Budgeting System," *Review of Economics and Statistics* 49: 32–3.

Rippe, R.D., and M. Wilkinson, 1974. "Forecasting Accuracy of the McGraw-Hill Anticipatory Data," *Journal of the American Statistical Association* 69, no. 348 (December): 849–58.

Robertson, H., and M. McDougall, 1982. "The Structure and Dynamics of RDXF: September 1980 Version," Bank of Canada, Technical Report 26.

Rose, D., and J. Selody, 1985. "The Structure of the Small Annual Model," Bank of Canada, Technical Report No. 42.

Rutenberg, D., 1985. "Playful Plans: Scenario Planning at Royal Dutch Shell," unpublished paper, School of Business, Queen's University, October.

Samuelson, P., 1976. "Is Real-World Price a Tale Told by the Idiot of Chance?" *Review of Economics and Statistics* 58, no. 1 (February): 120–3.

Sargent, T., and N. Wallace, 1975. "'Rational' Expections, the Optimal Monetary Instrument, and the Optimal Money Supply Rule," *Journal of Political Economy* 83 (April): 241–54.

Schelling, T.C., 1978. *Micromotives and Macrobehaviour*. New York: W.W. Norton.

Scherer, F., 1980. *Industrial Market Structure and Economic Performance*. Second edition. Chicago: Rand-McNally.

Schustack, M.W., and R.J. Sternberg, 1981. "Evaluation of Evidence in Causal Inference," *Journal of Experimental Psychology: (General)* 110: 101–20.

Shefferin, S., 1983. *Rational Expectations*. Cambridge: Cambridge University Press.

Shiller, R.J., 1978. "Rational Expectations and the Dynamic Structure of Macroeconomic Models: A Critical Review," *Journal of Monetary Economics* 4, no. 1 (January): 1–44.

Siedule, T., N. Skoulas, and K. Newton, 1976. *The Impact of Economy-Wide Change on the Labour Force: – An Econometric Analysis*. Ottawa: Supply and Services Canada.

Simon, H.A., 1954. "Spurious Correlation: A Causal Interpretation," *Journal of the American Statistical Association* 49: 467–79.

– 1955. A Behavioral Theory of Rational Choice," *Quarterly Journal of Economics* 69 (February): 99–118.

– 1979a. *Models of Thought*. New Haven: Yale University Press.

– 1979b. "Rational Decision Making in Business Organizations," *American Economic Review* 69, no. 4 (September): 493–513.

Sims, C., 1969. "Evaluating Short-term Macro-Economic Forecasts: The Dutch Performance," *Review of Economics and Statistics* 49: 225–39.

– 1977. *New Methods in Business Cycle Research*. Minneapolis: Federal Reserve Bank.

Smirlock, M., T. Gilligan, and W. Marshall, "Tobin's q and the Structure-Performance Relationship," *American Economic Review* 74, no. 5 (December): 1051–60.

Smyth, D., 1966. "How Well Do Australian Economists Forecast?" *Economic Record* 42: 293–311.

Statistics Canada, 1974–81. *Corporate Financial Statistics*. 61–207, Government of Canada.

– 1977. *The Input-Output Structure of the Canadian Economy*. Catalogue 15–506E (occasional). Ottawa: Information Canada.

Steiner, G.A., 1979. *Strategic Planning*. New York: The Free Press.

Stephan, F., and P. McCarthy, 1958. *Sampling Opinions*. New York: Wiley and Sons.

Stephenson, D., 1985. "The Colorful History of RDX: Notes on the Evolution of Our Model," Bank of Canada mimeograph, March.

Stigler, G.J., 1961. "The Economics of Information," *Journal of Political Economy* 69 (June): 213–25.

Stokes E., 1982. "The Nature and Predictive Accuracy of the Quarterly Canadian Forecast," *Canadian Business Review*, Conference Board.

Su, V., and J. Su, 1975. "An Evaluation of ASA/NBER Business Outlook Survey Forecasts," *Explorations in Economic Research* 2, no. 4 (Fall): 588–618.

– 1978. "An Error Analysis of Econometric and Noneconometric Forecasts," *American Economic Review* 68, no. 2 (May): 12–21.

Suits, D., 1962. "Forecasting and Analysis with an Econometric Model," *American Economic Review* 52, no. 1 (March): 104–32.

Taylor, J., 1979. "Estimation and Control of a Macro Economic Model with Rational Expectations," *Econometrica* (September): 1286–97.

Theil, H., 1955. "Who Forecasts Best?" *International Economic Papers* 5: 194–9.

– 1966. *Applied Economic Forecasting*. Amsterdam: North Holland.

– 1975. *Economic Forecasts and Policies*. First edition 1958. Amsterdam/ New York: North Holland/American Elsevier.

Theil, H., and S. Wage, 1964. "Some Observations on Adaptive Filtering," *Management Science* 10, no. 2: 198–224.

Thomopoulos, N.T., 1980. *Applied Forecasting Methods*. Englewood Cliffs, NJ: Prentice-Hall.

Thompson, H.E., and G.E. Tiao, 1969. "Analysis of Telephone Data: A Case Study of Forecasting Seasonal Time Series," *Proceedings of the Conference on Time Series Models for Marketing Forecasts*, University of Wisconsin, May.

Toffler, A., 1979. *Future Shock*. New York: Random House.

Tsurumi, H., 1970. "A Four-Sector Econometric Model of the Canadian Economy," Discussion Paper No. 8, Institute for Economic Research, Queen's University.

– 1973. "A Survey of Recent Canadian Macro-Econometric Models," *Canadian Journal of Economics* 6, no. 3 (August): 409–28.

Turnovsky, S., 1970. "Empirical Evidence on the Formation of Price Expectations," *Journal of the American Statistical Association* 65, no. 4 (December): 141–54.

Tversky, A., and D. Kahneman, 1971. "The Belief in the 'Law of Small Numbers'," *Psychological Bulletin* 76, no. 2: 105–10.

Umstead, David A., 1977. "Forecasting Stock Market Prices," *Journal of Finance* 32, no. 2: 427–41.

Wachs, M., 1982. "Ethical Dilemmas in Forecasting for Public Policy," *Public Management Forum* (November/December): 562–8.

Wack, P., 1985. "Scenarios: Unchartered Waters Ahead," *Harvard Business Review* (September–October): 73–89.

Waslander, H.E.L., 1979. "The Dynamic Properties of CANDIDE Model 1.2M," *Canadian Journal of Economics* 12, no. 2 (May): 139–50.

– 1982. "Forecasting and Policy Planning – Some Recent Canadian Experience," unpublished paper, Ministry of State for Economic and Regional Development, Government of Canada.

Weintraub, E.R., 1975. "'Uncertainty' and the Keynesian Revolution," *History of Political Economy* 7 (Winter): 530–48.

Wheelwright, S.C., and S. Makridakis, 1980. *Forecasting Methods for Management.* Third edition. New York: John Wiley & Sons.

Wood, D., and R. Fildes, 1976. *Forecasting for Business.* London: Longman.

Yermilov, A., 1983. "An Analysis of the Accuracy of the Blue Chip Short-term Macroeconomic Forecasts," paper, Third International Symposium on Forecasting, Philadelphia.

Young, R.M., 1982. "Forecasting with an Econometric Model: The Issue of Judgemental Adjustment," *Journal of Forecasting* 1, no. 2: 189–204.

Zarnowitz, V., 1967. *An Appraisal of Short-Term Economic Forecasts.* Occasional Paper No. 104. New York: National Bureau of Economic Research.

– 1971. *The Business Cycle To-day.* New York: National Bureau of Economic Research.

– 1979. "An Analysis of Annual and Multiperiod Quarterly Forecasts of Aggregate Income, Output and the Price Level," *Journal of Business* 52, no. 1: 2–25.

– 1984a. "The Accuracy of Individual Group Forecasts from Business Outlook Surveys," *Journal of Forecasting* 3, no. 1 (January): 11–26.

– 1984b. "Major Changes in Cyclical Behavior," Working Paper No. 1395. New York: National Bureau of Economic Research, July.

Zellner, A., and F. Palm, 1974. "Time Series Analysis and Simultaneous Equation Econometric Models," *Journal of Econometrics* 2: 17–54.

Zwicky, F., and G. Wilson, 1967. *New Methods of Thought and Procedure.* New York: Springer Verlag.

Index